Synthesis Lectures on Human Language Technologies

Series Editor

Graeme Hirst, Department of Computer Science, University of Toronto, Toronto, Canada

The series publishes topics relating to natural language processing, computational linguistics, information retrieval, and spoken language understanding. Emphasis is on important new techniques, on new applications, and on topics that combine two or more HLT subfields.

Michael Flor

Automatic Question Generation

 Springer

Michael Flor ⓘ
Educational Testing Service
Princeton, NJ, USA

ISSN 1947-4040 ISSN 1947-4059 (electronic)
Synthesis Lectures on Human Language Technologies
ISBN 978-3-031-92071-4 ISBN 978-3-031-92072-1 (eBook)
https://doi.org/10.1007/978-3-031-92072-1

© The Editor(s) (if applicable) and The Author(s), under exclusive license to Springer
Nature Switzerland AG 2025

This work is subject to copyright. All rights are solely and exclusively licensed by the Publisher, whether the whole or part of the material is concerned, specifically the rights of translation, reprinting, reuse of illustrations, recitation, broadcasting, reproduction on microfilms or in any other physical way, and transmission or information storage and retrieval, electronic adaptation, computer software, or by similar or dissimilar methodology now known or hereafter developed.
The use of general descriptive names, registered names, trademarks, service marks, etc. in this publication does not imply, even in the absence of a specific statement, that such names are exempt from the relevant protective laws and regulations and therefore free for general use.
The publisher, the authors and the editors are safe to assume that the advice and information in this book are believed to be true and accurate at the date of publication. Neither the publisher nor the authors or the editors give a warranty, expressed or implied, with respect to the material contained herein or for any errors or omissions that may have been made. The publisher remains neutral with regard to jurisdictional claims in published maps and institutional affiliations.

This Springer imprint is published by the registered company Springer Nature Switzerland AG
The registered company address is: Gewerbestrasse 11, 6330 Cham, Switzerland

If disposing of this product, please recycle the paper.

Competing Interests The author has no competing interests to declare that are relevant to the content of this manuscript.

Contents

1	**Introduction**	1
2	**Types of Questions**	5
	2.1 Introduction	5
	2.2 Interrogative Forms	5
	2.3 Taxonomies of Questions	7
	2.4 Cloze Items	10
	2.5 Factual Questions	13
	2.6 Open-Ended Questions	16
	2.7 Questions—Depth and Difficulty	17
	2.8 Summary	19
3	**Evaluation Methods for AQG**	21
	3.1 Introduction	21
	3.2 Human Intrinsic Evaluation	22
	3.3 Comparing AQG to Human-Produced Questions	24
	3.4 Rater Agreement	26
	3.5 Automated Metrics for AQG Evaluation	27
	3.6 Extrinsic Evaluations of AQG	35
	3.7 Summary	37
4	**Classic Approaches to AQG from Text, Part 1: Syntax, Semantics and Discourse**	39
	4.1 Introduction	39
	4.2 AQG with Constituent Parse Trees	40
	4.3 Semantic Roles and Question Generation	43
	4.4 Classic Cross-Sentence AQG	48
	4.5 Summary	55

5 Classic Approaches to AQG from Text, Part 2: Templates 57
5.1 Introduction 57
5.2 Simple Templates 58
5.3 Automating the Acquisition of Templates 61
5.4 Deeper Questions with Templates 66
5.5 Summary 73

6 Neural AQG, Part 1: Early Models 75
6.1 Introduction 75
6.2 RNN, LSTM and Seq2Seq Models 76
6.3 Data Sets 78
6.4 Seq2Seq Models for Neural Question Generation 79
6.5 Semantic Drift and Hallucinations 85
6.6 Summary 87

7 Neural AQG, Part 2: Transformers 89
7.1 Introduction 89
7.2 Generating Questions with Transformers 92
7.3 Question Generation with Large Transformer Models 95
7.4 Summary 100

8 Content Selection for AQG 101
8.1 Introduction 101
8.2 Selection of Sentences 103
8.3 Keyphrase Selection 109
8.4 Specific Content Selections 113
8.5 Summary 119

9 Question Generation from Ontologies and Knowledge Bases 121
9.1 Introduction 121
9.2 Ontologies 121
9.3 Question Generation with Ontologies 124
9.4 Language Aspects 127
9.5 Selection of Distractors 131
9.6 Summary 135

10 Question Generation with Large Language Models and Generative AI ... 137
10.1 Introduction 137
10.2 Generation 139
10.3 Prompt-Engineering for QG 142
10.4 Question Selection 144
10.5 Summary 147

| 11 | **Conclusion** | 149 |

References 153

About the Author

Michael Flor is a senior research scientist at the ETS Research Institute, the research arm of the Educational Testing Service, in Princeton, New Jersey. He specializes in language technology for educational applications. At ETS, Dr. Flor has led, and co-led R&D projects focused on text complexity and readability, question generation, automated spelling correction, analysis of figurative language, automated scoring of essays and short answers, assessment of collaborative problem solving, sentiment analysis, and on psycholinguistic aspects of the lexicon. He serves as academic editor for the *PLOS ONE* journal and as guest associate editor for the journal *Frontiers in AI*. He is a long-time member of SIGEDU, and has been a committee member for multiple international conferences and workshops in the areas of NLP and language learning. Dr. Flor's research has appeared in major international journals, conferences, and workshops.

# Introduction

Automatic question generation (AQG) is a very prolific area of research that spans multiple disciplines. AQG is mostly rooted in computational linguistics, but is also related to other areas of linguistics, education, tutoring systems, computer science, knowledge representation, AI, Deep Learning, etc. This book intends to provide an introduction to AQG by describing its fundamentals, its linguistic and educational aspects, and by presenting the major technical approaches to AQG.

Automatic question generation is generation of questions by an automated process, usually implemented as a computer algorithm. The input for such generation is usually text. The input can also be formal knowledge representation and even images. The outputs are usually questions—interrogative linguistic forms (question phrases). AQG outputs also often include multiple-choice items, sometimes without interrogative forms. In that case it is sometimes called Automatic Item Generation (AIG). AQG and AIG are not always seen as the same thing,[1] but those areas are highly interrelated.

AQG is not a new area of research, it has existed in some form for about fifty years. Wolfe (1975) is often cited as the earliest published work on using automated methods to generate content questions from text. That study used syntactic transformations from sentences, in accordance with the prevailing linguistic theories of the time. Finn (1975) published a detailed algorithm for producing questions from text passages, using constituent syntactic analysis of sentences in combination with an early variant of linguistic case theory. Finn's work was intended for human test developers, presuming text analysis is done by trained linguists, whereas Wolfe presented a working computer-implemented prototype system. Even earlier, Carbonell (1970) described an implemented system for generation of questions from a formal knowledge presentation, a semantic network.

---

[1] For example, generation of arithmetic practice items belongs in AIG but not in AQG.

© The Author(s), under exclusive license to Springer Nature Switzerland AG 2025
M. Flor, *Automatic Question Generation*, Synthesis Lectures on Human Language Technologies, https://doi.org/10.1007/978-3-031-92072-1_1

The modern era of AQG can be roughly divided into three phases. From about 2004–2010, studies began to appear dealing with automated generation of questions and gap-filling items for educational purposes. Using rule-based and statistical approaches (Kunichika et al. 2004; Brown et al. 2005; Hoshino and Nakagawa 2005; Mitkov et al., 2006; Goto et al. 2010). In 2008, members of the research community decided to organize around a set of joint tasks and benchmark competitions. Part of the interest that sparked this phase of research was interest in AQG for tutorial applications, especially Intelligent Tutoring Systems (Graesser et al. 2008; Boyer et al. 2009). This has led to three workshops on AQG (Rus and Lester 2009; Rus et al. 2010, 2011). The first phase of AQG research lasted until approximately 2018, with an intense focus on how to convert declarative statements into interrogative forms for the purpose of question generation. This can be considered the era of classic AQG, with rule-based and statistical methods that utilized templates, syntactic analyses (constituency and dependency parsing), semantic role labeling (SRL), and some other linguistically motivated approaches to AQG. During this era, AQG was considered to depend crucially on some forms of explicit computational analysis of text, with parse trees or other formal structures being the backbones of AQG algorithms. Although it is sometimes claimed that the approaches in this era were purely rule-based, statistical methods and machine learning were crucial components in those systems from the beginning. With the considerable success of the various method of converting statements to interrogative forms, there came the additional important issues, such as how to evaluate the AQG results, how to develop applications with AQG technologies, and how considerations from potential applications may influence the selected algorithms. Another important aspect that arose during that phase was how to focus the AQG process, how to decide what is question-worthy. The first phase can be considered classic in the sense that it introduced AQG as a major research area, demonstrating significant achievements. After 2018, AQG research rarely focused on classic AQG methods, except for comparison purposes. However, some component methods and approaches from that phase are still used in later research (and shown in this book).

The second phase of AQG research began in 2016 and was marked by transition to deep learning neural architectures, in step with the rest of the computational linguistics field. It largely dispensed with formal analytic structures (such as parse trees) as a basis for question formulation, and instead switched to training neural network models to directly generate questions from declarative texts and knowledge graphs. The transition from analysis to training was a major paradigm shift in AQG. With the rise of transformer-based pretrained models in NLP after 2018, such models were quickly adapted and became a major factor in AQG research. The third phase of AQG began after 2020, with the introduction of large language models (LLMs) and the transition from model training to prompt engineering.

This book introduces major approaches to automatic question generation by providing general introductions for each approach and then presenting select case studies that illustrate those approaches, with their advantages and complexities. The book is not intended to provide complete coverage of AQG—the research field is wide and is constantly changing, as AQG continues to be an active area of research. There are many good review papers about automatic question generation. For the historical outlook of the early approaches, see Boyer and Piwek (2010), Piwek and Boyer (2012), as well as Rus et al. (2012). Le et al. (2014) provided an overview of AQG during the heyday of the classic AQG approaches, with a focus on educational applications. A dedicated review of the first wave of neural question generation systems was presented by Pan et al. (2019). Kurdi et al. (2020) provided an extensive overview of both classic and neural approaches. Lu and Lu (2021) and Das et al. (2021) described more recent advances in AQG. Mulla and Gharpure (2023), as well as Zhang et al. (2021), provide rich and detailed reviews on current trends in neural question generation, including listing of the datasets that are used for training and descriptions of network architectures. Amidei et al. (2018b) presented a review of evaluation studies of AQG. Horbach et al. (2020) provided an update on evaluation methods and also compiled a reference for the many question–answer datasets that were produced by researchers in the last decade. Tan et al. (2024) presented a review of question and item generation with large language modes.

Many research papers presenting various AQG system stress the relevance and importance of AQG for educational applications. In the domain of education, questions are a tool for a variety of purposes. One of those purposes is assessment: questions posed to students/examinees are used to elicit information about reading comprehension or the students' knowledge and abilities. Questions not only assess the acquisition of knowledge, but can also facilitate learning, including critical thinking, retention, and engagement (Glass and Sinha 2013; Gall 1970). End-of-chapter questions are often included in textbooks to allow students to test their understanding and also guide students as to the important aspects in the text. Similarly, *adjunct questions* are questions that are provided together with a reading passage or book, either before reading or in the middle or at the end of the text, to guide readers attention, help them explore the text, and promote memory and retention of the materials (Hamaker 1986; Carrier and Fautsch-Patridge 1981). The wider domain of education includes not only organizations focused on learning, such as schools and universities, but also organizations dealing primarily with certification and licensure. All of them use forms of assessment involving questions and test items, and thus can benefit from AQG technologies, automating the creation of questions for learning and assessment.

Types of Questions 2

2.1 Introduction

Questions are everywhere. They have many uses and many forms. We begin this book with a short reflection on what kinds of questions there are in human communication, just to outline the general territory. We start with a focus on form and then consider various classifications of questions. For a multifaceted modern treatment of questions in the field of Linguistics see Dayal (2016).

2.2 Interrogative Forms

The most obvious forms of questions are interrogative forms. There are several interrogative forms of sentences in English (Krifka 2011). The most common types are constituent questions, polar questions, and choice questions.

- **Yes/no questions**, also called **polar questions**. Polar questions can be formulated in positive form (*Did England win the FIFA World Cup in 1966?*), or in negative form (*Didn't England win the FIFA World Cup in 1966?*). Polar questions in English use the verbs *do* and *be* (*Is it too late for breakfast?*), and the modal verbs *can, may, should*, etc. (*Can ice melt below 0 °C?*).
- **Constituent questions**, also called **Wh-questions** (Erteschik-Shir 1986). Those questions feature the question words *what, who, where, when, whose, which, why, how, how much*, etc.
- **Choice questions** have interrogative form, but include the potential answer choices in the question: *Does he like ice cream or sweets? Where was she born, in Italy, Austria or in Switzerland?* Such questions are also called alternative questions, as they include

the alternative answer options. Yes/no questions can also appear in a form similar to choice questions: *Did she go to Paris or didn't she?*

There are some additional question types in English, including fragments, tag questions, and declarative-form questions. Fragmental questions are fragments such as *What?*, *Who did?*, *Go where?* They often appear in conversational context. Usually, human interlocutors have little problem interpreting them in context. Tag questions are a form or construction in which an interrogative component is added to a declarative clause. Tag questions usually involve a negation twist between the main clause and the added tag-question: *John is in his office, isn't he? He doesn't intend to resign, does he?*. Tag questions have a variety of pragmatic uses (Cuenca 1997).

Like many natural languages, English allows the formation of simple questions in speech by just changing the intonation over standard declarative sentence forms, as illustrated below.

The house is purple. → *The house is purple? Mr. Smith drove to the park.* → *Mr. Smith drove to the park?*

Such questions are typically used to express surprise or bewilderment with either the whole proposition (equivalent to *Is it true that Mr. Smith drove to the park?*) or with some salient parts of it. Informationally salient parts of the question are usually stressed, hinting to the listeners which part of the question is of particular interest. In MR. SMITH drove to the park? The focus is on the agent—was it indeed Mr. Smith or maybe someone else. In *Mr. Smith drove to the PARK?*, the focus is on the location/destination—did he indeed drive to the park, or maybe somewhere else. In *Mr. Smith DROVE to the park?*, the focus is on the mode of transport—did Mr. Smith indeed drive to the park, rather than walk there? Similar nuances can be imposed (via stress) on the original declarative sentence; or be expressed as declarative cleft-sentence formations: *it was Mr. Smith who drove to the park; It was to the park that Mr. Smith drove; What Mr. Smith did was drive to the park.*

Nuances similar to the intonational declarative form can be expressed by constituent questions: *Who drove to the park?, Where did Mr. Smith drive?, How did Mr. Smith arrive at the park?* Note that the last question involves a presupposition, by presuming that Mr. Smith completed his driving activity as intended and arrived at the park. If Mr. Smith did not complete his action as intended (he got lost or had an accident), the question is not felicitous. The infelicity might not be a problem in a human conversation; an interlocutor might just note "*He never arrived there*". The intonational version of the question, *Mr. Smith DROVE to the park?*, does not have a problem of infelicity, as it preserves the ambiguity of the original declarative sentence.

But why do we delve on this issue here? There are two reasons. First, it provides an illustration of how a single simple sentence/statement/proposition can lead to variety of questions via focusing on the different aspects (semantic arguments) involved in a proposition. The abundance of possibilities poses a challenge for AQG systems as to what question to generate, or how to generate the different questions. Second, it illustrates some issues with formation of constituent questions (e.g. from declarative text). Automatic formation of constituent questions is one of the most common tasks in AQG. Some of them may look like transformations *"Mr. Smith drove... → Who drove...?"*, and seem relatively safe, but others may involve considerable rephrasing and may involve various infelicities. Such infelicities can be problematic or unacceptable in many settings, for example in educational applications of AQG.

2.3 Taxonomies of Questions

Various kinds of classification for questions have been proposed by researchers in different disciplines. Such classifications reflect a variety of approaches and also a variety of uses for questions. In the field of Cognitive Science, Graesser et al. (1988, 2008) proposed a multi-aspect taxonomy of questions. That taxonomy was based on a review of past research, and on studies of questions generated by adults in different contexts, especially by students during tutoring sessions (Graesser and Person 1994). The taxonomy included semantic categories and pragmatic categories. The semantic categories (Table 2.1) map the various kinds of information that the questions addressed. The pragmatic categories (Table 2.2) map the social, personal and communicative goals of people asking questions.

Within computational linguistics, classification of questions into various types has long been a staple in the research area of Question Answering (QA). Early question-answering systems (Lehnert 1978) answered questions by first detecting the question type, and then using type-specific search and answer procedures. Consequently, in traditional QA research, before the advent of neural systems, question classification was utilized for selection of optimal strategies/algorithms for question handling and answering (Loni 2011). The architectures of traditional QA systems typically used a three-stage architecture: Question Analysis, Document Retrieval, and Answer Extraction (Harabagiu et al. 2003). Question Analysis often incorporated a Question Classification step, using a predefined taxonomy of questions (e.g., Hovy et al. 2002; Li and Roth 2002). For QA, the question type (for example *who, what, where, when*) can be indicative of the type of answer that needs to be found (so called Answer Type Classification). For example, for a question *When was X born?*, the answer type is a date, and so the QA system would use such information looking for a year/date. A popular taxonomy of question types was proposed by Li and Roth (2002)—a hierarchical taxonomy of questions with a coarse level and a fine-grained level (Table 2.3). However, it is fairly easy to see from the table that this taxonomy is more oriented towards potential classes of answers. Pomerantz (2005) presented a review of question taxonomies from the perspective of library reference services. Those taxonomies included syntactic forms of questions, forms of expected answer-types (semantics), functions of expected answers (pragmatics) and even sources from which

Table 2.1 Semantic categories of questions (adapted and reworked from Graesser et al. 1988, 2008)

	Category	Examples
1	Verification	Is X true or false?
2	Disjunctive	Is X or Y the case?
3	Concept completion	Who? What? When? Were? (seeking a 'missing' aspect/component)
4	Example	What is an example of X?
5	Feature specification	What are the properties if X? E.g. What color is the new shirt?
6	Quantification	How much? How many? How long? How much does the shirt cost?
7	Definition	What does X mean?
8	Comparison	How is X similar to Y? Are X and Y different?
9	Interpretation	What does X imply? What can be inferred from X?
10	Causal antecedent	What caused some event to occur?
11	Causal consequence	What happened as a result of X occurring? What may happen next?
12	Goal orientation	Why did an agent do some action?
13	Enablement	What enabled X to occur? How was X possible?
14	Instrumental/procedural	How did an agent perform the action?
15	Expectational	Why isn't X occurring? What may happen to Y?
16	Judgmental	What should X do? What do you think of Y?

answers may be drawn (e.g. books, websites, experts, etc.). It should be noted that with the spread of deep learning approaches in computational linguistics and the development of very large datasets of questions and answers, question taxonomies play lesser and lesser role in QA research, which has become almost totally data-driven, though taxonomies still play an important role for theoretical understanding (Rogers et al. 2023).

Nielsen et al. (2008) presented a taxonomy of questions for automated tutoring systems (Table 2.4). Such a taxonomy combines aspects of semantics (what is the question about) and pragmatics (for what educational purpose is the question applicable). Boyer et al. (2009) have emphasized that in task-oriented tutoring, the tutorial goals (what needs to be learned) may take precedence, and semantic categories of questions might be nested inside the pragmatic categories.

2.3 Taxonomies of Questions

Table 2.2 Pragmatic categories of questions (adapted and reworked from Graesser et al. 1988)

Category	Use cases and examples
Information acquisition	
Clarify common ground	This commonly occurs in dialogs, where participants clarify their mutual understanding. (*How much time do we have?*)
Goal blockage	This reflects situations when a questioner asks someone (possibly an expert) on how to solve some problem or attain a goal. (*How do we solve this situation?*)
Glitch in explanation	Questions that are asked when some explanation or assertion does not make sense, and some resolution is sought. (*Given that, haven't we found the solution?*)
Asking permission	Usually for some action (or inaction). (*May I call you tomorrow?*)
Knowledge elicitation	Seeking knowledge or understanding. This is a wide category, that may cover anything from learning environments to casual information exchange (*What would you like to eat?*). A subcategory here are questions asked for testing someone's knowledge
Assertions (question forms can be used to make statements and assertions)	
Express opinions	The question form allows to express opinions indirectly, possibly reducing tension. (*Is the company policy in this case mistaken?*)
Rhetorical questions	Such question are not requests for information, but rather a form emphasis for stating facts and opinions. The answer to such question is supposed to be widely obvious. (*Who enjoys doing such chores?*)
Indirect request for non-verbal behavior	The classic example for this category is when someone at a dining table asks *Can you pass the salt?*. The question is not intended to produce a yes/no answer, but rather to facilitate passing the salt
Conversation monitoring	
Greetings	Question forms can be used as ritualized greetings that do not imply seeking an answer. (*How are you?*)
Change topic or speaker	Question forms can be used to signal a switch of topic (*Can we switch to the next topic?*) or moving to another speaker in a conversation

Table 2.3 Question taxonomy (adapted) from Li and Roth (2002), questions are classified by the type of answer that would be expected

Coarse classes	Fine classes
Abbreviation	Abbreviation, expansion
Description	Definition, description, manner, reason
Entity	Animal, body, color, creation, currency, disease, event, food, instrument, language, letter, other, plant, product, religion, sport, substance, symbol, technique, term, vehicle, word
Human	Description, group, individual, title
Location	City, country, mountain, other, state
Numeric value	Code, count, date, distance, money, order, other, percent, percent, period, speed, temperature, size, weight

2.4 Cloze Items

Cloze items are the other very popular format of presenting questions. Instead of using an interrogative language form, a cloze item just deletes (blanks out) some portion of the original sentence/text, leaving a blank/gap, and the examinee/test-taker is required to fill in the missing text. For this reason, cloze items are also known as *cloze questions*, *gap-fill*, *gap-filling*, *fill-the-gap*, *fill-in-the-blank(s)*, the last term also abbreviated as *FITB*. Also note the use of the term 'item'. This comes from the domain of educational assessment (testing), where any question prepared for assessment, be it in mathematics, language proficiency, or any subject-matter knowledge, in interrogative form or a gap-fill form, is called an **item**.

As a procedure, word deletion from text, with the intent of checking how well people can complete the gap, was used from the early days of psychological research in the nineteenth century (Rankin 1959). Word-deletion in text passages, or in single sentences, with a purpose of completion, has been, and still is, widely used in psychological and educational testing.

Deletion of multiple words in a text passage (replacing each one with a blank) was introduced by Taylor (1953) as a technique for measuring text readability, which he named the *cloze procedure*. The application to readability was empirical: if many people can correctly fill in the blanks, the text is probably very readable, the missing information can be easily guessed from context; if many people cannot correctly fill most of the blanks, then the text can be considered difficult. In addition to readability, the text cloze procedure has been utilized as a measure of reading comprehension, vocabulary knowledge, and as tool for instruction (gap-filling as a practice activity). Recently, the cloze procedure has been rediscovered in computational linguistics as a very powerful method for (self)-training of large language models utilizing deep learning (Devlin et al. 2019). The cloze procedure is used not only for research and education. At about the same time Taylor

2.4 Cloze Items

Table 2.4 Question taxonomy adapted from Nielsen et al. (2008)

	Category	Examples
A	Description questions	Questions that ask for descriptions
A.1	Concept completion	Who, what, when, where?
A.2	Definition	What does X mean? What defines Y?
A.3	Feature specification	What features does X have?
A.4	Composition	What are the components of X?
A.5	Example	What is an example of X?
B	Method questions	Focus on methods and procedures
B.1	Calculation	Compute or calculate X. (imperative form)
B.2	Procedural	How do you perform X?
C	Explanation questions	Causal reasoning
C.1	Causal antecedent	What caused X?
C.2	Causal consequence	What will X cause?
C.3	Enablement	What enables the achievement of X?
D	Rationale questions	Goals and motivations
D.1	Goal orientation	What is the goal of X?
D.2	Justification	Why is X the case?
E	Comparison questions	
E.1	Concept comparison	Compare X to Y
E.2	Judgment	What do you think of X?
E.3	Improvement	How could you improve X?
F	Preference questions	
F.1	Free creation	Calls for a subjective response
F.2	Free option	Select from a set of presented valid options

introduced the cloze as a research tool, a similar procedure of word omission was utilized as a form of entertainment, leading to the popular Mad Libs game.[1]

A **cloze item**, whether a single blank in a single sentence, or multiple blanks in a passage of text, can be presented in two major modes. In one mode, no potential answer options are provided, and the students have to complete the missing material from their own memory or knowledge. This format is often called *open cloze*, alluding to the notion that the set of potential answers is 'open'. Examples are presented below.[2]

---

[1] See https://en.wikipedia.org/wiki/Mad_Libs.
[2] The respective correct answers are 'Corsica' and 'organisms'.

Table 2.5 Cloze (left) and interrogative (right) forms of the same MCQ

Napoleon Bonaparte was born in _____	Where was Napoleon Bonaparte born?
(a) France	(a) France
(b) Corsica	(b) Corsica
(c) Belgium	(c) Belgium
(d) Italy	(d) Italy

Napoleon Bonaparte was born in _____

Eukaryotes are _____ *whose cells have a nucleus enclosed within a nuclear envelope.*

The other mode or format of presentation is one where the answer options are provided, with the correct answer among them, and the examinees need to select the correct option. This mode is the well-known multiple-choice format, also abbreviated as multiple-choice question (**MCQ**), multiple-choice item (MCI), or multiple-choice test item (MCTI). However, note that multiple-choice items can appear with interrogative questions, and so one should distinguish between Cloze MCQs and Interrogative-form MCQs. An example of both forms for essentially the same content, is presented in Table 2.5.

The part of the item that contains the question or the text with a blank is called an **item stem**. In some cases, a stem may include not only the question, but also instructions for examinees (in the simplest case, something like *Please indicate...*). Thus, an item often can have much more content than just a question, though the term *question* is often used interchangeably with *item*, in everyday use and in research literature, including literature on AQG. In addition, when items are not intended for testing, but rather for practice and learning activities, they are often called *gap-filling exercises*.

A multiple-choice item presents a finite set of response options. The incorrect options are called **distractors**, as they presumably distract the examinee from the correct answer. The correct option/answer is often called the **key**. The most widely used form of MCQs is the form with four response options, of which only one option is the key, and the others are distractors. In educational assessment, MCQs in which more than one option turns out to be acceptable, are called double-keyed or multi-keyed. Such items are generally unacceptable for assessment, unless an item was intentionally designed to have multiple correct answers.[3]

The basic requirements for cloze items differ somewhat from interrogative form items. Text-based items are usually (but not exclusively) generated from a single sentence, which is called the **carrier sentence**. For a cloze item, the carrier sentence does not need to be

---

[3] This is also different from items with an option like *all of the above*, which can be a distractor, but, when it is intended as a correct option, all other options are incorrect or give only partial credit. Another special type of MCQ is called *odd-one-out* where only one option is incorrect, and the student needs to indicate which one.

significantly changed. In most cases, the focal word/term/phrase/span is extracted (blanked out), producing a gap. The extracted material automatically becomes the correct potential answer (also called *answer-key* or *key phrase*). It can be convenient to think of the extracted material as a target while we are searching for the suitable phrase to extract, and as an answer key once it has been designated. For interrogative-form items, unlike cloze items, a conversion of the sentence is required, from a declarative form into an interrogative form.

The answer-key is a very valuable 'by-product' of the question generation process. For MCQ items, the answer-key usually becomes one of the response options (as extracted, or possibly with some rephrasing). Examinees' responses to MCQs can be scored automatically, as generation of MCQs also provides the key for automated grading/scoring of responses. For open-response items, the answer key can be used for automatically scoring potential responses, by checking to what desired degree they approximate the answer-key.[4] In addition, the answer-key can be used as a basis of feedback to students/examinees, providing indication of what the expected correct answer would be. This can be especially valuable when questions are generated as exercises for student learning/practice activities.

The discussion above introduced two distinctions: one is between the cloze format and the interrogative-form format, the other between multiple-choice and open questions. Those distinctions are independent and thus allow four different combinations. All four combinations can be found in educational use and in other applications. All four are also addressed in AQG literature, though cloze MCQs and open interrogative items are the two most popular types in AQG research.[5]

2.5 Factual Questions

The term **factual questions** is widely used in the AQG research literature, often without clarification. Technically, factual questions are questions/items that can be answered (by examinees, students) directly from a reading passage text, or from the learning materials. Factual questions (also called *factoid* questions or *literal* questions) are 'based on the text', or on the 'facts in the text', they *"ask a learner to repeat or recognize some information exactly as it was presented in instruction"* (Andre 1979). Factual questions, of course, do not presuppose any specific text type or type of content, and can be asked about any

---

[4] In the simplest case, student-supplied response must match the answer-key exactly. With some relaxation, misspellings, synonyms, and paraphrases might be acceptable. In the general case, automatic scoring of short student responses to open-ended items (also known as *constructed responses*) is a whole separate area of research (Bai and Stede 2022).

[5] This is possibly so due to their popular applications. Cloze MCQs are widely used in educational applications, open interrogative-form questions have found a novel kind of use: they are utilized in computational linguistics for training automatic question answering systems (Rajpurkar et al. 2016; Hermann et al. 2015).

text, including works of fiction (*What was the name of Harry Potter's owl?*). The notion of factual questions does have some nuances, though. In educational literature this notion is often invoked in question classifications that distinguish between factual questions and higher-order questions, which include inferential, interpretative, and evaluative questions. **Interpretative questions** require the respondent to provide a certain (subjective) interpretation of a text, and there can be multiple correct answers, although they need to be supported by some textual evidence. **Evaluative questions** require the respondent to form an evaluation and offer an opinion, which can be very subjective. In contrast to those, factual questions are considered to be objective, having the following attributes: (a) the answer is in the text, (b) there is only one correct answer, (c) people (teachers/students, etc.) usually can agree on the correct answer, although the answer might be phrased in different ways.

Inferential questions require the respondent to make some inferences from the text, in order to answer the question correctly. However, unlike interpretive questions, for inferential questions the answer is not supposed to be subjective, and there should be a consensus as to where the answer is inferable from the text, or on which statements it is based. In educational applications, inferential questions are used to measure reading comprehension (Day and Park 2005), because the correct answer is not directly found in the text. The notion of inferential questions can be quite broad and can mean different things in different contexts. In some cases, inference implies connecting separate statements in a text, even simply resolving anaphoric pronouns. In other cases, it can be a summative generalization, like *Why does salt cause ice to melt?* → *chemical reaction*. For example, in most settings, anaphora resolution would not be considered an inference, but rather a normal part of human text-comprehension. But when working with struggling readers in elementary school, even anaphora resolution can be considered as a kind of inference that needs special treatment (Mesmer and Rose-McCully 2017). So, what counts as an inferential question rather than simply factual? If an AQG process involves anaphora resolution, or coreference resolution, are the resulting questions then factual or inferential? What about cases when original words from the text are substituted with synonyms or some other means of paraphrase? Is the resulting question a factual question (technically, after paraphrase, the answer is not verbatim in the text) or is it an inference question? The proper label depends on what is considered as inference for the intended application of questions. A question can be considered as factual if the answer can be wholly found in the content of a text, even in a somewhat modified form. In computational linguistics, a large amount of research has revolved around the notion of how to accurately retrieve information and also automatically answer questions from texts and data sets that do not repeat the query verbatim. Answering questions as well as generating questions, often involves use of information or knowledge that is not verbatim in the text, and using knowledge and abilities that are not part of the text (Dunietz et al. 2020). Consider the following mini-example:

2.5 Factual Questions

Text: Mr. X is married to Mrs. X. Mrs. X is the heiress of a large fortune. Question: Whose wife owns a large fortune?

The relationships between 'marriage' and 'wife', and between 'heiress' and 'own', are not in the text but are normally considered part of the background knowledge that most people have. Under tacit default assumptions, this question is factual, while some may consider it mildly inferential. Whether an AQG system can generate such questions from text depends on the knowledge that the system is equipped with, either explicitly, as in older AQG systems, or implicitly, via training, as in modern neural AQG systems. A lot of valuable AQG research is focused on dealing with informational texts (e.g. Wikipedia articles) and generating factual questions. It should be useful to keep in mind that the designation of questions as factual or inferential depends on the intended use of the questions and the often-tacit assumption as to what level of comprehension is presumed as relevant for the intended audience of the questions. Although the notions of *factual information* and *factual questions* pertain to information that is directly and explicitly stated (e.g. in a text), this should not be taken as a clear-cut definition. In many cases what is taken as factual statements may involve some inference and reasoning, such as reference resolution, paraphrase, and integration of general or specific knowledge.

As noted above, some questions require inference and reasoning. There are various types of inferences, and the amount of required reasoning can vary greatly. For some questions we can barely notice that they involve inference (like the wife/married example above). For other questions considerable knowledge and deductive skills might be needed. This is of course well known to educators. But the need to integrate reasoning with questions has also attracted researchers in computational linguistics. Researchers in the field of automated question answering have long noted that in order to enable their systems to answer some questions, systems need to be able to reason and infer from diverse information (Mavi et al. 2023). One particular distinction that has attracted researchers is how many inferences are needed and how many sources for information are involved. In computational linguistics this is known as **multi-hop** question answering, where 'hops' are the presumed number of inference steps. A question is considered as multi-hop (or multi-step) if intermediate information or conclusions are needed before reaching the final answer. Mavi et al. (2023) provide several examples that demonstrate different types of multi-step reasoning for questions. A question like '*Which country has won more soccer world cups—Argentina or Brazil?*', requires finding the number for each country and then comparing them. A question like '*Who is the only person to win an Olympic medal and a Nobel prize?*' may call for intersecting two specific lists of medal winners. Another distinction is where the relevant information comes from. Sometimes the relevant information for inference belongs to what we call 'common sense' or general knowledge. Some inference questions, for example in reading comprehension, can be answered by integrating information from different places in the same document. Finally, some inference questions require integrating information from multiple sources—different documents, books, databases etc.

2.6 Open-Ended Questions

Another important contrast in research on questions is the distinction between close-ended and **open-ended questions**. This contrast may seem as a very simple one. Close-ended questions are often portrayed as questions for which the number of correct-response options is strictly limited; the ultimate case being questions with a simple yes/no answer. Multiple-choice questions are technically also close-ended as the number of response options is prespecified. Many open-response questions are close-ended in the sense that the kind of a valid response is 'closed'; for example, questions such as '*What is your name?*' or '*What is the capital of France?*'. Intuitively, we may feel that there is only one kind of correct response to such questions. While that is often true, it is not always the case. For example, for '*What is your name?*', instead of giving a specific name, a valid answer (in some circumstances) could be "the same as the name of your aunt". Similarly, "the largest city on the Seine river" might be an acceptable answer for the capital-of-France question. This is not a mere sophistry. Even when the expected type of valid answer is more-or-less obvious, there is often a large variety of ways in which it can be expressed, including coreferences and paraphrases. In fact, detection of equivalent responses is a major topic of research for automatic scoring of short student responses (Bai and Stede 2022).

The notion of open-ended responses extends well beyond what is outlined above. Factual questions with an obvious outline for a valid answer are just a part of the very diverse universe of open-ended questions. In educational settings, factual open-ended questions are typically used for assessing student knowledge on particular topics, but they can vary from very specific to more encompassing (e.g., *What were the major factors for the French Revolution in 1789?*). Interpretative questions and evaluative questions are open-ended questions that call for rather lengthy responses with no predefined valid answer. Open-ended questions are used in educational settings as topics for essays (e.g., *What did you do on your summer vacation?*; *What is your favorite book?*) and as setters for discussions in class (e.g., *Should uniforms be mandatory in schools?*) (Dillon 1982). They are intended to elicit from respondents more of their own information and from their own point of view (Godfrey 2001). They are often intended to promote student learning and deeper thinking (Wilkinson and Son 2009; Newton 2013). Worley (2015) has noted that the intended use of questions distinguishes between questions that are primarily used for testing specific knowledge, and questions that are intended to elicit longer responses. According to Worley, even some close-ended questions can and often are used for elicitation of long responses and debates, while seemingly asking for a restricted type of answer. Beyond educational settings, open-ended questions are widely used for generating ideas and for collecting opinions, such as in surveys, brainstorming sessions, and in public opinion polls (Neuert et al. 2021).

2.7 Questions—Depth and Difficulty

Researchers in education have long been concerned with levels of difficulty or complexity of questions—what difficulty they pose to students. Distinctions between question levels are usually designed to correspond to the levels of some hierarchical taxonomy of cognitive skills, strategies, and processing mechanisms necessary for knowledge or comprehension (Carrier and Fautsch-Patridge 1981). The levels of cognitive complexity may range from simple forms (e.g., factual recall from text) to more complex forms (integration of information across a text and analysis of the content).

Bloom's taxonomy is a framework for categorizing educational goals—objectives of student learning, what students need to learn from a given program or instructional activity. The full taxonomy includes three domains: cognitive, affective, and psychomotor. The most famous and most influential of them is Bloom's taxonomy for the cognitive domain (Bloom et al. 1956). It proposed six general cognitive processes in which a human learner may engage, or abilities that a learner can demonstrate. The six abilities are organized hierarchically with increasing sophistication or complexity from level to level (see Table 2.6). The most basic level of the taxonomy is knowledge. As described by Scully (2017), *"Within any subject area, a learner can possess mere knowledge, and may demonstrate the ability to recall this learned knowledge in an assessment."* Each subsequent level is considered to be a higher level of thinking and reasoning. It has been often assumed that a learner must master the lower levels before moving on to the higher levels (Krathwohl 2002; Scully 2017). Bloom's taxonomy has been formally revised (Anderson et al. 2001), to address some shortcomings of the original, and to adjust it to new developments in cognitive psychology. One of the most important changes was changing the level labels from nouns to verbs, to emphasize the skills as actions and processes (Krathwohl 2002; Scully 2017).

In addition to being a framework for describing learning objectives and the progression in which materials might be taught, Bloom's taxonomy is also seen as framework of describing assessment. It is sometimes used by teachers and instructors to classify curricular objectives and test items, including questions, to define their relative level of complexity (Krathwohl 2002; Crowe et al. 2008; Scully 2017). Questions corresponding to deeper/higher levels on the taxonomy are likely to require higher-order reading abilities or cognitive skills. Given the utility of Bloom's taxonomy for classifying educational assessments (questions and test items), there has been some research on automatically classifying questions into levels of Bloom's taxonomy (Wang et al. 2021; Mohammed and Omar 2020). For a review of studies on automated evaluation of question difficulty,

Table 2.6 Bloom's original and revised taxonomies of cognitive aspects of educational objectives

	Original Bloom's taxonomy		Revised taxonomy	
	Level	Description	Level	Description
1	Knowledge	Recall or recognition of learned knowledge (without necessarily having the ability to apply this knowledge)	Remember	Retrieving relevant knowledge from long-term memory
2	Comprehension	Describing and explaining learned knowledge	Understand	Determining the meaning of instructional messages, including oral, written and graphic communication
3	Application	Using learned knowledge to solve problems in new contexts	Apply	Carrying out or using a procedure in a given situation
4	Analysis	Using learned knowledge to decompose situations into components, recognize unstated assumptions and identify motives	Analyze	Breaking material into its constituent parts, detecting how the parts relate to one another and to an overall structure or purpose
5	Synthesis	Combining elements of learned knowledge into new integrated wholes	Evaluate	Making judgments based on criteria and standards
6	Evaluation	Critiquing or judging the value or worth of learned knowledge	Create	Putting elements together to form a novel whole

Levels 1–6 are in increasing level of complexity. Levels 5 and 6 were switched in the revised taxonomy. (Adapted from Krathwohl 2002 and from Scully 2017)

see Benedetto et al. (2023). However, classifying questions to levels just by their content can be problematic, as exemplified by Huang and He (2016): "*given a sentence that states an explicit causal relationship (e.g., it is dark because it is raining), a deep question (e.g., why is it dark) that merely rearranges the words from the sentence, can be answered correctly by matching the surface words.*" While understating causal relations may require considerable cognitive effort, recognizing a mention of a causal relation in a text might be a much less sophisticated skill. Research in automated question generation is not yet fully guided by levels of Bloom's taxonomy, but there is much appetite for questions to target higher-order thinking and not just factual recall (Gao et al. 2022; Ko et al. 2020; Labutov et al. 2015).

2.8 Summary

Questions come in different types and forms. On the side of form, natural languages have many different interrogative forms, most commonly yes/no and wh-questions. In addition, questions in speech can be posed by using declarative forms with different intonation. Questions can also be presented in declarative form as fill-in-the-blanks format. Question can also be open-ended or they can present response options (multiple-choice). Multiple choice questions typically have one key (answer) and several distractors.

There are many typologies of questions, analyzing them from semantic, pragmatic, and other aspects. One important type of questions are factual questions, questions about what explicitly is asserted in a text. Other types in this line of typology are inferential, interpretative, and evaluative. Factual and inferential questions are most widely used in AQG. Inferential questions may involve various types of reasoning and multiple steps of inference. The notion of open-endedness may also refer to how much restricted is the expected answer and may depend on the pragmatics of question use. Another way to consider questions is by the level of difficulty they might pose to respondents. Bloom's taxonomy is a common framework for categorizing levels of educational complexity, and it is often applied to categorizing questions by cognitive aspects of content.

Evaluation Methods for AQG

3.1 Introduction

This chapter introduces methods for evaluation of automatic question generation. There are two reasons for presenting evaluation before we discuss AQG techniques. First, we will mention evaluation results when we present the various AQG methods in subsequent chapters, so familiarity with evaluation methods will be needed. Second, evaluation methods involve not only strict methodology; they highlight the more general approaches toward what is important, what are the valued outcomes in the generation process. It may be useful to become acquainted with this variety before we delve into the specific generation methods. In this chapter we describe common human-based intrinsic evaluation methods, common intrinsic automated evaluation methods, and some approaches to extrinsic evaluation of AQG.

A classic distinction in evaluation of NLP systems is that between intrinsic and extrinsic evaluations. According to Galliers and Sparck Jones (1993, p. 22), *"Intrinsic criteria are those relating to a system's objective, extrinsic criteria those relating to its function i.e., to its role in relation to its setup's purpose."*

An intrinsic evaluation of an NLP process or component estimates the quality of the outputs of the process. In the case of AQG, an intrinsic evaluation asks whether the AQG system was able to generate any questions, what was the quality of the questions (are they grammatical, are they related to the content of the input, etc.). An extrinsic evaluation estimates the impact of the NLP component in the broader task in which it is used, and in the case of AQG—are the generated questions useful for their intended purpose.

The relations between intrinsic and extrinsic evaluations of a given system may be more complex than expected. If an intrinsic evaluation indicates that the outputs (questions) are quite problematic, one might expect that the extrinsic value of such questions would also be considered as inadequate. However, for some uses (e.g., training question-answering systems), even so-so quality autogenerated questions might be useful (Duan et al. 2017). On the other hand, a system that generates good quality questions (as rated in an intrinsic evaluation), might still be considered problematic in extrinsic evaluations, depending on the criteria used in the extrinsic evaluations (for example: questions are too simple, or not enough variety is produced). The evaluation criteria usually depend on the specific task, reflecting the variety of goals defined by researchers or users.

3.2 Human Intrinsic Evaluation

The most fundamental evaluation of AQG has been direct human evaluation of the outputs of AQG systems, i.e. by reading and evaluating the produced questions. The earliest proposals for human evaluation of generated questions laid the groundwork for all later uses of such approaches (Rus et al. 2010, 2012; Boyer and Piwek 2010; Heilman and Smith 2010b). The underlying idea of such evaluations is that every generated question or item must be separately judged about its quality. The rating is performed by a human annotator/rater. It is often tacitly presumed that the human rater must be a native speaker of the language in which the texts (and questions) are written. Sometimes, a suitable level of education is also expected for question raters. In some case the human evaluators need to be experts in the content domain for which questions are generated (e.g. questions about medical procedures). However, in many cases human evaluators are just ordinary people, enlisted via crowdsourcing platforms. Wong et al. (2021) have noted a considerable shift in human evaluation practices of natural language generation (NLG[1]). One aspect is annotator diversity. Before crowdsourcing became commonplace, NLG data were typically evaluated by graduate students, following detailed guidelines. In recent times crowdsourcing evaluations became ubiquitous, since they are often cheaper and allow unprecedented scalability. However crowd workers come with considerable cultural and training variances, and their command of the target language may vary greatly. Methodologies have been developed to mitigate potential influences of such variability, such as limiting the crowdworkers to certain groups, prescreening language proficiency, and prescreening work accuracy with pilot tasks. Another shift in NLG evaluations is task diversity (Wong et al. 2021)—the generation tasks become more diverse and specialized, and evaluations become more sophisticated and more complex. Similarly in the domain of AQG, the diversity of AQG applications has led to a variety of evaluation criteria.

The classic human-based evaluation of AQG involves rating each generated question along several traits, or dimensions. The ratings are usually numeric, expressed on Likert scale with three (1–3) or five (1–5) discrete points, often with higher values for better rated questions. However sometimes the evaluation scale is just a binary yes/no (Amidei et al. 2018a). The typical dimensions of AQG evaluation are:

---

[1] Within computational linguistics, AQG is considered a proper subfield of NLG.

3.2 Human Intrinsic Evaluation

Grammar: Does the question seem syntactically correct? is it grammatically well-formed?
Semantics: Does the question make sense, semantically? (within the question itself, and also with respect to the text on which the question is drawn.)
Relevance: Does the question seem relevant to the source? (even well-formed and semantically adequate questions might be not quite relevant to the given text.).

Those dimensions were originally oriented for factoid questions generated from informational texts, which were the main focus of early AQG research. In later research additional dimensions were added, which may sometimes complement or even replace some of the dimensions above. The additional dimensions are:

Answerability: is the question answerable from the text? Answerability might be compromised by different factors—being ill-formed, nonsensical, irrelevant, or maybe the answer is simply not stated in the text.
Fluency: Does the question seem fluent and natural, or does it seem awkward and unnatural? (Even grammatical and sensible questions might be posed in awkward ways).
Interestingness (or inquisitiveness). Does the question show inquisitiveness to learn more about the topic? This type of evaluation does not apply to factual questions, but is geared for questions that are supposed to promote interest in a text or engagement with a topic.

The rating dimensions in human-evaluation studies sometimes use similar labels for related but non-identical criteria, and in some cases use different labels for rather similar criteria (e.g. grammatical correctness and fluency). Sometimes a dimension (aspect) of evaluation includes multiple and complex criteria. For example, Chali and Hasan (2015) used two dimensions for AQG evaluation, topic relevance and syntactic correctness, each on a 5-point scale. For topic relevance, the criteria included: (a) *Semantic correctness*—is the question meaningful and related to the topic? (b) *Correctness of question type*—is a correct question word used? and (c) *Referential clarity*—is it clearly possible to understand what the question refers to? On the other hand, their dimension of syntactic correctness asked just to what extent a question seems grammatically correct. One might consider that their second dimension was rather simple, while the first one was overloaded and overly complex.

The context in which an evaluation is performed can also be varied. Lindberg et al. (2013) enlisted an education expert to evaluate automatically generated questions (from educational texts), with binary judgments for grammaticality, semantic validity, vagueness, answerability, and learning value. Two different judgments of answerability were employed: (a) is the question answerable from the source sentence from which it was generated; and (b) is the question answerable given the whole source document. Only

14% of the questions were rated as answerable from the sentence, while 20% of the same questions were marked as answerable in context of the document.

Amidei et al. (2018b) presented an extensive review of evaluation approaches for AQG. They have collected a list of different evaluation aspects that were used in studies with human evaluation of AQG outputs, including labels such as *naturalness, clarity, coherence, importance,* and *specificity*. Some such dimensions stem from the intended use of generated questions. For example, question clarity might be a relevant aspect for educational purposes (for students), but much less so when generated questions are used to train a question-answering system.

3.3 Comparing AQG to Human-Produced Questions

Instead of rating generated questions, a different type of evaluation is to compare automatically-generated questions to human-authored questions. The idea is that if they are not well-distinguishable, that may give credit to the quality of AQG. This presumes that human-authored questions are of good quality, which might not always be the case, for example when questions are authored via a crowdsourcing effort.

Person and Graesser (2002) devised a Bystander Turing Test (BTT), for the purpose of a holistic evaluation of their Intelligent Tutoring System (ITS). The original Turing test states that an evaluator must decide whether they are conversing with a human or a computer, solely from the responses a system gives to the interrogator. In a BTT, the evaluator is not a participant in a dialog. Evaluators read a transcript of a tutorial dialog of human student and a tutor, and need to decide whether particular dialog moves were made by a human tutor or a computer. Note that with the technology available at that time, computer responses were not entirely generated by the system, rather *"the dialog move generator selects one or a combination of pedagogically appropriate dialog moves from the curriculum script."* Some dialogs included human-authored dialog moves. Evaluation responses were given on a Likert scale from 1 (definitely human) to 6 (definitely computer). Person and Graesser have shown that college students could not discriminate whether particular dialog moves in tutoring transcripts were generated by the AutoTutor intelligent tutoring system (ITS) or by skilled human tutors. They concluded that the results were compelling evidence that *"AutoTutor's dialog move selections are on par with those of human tutors."* This kind of evaluation can provide elegant holistic evidence for the quality of computer outputs for materials that are typically routinely created by humans.

A similar kind of evaluation was adopted in several studies of AQG. The general outlook is that if human evaluators cannot distinguish computer-generated questions from human-generated questions, then computer-generated questions are probably pretty good. Liu et al. (2012) had an AQG system generate questions from student academic practice-essays. The questions were compared to questions manually prepared by the tutor and lecturer of the academic course, for the same essays. Students who wrote the essays were

3.3 Comparing AQG to Human-Produced Questions

shown human-written and auto-generated questions and were asked to state whether a question was written by the tutor, the lecturer, or an AQG system. Participants' average performance on the classification achieved F1 scores of 0.18, 0.24 and 0.43 respectively.[2] The authors interpreted this as *"writers found it moderately difficult to distinguish between questions generated by humans and automatically generated questions."*

Establishing that automatically-generated questions are (almost) indistinguishable from human-generated questions is not, by itself, a guarantee for the quality of the questions, or their adequacy for the task that the questions are supposed to support. In the limiting case, one could compare bad AQG outputs with bad human-composed questions, and still conclude that AQG outputs are on a par with human-sourced ones. The logic of the human-vs-AQG evaluation relies on the assumption that the human-generated questions are of good or adequate quality by design. Such presumption is often supported by having the human-generated questions prepared by educational experts (or other task-specific experts) with relevant knowledge and good command of the subject domain. Such experts are often teachers, lecturers, tutors, or other educational experts. If we presume that the human-written questions are quality questions, then establishing that computer-generated questions are on a par with human written questions provides good evidence for the quality of AQG. Instead of presuming the quality of human-constructed questions, they can be explicitly evaluated, just as the automatically-generated questions are. The common approach in AQG studies is to evaluate all questions on aspects of well-formedness (grammaticality), and also semantic fit and/or appropriateness for the task. Note that well-formedness can often be judged by native speakers of the language involved. Some aspects of semantic fit and relevance can also require just good command of the language (and understanding of the context, e.g. the source text). However, some other aspects of semantic fit, relevance and appropriateness for the task may depend on the task itself and may require (that evaluators have) expertise in the given task or knowledge domain.

Chinkina and Meurers (2017) evaluated a syntax-driven AQG system that was designed to produce grammar-oriented questions for English language learners, based on snippets from source-texts. Evaluation involved a comparison with questions of the same type that were written by a human educational expert. The goal of the evaluation was to find out whether computer-generated questions were on a par with human-written ones. Evaluation was performed by crowdsource workers, who were thoroughly selected on being well-proficient speakers of English and passing an accuracy test threshold of 70%. The evaluators were shown the source-text-snippet and the question being evaluated. The evaluation involved three aspects. Two aspects of the questions were selected: (1) well-formedness—whether a question is written in acceptable English form; and (2) whether a question can be answered from the information in the source text. Each of these were scored on a 5-point Likert scale. In addition, evaluators were asked also who, in their opinion, wrote the question— human or computer (binary choice). It turned out that 74%

---

[2] F1 scores are explained in Sect. 3.5.

of human written and 67% of computer-generated questions were thought to be written by an English teacher.

3.4 Rater Agreement

As with many human annotation tasks in computational linguistics, inter-rater agreement[3] is often needed to assess the quality of annotations, or at least their consistency/reliability (Artstein and Poesio 2008). Not many studies with human evaluation of AQG report inter-rater agreement. The simplest measure is percentage of rater agreement (in how many cases raters assigned the same score), which is also the easiest metric to comprehend. A problem with simple agreement percentage is that it does not account for chance agreement. Measures that do account for chance agreement include Cohen's Kappa (Cohen 1960) and, for multiple raters, Fleiss Kappa (Fleiss 1971) and Krippendorf alpha (Hayes and Krippendorff 2007); for a tutorial, see Hallgren (2012). For ratings on interval scales, such as Likert scales, Quadratic Weighted Kappa (QWK) (Cohen 1968) can be suitable as it emphasizes closer ratings and more strongly penalizes discrepant ratings. All kappa statistics values have a range of -1.0 to 1.0.

The interpretation of the goodness of agreement for kappa values typically follows the guidelines proposed by Landis and Koch (1977). According to Landis and Koch, Kappa values below 0.0 indicate poor agreement, values in the range 0.0–0.20 indicate slight agreement, values between 0.21 and 0.40 indicate fair agreement, values between 0.41 and 0.60 indicate moderate agreement, values from 0.61 to 0.80 are substantial agreement, and 0.81–1.0 is near perfect agreement. It has been suggested that kappa values above 0.67 are needed for adequate reliability (cited by Hallgren 2012), however Artstein and Poesio (2008) claim that the minimal acceptable agreement should be 0.8. Amidei et al. (2018a) noted that in NLG studies, the human evaluation agreement is often below 0.6 and stronger agreement is difficult to obtain. For discussion of inter-rater agreement in NLP see Artstein and Poesio (2008) and Wong et al. (2021), for a comprehensive general treatment see Gwet (2014).

Godwin and Piwek (2016) described an interactive process where evaluators discuss their opinions about the criteria they used for evaluation of automatically generated questions, in order to reach better consensus. They reported that such a method can boost agreement up to 0.9. However, this type of process is time consuming and not suitable for crowdsourcing evaluations where raters work on their own, in their own time.

Flor and Riordan (2018) have demonstrated that quite high inter-rater reliability can be achieved for AQG evaluations with traditional dimensions of grammar, semantics, and relevance. They had 1060 automatically generated questions rated by two trained annotators. The annotators were given the full texts and the generated questions. Ratings for

---

[3] Inter-rater agreement is also often called inter-rater reliability (IRR) or inter-annotator agreement (IAA).

grammar and semantics used 5-point scales, while rating of relevance used a 4-point scale. The inter-annotator agreement levels were substantial: QWK = 0.75 for grammar, and QWK = 0.77 for semantics. The agreement value for relevance was only moderate, QWK = 0.48. They noted that lower agreement on relevance stemmed from the tendency of one of the annotators to lower the relevance rating when a question was syntactically and/or semantically ill-formed. This case indicates that human ratings on supposedly separate dimensions might be correlated, because when generated questions are considerably ill-formed, it may impair their interpretation and scores on other dimensions.

Amidei et al. (2018a) describe some of the reasons for disagreements in human evaluations of generated questions. One source of differences are preferences for style. Given the question *Jean De Rely's illustrated French-language scriptures were first published in what city?*, which adheres to American English, British annotators deemed it less fluent, and preferred *which city* instead of *what city*. In another case, an evaluator judged the question *The adaptive immune system must distinguish between what types of molecules?* as less fluent, because he preferred the reversed 'standard' word order: *Which types of molecules must the adaptive immune system distinguish between?* Another source of differences is background knowledge of the evaluator. For example, a question *How many Time incarnations can a Lord have?* might seem nonsensical or incomprehensible, unless one knows that it refers to the *Doctor Who* television program. Individual differences in interpretation and inference may also lead to evaluation disagreements. In Amidei et al. (2018a) study, one of the texts said that early French-language scriptures *"were printed in Paris"*. An automatically generated question was *"...French-language scriptures were first published in what city?"* One of the annotators disagreed on whether the question is answerable from the text, because place of printing and place of publishing might not be the same. Such sources of disagreement may influence the outcomes of evaluation studies in addition to factors such as the number of categories used in the annotation, the use of experts vs. non-experts, and evaluators' training, motivation, and attention. Amidei et al. (2018a) even suggested that striving for very high agreement levels in NLG (and AQG) evaluations might be counterproductive, because it runs counter to the variability and diversity of human language.

3.5 Automated Metrics for AQG Evaluation

Kalady et al. (2010) presented one of the first uses of information retrieval (IR) metrics for QG evaluation. This methodology is applicable if a large quantity of questions is available for the given corpus of text. The idea for evaluation is then to assess how many of such human-authored questions were replicated by the AQG system. The classic measures for information retrieval are Precision, Recall and the F1 score (Van Rijsbergen 1979). They are defined as follows.

- **Precision.** For IR, precision is the amount of correctly retrieved documents out of the total amount of retrieved documents. For AQG: the number of generated questions that replicate manually authored questions, divided by the total amount of AQG generated questions.
- **Recall.** For IR, recall is the amount of correctly retrieved documents out of the total amount of *relevant* documents that should be retrieved. For QG: the number of generated questions that replicate manually authored questions, divided by the total amount of *manually* generated (reference) questions.
- **F1 measure.** The F1 score is a harmonic mean of precision and recall. The standard widely used form is:

$$F1 = 2 \times \frac{\text{Precision} \times \text{Recall}}{\text{Precision} + \text{Recall}}$$

For a review of the F1 measure and its variants see Christen et al. (2023). Note that Precision, Recall, and the F1 measure, take values in the range 0–1. However, for convenience, their values are often presented on a 0–100 scale, since precision and recall can be interpreted as percent values.

In the limiting case, when no prior questions are available, it is possible to ask independent judges to generate all possible questions for the (reasonably small) corpus of texts under investigation. For their corpus of twenty sentences, with questions generated by judges, Kalady et al. obtained Precision of 0.46, Recall of 0.68, and F1 score of 0.55 for their syntax-driven AQG system. That early study already noted one of the problems with IR-based approach to AQG evaluation: for the same texts, an AQG system often generates many more questions than human authors. Some of those questions might be good and valid, but having no counterparts among the human-generated questions, some automatically generated questions will not be counted as hits. This might lead to underestimating the quality of the AQG system output.

A related issue is this: how do we ensure that human authors generate many possible questions for a given set of texts? This may strongly depend on the instructions given to the human authors. One potential solution to this issue is crowdsourcing the question-generation task—with lots of people involved a greater variety of questions can be expected. This indeed has led to creation of large-scale textual resources annotated with lots of different questions, such as the SQuAD data set (Rajpurkar et al. 2016). Although such resources were not produced directly for the purpose of evaluating AQG systems (but rather for evaluating question-answering systems), their utility for evaluating AQG was obvious. We will come back to this aspect in Chap. 6.

Automated evaluation of AQG systems is a very appealing proposition, as it promises to handle three major aspects: it is very quick (unlike the time-consuming human evaluation), cheap (no need to hire expensive annotators or pay the crowdsourcing agencies), and hassle-free (no need to train evaluators and monitor the quality of their work). In

3.5 Automated Metrics for AQG Evaluation

addition, automated evaluation is very stable, in the sense that rerunning the same evaluation code on the same input data would produce the same results again, which is not always the case for evaluations carried out manually by human raters. Historically, automated evaluation of AQG has borrowed from automated evaluation of other NLG tasks, specifically machine translation and automatic summarization.[4] Presently, we may distinguish two waves of automatic evaluation approaches to AQG. The first wave began approximately in 2017, adopting and extending the classic metrics of automated evaluation, such as BLEU and ROUGE. The second wave began in 2020, with the introduction of deep-learning based evaluation metrics, such as BERTScore (Zhang et al. 2020).

Automated evaluation in NLG presupposes comparison and thus carries a basic requirement—one must have data (reference materials, also called *ground-truth* or *gold standard*) against which the outputs generated by a system would be compared. The idea of automated evaluation is to compare how close, on average, are the system outputs to the outputs produced by humans. The comparisons are usually defined in terms of some metric that defines how to measure the similarities or differences between the NLG system output and the standard materials. The evaluation takes the reference and NLG output and computes a score on how well the NLG output matches the reference. In the case of machine translation, the reference materials are human-produced gold-standard translations of the relevant texts. In the case of automated summarization, the reference materials are text summaries produced by human experts. For evaluation of AQG, the reference materials are questions produced by human authors for the texts under investigation.

In the following sections we present some of the most popular metrics for NLG evaluation that have been adopted in AQG research. For a recent overview of automated evaluation metrics for machine translation see Lee et al. (2023). For surveys of automated evaluation methods of NLG, see Celikyilmaz et al. (2020), section. 7 in Gatt and Krahmer (2018), as well as section. 7 in Dong et al. (2022). For a critical appraisal of NLG evaluation see van der Lee et al. (2021), van Miltenburg et al. (2021), Howcroft et al. (2020).

BLEU (BiLingual Evaluation Understudy) was first proposed by Papineni et al. (2002) for evaluation of machine translation. The BLEU measures how similar is the generated text to one or more reference texts, by counting word overlaps. The BLEU metric uses exact n-gram matches between NLG outputs and reference materials. For a given value of n, BLEU computes the fraction of n-grams in the generated text which match the n-grams in the reference text. BLEU score is calculated as the ratio of reference-shared n-grams to the total number of NLG output n-grams (thus it is oriented to measure precision). A final BLEU score is computed as the geometric mean of the n-gram scores obtained by varying the number of words in n-grams from 1 to n, where n is usually 3 or 4. It

---

[4] As noted by Gatt and Krahmer (2018), many NLG tasks use evaluation of generated output against reference materials, including machine translation, text summarization, text simplification (text-to-text tasks), AQG, image captioning. and data-to-descriptive-text generation.

also has a brevity penalty to penalize outputs that are too short (relative to the length of reference text). In some papers, BLEU metric is reported with a numeric index, indicating the largest value of n used, e.g. BLUE-4. A special variant, BLEU-1, simply measures the proportion of shared single words. This variant is useful for evaluating very short outputs. BLEU scores are usually computed at the sentence level. BLEU scores take values between 0 (no match) and 1 (perfect match), and sometimes they are reported on the scale 0–100.

BLEU has several important advantages. Most important, BLEU can be computed quickly. This is important when multiple evaluations are computed or when BLEU scores are used to tune a learning system. A second advantage is that BLEU is language-independent, i.e. it can be computed for data in almost any natural language, with the only caveat that text segmentation into words (tokenization) may vary. BLEU is also resource-independent—it needs only reference data and a segmentation routine; it does not use any lexical or other resources. This contributes greatly to its simplicity. Another advantage of BLEU is that it can be computed with multiple reference texts (more than a single reference translation or more than one original question).

NIST. The NIST metric (Doddington 2002) also calculates the relative overlap of n-grams between NLG output and reference data. Unlike BLEU, NIST computes the arithmetic mean of n-gram overlaps. Additionally, instead of weighting each n-gram equally, NIST gives more weight to n-grams that have a lower frequency in a corpus (rare n-grams), which might be more informative pieces. The corpus for estimating n-gram probabilities can be the reference data itself, or a larger corpus of texts. The latter option can make it difficult to compare results from different studies that use different estimation corpora.

The **ROUGE** metric (Recall-Oriented Understudy for Gisting Evaluation) was proposed by Lin (2004) for evaluation of automatic summarization systems. ROUGE measures the similarity between the generated and reference summaries with a focus on the recall score. The ROUGE approach has several variants. ROUGE-N measures the n-gram overlap statistics; ROUGE-S measures the skip-bigram overlap; ROUGE-L measures the longest common subsequence; ROUGE-W measures the weighted longest common subsequence. ROUGE has the same advantages as BLEU: it is quick and is resource and language independent (except for text segmentation).

The **METEOR** metric (Metric for Evaluation of Translation with Explicit ORdering) is another approach for automatic evaluation of machine translation (Lavie and Agarwal 2007; Banerjee and Lavie 2005). It considers both the similarity of the generated text to reference text and the similarity of the reference text to the generated text. Thus, it is symmetric (at least in principle), as it combines both precision and recall. The METEOR score is the harmonic mean of the precision and recall, calculated based over weighted n-gram matches. While the classic BLEU considers only exact matches, METEOR also uses matches with stemmed words, synonyms, and paraphrases. Note that for stemming, obtaining synonyms and paraphrases, different lexical resources might be used, and this, may make METEOR a less stable metric, as the resources for those enhancements may

3.5 Automated Metrics for AQG Evaluation

vary. METEOR also gives different weights to function words and content words. It also penalizes for gaps and differences in word order. METEOR is a parametric metric, its parameters are a) fragmentation penalty, b) weights of different matches (exact, stemmed, synonyms, paraphrases), and c) weights of function and content words.

Metrics like BLEU and ROUGE presume that good NLG outputs should have significant word overlap with the reference data. In many cases this is a too-strong assumption that tends to underestimate the quality of outputs—even outputs that are not similar to reference data can be good and valid outputs. Such productions are not recognized by BLEU and ROUGE, while METEOR, tries to address this issue, at the expense of much more complicated procedure and dependence on resources.

Numerous studies have indicated that metrics like BLEU and ROUGE often have poor correlation with human judgments, for machine translation (Callison-Burch et al. 2006), automated summarization (Graham 2015) and for other areas of NLG (Reiter and Belz 2009; Liu et al. 2016). Some modifications have been proposed for the BLEU metric (Galley et al. 2015; Chen and Cherry 2014), but not widely adopted. Reiter (2018a) discusses the validity of the BLEU metric, suggesting that it can be useful for diagnostic/indicative purposes, but not for validity claims. Despite those shortcomings, BLEU and ROUGE remain popular in NLG evaluation in general and in AQG evaluation in particular.

Nema and Khapra (2018) introduced a notion of *answerability* for AQG evaluation. They define a dimension of answerability as the extent that a question is perturbed, i.e. the degree of change that makes the question not answerable and maybe even not recognizable. In other words, how to quantify ill-formedness of generated questions with respect to well-formed questions. They define four types of perturbations: dropping function words from a question, dropping named entities, dropping (some) content words, and changing the question type (changing and dropping the question words). To illustrate their approach, they took human-authored questions from three large question-answering datasets. For each question they automatically applied some such perturbations and gave the results to human evaluators to score how answerable the resulting 'questions' are (on a five-point scale). They further applied the traditional evaluation metrics (BLEU, NIST, ROUGE and METEOR), comparing the original questions and the perturbed results. They then computed correlations between human scores and automated scores for questions, for the different datasets. All correlations were frustratingly low, all Pearson r values were below 0.2, and many lower than 0.1, indicating little correspondence between human estimations and automated estimations. The authors further proposed to incorporate those kinds of perturbations into a new evaluation metric, QBLEU, that could account for occurrence of such perturbations. They proposed a quantitative metric of answerability, that can be linearly combined with a traditional metric. For answerability, they compare a generated question with the reference question, counting separately the numbers of matching and non-matching function words, named entities, content words, and question words. For each type they compute precision and recall scores, and take weighted averages, which are then combined as a harmonic mean. This notion of answerability thus combines both the notion of grammaticality and semantic quality of questions.

The metrics described above compare generated questions to gold-standard questions by using a variety of word-overlap methods. With the advancement of embedding-vector-based methods in NLP and availability of word-embeddings, and since embeddings reflect semantics of words and phrases, a new approach to evaluation is to compare the embeddings of generated and gold-standard questions. The advantage of this type of approach is that matches need not be verbatim, paraphrases and closely related words can be accommodated. This situation is actually just a particular case of a more general problem of semantic similarity matching for sentences. Rus and Lintean (2012) explored this problem by using word-to-word similarity scoring (with LSA vectors[5]), which is then combined to produce a sentence-to-sentence similarity score. Liu et al. (2016) describe several variants of sentence-to-reference evaluation metrics for NLG that utilize static embeddings, such as word2vec (Mikolov et al. 2013) or GloVe (Pennington et al. 2014). The most common method is using embedding average: an average embedding for a sentence is created by averaging the embeddings of individual words (or alternatively, training a neural network to average the embeddings), and then the average embeddings of the generated output and the gold-standard reference are compared by computing the cosine between the embedding vectors. The method is also called 'cosine of bag-of-words embeddings', because naive averaging is not sensitive to word order. If several references are available, the average cosine with the generated output can be used as the metric. The higher the cosine value, the greater is the semantic relatedness between the generated text and the ground truth.

RUBER. Tao et al. (2018) proposed RUBER (Referenced metric and Unreferenced metric Blended Evaluation Routine) for automated evaluation of responses produces by open-domain dialog NLG systems. The dialog situation consists of a user-posed query, a ground-truth reply, and a system-generated reply. In order to evaluate the NLG reply, they proposed to combine two components: the similarity of NLG output to the reference reply (reference metric), and the similarity of the generated reply to the original query (unreferenced metric). To obtain the former, they calculate the cosine similarity between embedding vectors representing the NLG output and the reference sentence. For the unreferenced metric they design a neural network that learns to compare query sentences to the reply sentences. RUBER allows two methods of combining the two scores. RUBER-A takes an arithmetic average, while RUBER-G takes a geometric average. An important aspect of RUBER approach is in using neural representations (pre-trained word2vec embeddings) for comparing the NLG output to the reference data, unlike the BLEU and ROUGE metrics. The RUBER metric has been used in evaluation of AQG for conversational systems (Shen et al. 2021; Wang et al. 2019).

---

[5] Latent Semantic Analysis.

3.5 Automated Metrics for AQG Evaluation

With the development of Transformer architecture of neural networks, several metrics were proposed that incorporate large transformer language models to compute similarity of NLG outputs to gold-standard reference sentences.

BERTscore (Zhang et al. 2020) uses BERT-based contextual embeddings to compute word-to-word similarities. Contextual embeddings *"generate different vector representations for the same word in different sentences depending on the surrounding words"*. Each token in the generated sentence is compared to each token in the reference and the sum of those comparisons represents the 'recall' (how well the generated texts match the reference). In addition, each token in the reference is matched against each token in the generated text, and the sum of those matches represents 'precision'. Unlike Rus and Lintean (2012) who used the arithmetic average of two such scores, BERTscore uses the F1 (harmonic mean) of such values. BERTscore also optionally incorporates importance weighting, with a traditional assumption that matching of rare words can be more important than similarity of more common words. BERTscore uses inverse document frequency (IDF) computed from a separate text corpus. Zhang et al. have demonstrated that BERTScore is one of the best metrics in multiple comparisons for several NLG tasks. Hanna and Bojar (2021) have analyzed the performance of BERTScore. They point out that systems that use large pre-trained language models take advantage of the linguistic capabilities of such models. However, they also pointed out some of shortcomings. For example, representations derived from BERT can be insensitive to negation, named entities and function words. For example, a negation of a sentence might be judged as very similar to the original sentence (Ettinger 2020). If the negation (or a modal verb) is crucial in a comparison, a BERTScore might be inadequate.

MoverScore (Zhao et al. 2019) is another metric for calculating semantic similarity between text segments; it also utilizes contextual embeddings from large language models like BERT. Its major difference from BERTScore is in the method of aggregating word to word similarity. Instead of using greedy calculations like BERTScore, MoverScore tries to optimize word matching by computing the minimum cost of transforming one text into the other—the smaller the score the more similar those texts are.

The evaluation metrics described above use specific fixed calculation methods for computing similarity (such as sum of matches, etc.). Another family of approaches to evaluation metrics proposes to avoid fixed calculation methods and replace them with learned functions. For example, RUSE (Shimanaka et al. 2018) uses regression over sentence embeddings to learn how to compute the similarity between generated text and reference texts. Such learning requires a large dataset with gold-standard scores of similarity (usually assigned by human raters), and is available, for example, in evaluation datasets for machine translation. Notably, such data is rarely available in large quantities for the AQG tasks. Sellam et al. (2020) proposed BLEURT as a general learned metric for NLG tasks. Instead of learning the scoring function from a large collection of human scores (which is rarely available), BLEURT uses a large pre-trained language model (BERT) and learns an approximation to such a function from synthetic data (that can be relatively easily generated), and only after that it fine-tunes the scoring function on a smaller set of task-specific human-produced similarity scores.

Perplexity. Perplexity metric computes the probability of a given sequence of words by using some prior accumulated knowledge, typically a statistical language model. From a different perspective, it is sometimes stated that perplexity quantifies how 'surprised' the model is when it sees a given piece of text. Technically, perplexity metric of a text segment S is the inverse probability of the segment, normalized by the number of words (Jurafsky and Martin 2023, Chap. 3):

$$perplexity(S) = P(w_1, w_2, ...w_N)^{-\frac{1}{N}}$$

where w_1 to w_N are the words in segment S, and N is the word count. The probability of segment S is usually computed with reference to a given language model.

Originally, perplexity was proposed for evaluation of language models, with the rationale *"do language models exhibit the statistical tendencies of human language?"* (Meister and Cotterell 2021). Lower perplexity values indicate better model predictions. Modern neural language models achieve better perplexity values than traditional n-gram language models. If a language model is taken to represent the statistics of the language, then the role of perplexity can be flipped; one can use corpus-based perplexity measure to evaluate texts. Perplexity measure has been proposed to evaluate the grammaticality and fluency of NLG outputs (Vinyals and Le 2015; Niu and Penn 2020), and the performance of grammar error-correction systems (Islam and Magnani 2021). The basic idea is that a grammatically well-formed and fluent output should have lower perplexity value than a non-grammatical or disfluent one. However, it is not yet a well-established measure for fluency and grammaticality, with some studies indicating that it is problematic (Keukeleire et al. 2020). In AQG, perplexity is sometimes used for estimating the relative grammaticality and fluency of generated questions, in lieu of human evaluations (Wang et al. 2018b; Zhao et al. 2018).

Diversity. A measure of diversity is intended to estimate whether the outputs of an NLG system are repetitive and, in a sense, 'non-interesting'. This issue arises especially in the domain of conversational NLG where researchers are interested in developing systems that produce more diverse and interesting responses. Li et al. (2016) have proposed a simple metric for estimating the diversity of NLG outputs. They proposed to compute the degree of diversity by calculating the number of distinct unigrams, bigrams and trigrams in the generated responses. Such value is scaled by the total number of generated tokens, or n-grams, respectively. The resulting metrics are called *distinct-1*, *'distinct-2*, and *distinct-3* correspondingly. Those metrics have been used in some research about conversational AQG, where diversity of outputs is of interest (Shen et al. 2021; Wang et al. 2018b).

Note that this measure targets lexical diversity and is opposed to lexical similarity that is favored by metrics like BLEU and ROUGE. Diversity metrics can be compared between AQG data and reference data, to consider whether AQG data is more, or less diverse than the reference. Even in the absence of reference data, the metric can be used to compare the diversity of outputs of different NLG systems.

Another approach to evaluation of AQG when reference answers are available is to use a round-trip processing with a question-answering system. The basic idea is to feed a text and a generated question to a good-quality automated question-answering system. The resulting answer can be compared to the original answer, using any of the similarity metrics. If the resulting QA answer is quite similar to the original answer, one might consider that the question was good. If the question results in a very dissimilar answer, it might be that the question was rather bad. This indirect approach was used in some studies (Ji et al., 2022; Stasaski et al. 2021; Yuan et al. 2023; Zhang and Bansal 2019) as an additional indicator of quality. This method may not work well if the QA system was trained on different kinds of texts or different kinds of questions than those used in the evaluation.

With the emergence of large language models (LLMs) and generative AI, researchers have turned to LLMs for evaluating the quality of generated questions. Maity and Deroy (2024) proposed to use two LLMs to iteratively score questions generated by an AQG system. The process uses textual descriptions of dimensions/aspects used in human evaluation, such as grammaticality, relevance, and novelty. The question, the question context, and the evaluation rubrics are provided to an LLM and the LLM is prompted to produce initial scores on each aspect, and in addition to find the flaws and strengths in each question. Those results are fed into a second LLM, which uses them to refine the score and update the lists of flaws and strengths. Such feedback process is used iteratively between two LLMs until convergence (scores don't change in subsequent iterations). Evaluation results indicated that such method can achieve results close to human evaluations.

3.6 Extrinsic Evaluations of AQG

For AQG systems that are aimed for educational applications, the obvious extrinsic evaluation is whether automatically generated questions can have any educational use or value. Researchers have made a variety of efforts to estimate educational value of AQG.

Mazidi and Nielsen (2014b) evaluated questions generated by three different AQG systems. They compiled two sets of reading materials, one from social science texts and one from science textbooks, both sets were at middle-school to high-school level. For each AQG system, for each set, 250 questions were randomly selected for evaluation. Questions from all systems were presented to human raters (crowdworkers). Each question was rated on two aspects. A 1–3 point scale (higher is better) was used for grammaticality and clarity, as a linguistic quality evaluation. The raters were also asked whether the question would help them remember or understand the meaning of the sentence (also on a scale 1–3). This aspect was considered as the pedagogical value of the question. Each question was rated by two raters. For each aspect, questions that received a score of 5 or 6 (from the two raters) were considered acceptable. The authors then showed that their AQG system produced acceptable questions at a higher rate than the two other systems, both on linguistic quality and for the pedagogical value. Note that this evaluation did not measure actual pedagogical value of AQG questions, only the subjective opinions of raters.

Zhang and VanLehn (2016) investigated whether machine-generated questions can be as good as human-authored questions for the same content domain. They collected three sets of questions intended for college students in introductory biology classes (specifically for the topic of photosynthesis). One set of questions was collected from the web (the authors conjectured that most of those questions came from students). Another set of questions came from biology textbooks, those questions were authored by professional authors. The third set of questions were generated by an AQG system, using a knowledge base of biology facts as its source.[6] Forty AQG questions and 20 questions for each of the other sets were selected for evaluation. Twelve raters (college students) were asked to evaluate each question on four aspects, each on a 5-point scale. The aspects were fluency (grammatical correctness), semantic ambiguity, pedagogy, and depth. The raters were asked to answer the questions and then consider whether answering the question helped them understand the relevant biological concept—that was the pedagogical rating, i.e. estimated usefulness for learning important concepts. The rating for depth asked how much thinking was needed to answer the question. Upon analyzing the ratings, the authors concluded that all three sources of questions were *"equally beneficial on the whole"*.

Syed et al. (2020) compared the effect of AQG questions vs. human-authored questions on learning from texts. Participants in the experiment were given Wikipedia articles to read and some adjunct practice questions to answer. They were then tested (with a post-test in writing) on their comprehension of the articles. The post-test answers were graded by raters. For the practice questions (about those articles), some participants received human-authored questions, and some received questions generated by a neural AQG system, about the same sentences. The researchers found that participants that received AQG practice questions had better scores in the post-test than participants who received human-authored practice questions. According to the researchers, the AQG questions were longer than human-authored questions (average word count 12.72 versus 11.43). The authors conjectured that the longer AQG questions may have been more detailed and thus encouraged better comprehension by the readers.

Van Campenhout et al. (2022) presented a study about student engagement with automatically generated questions. The study involved practice questions for a college level

---

[6] Chapter 9 presents question generation from knowledge bases.

textbook materials in psychology. An AQG system generated concept-recognition questions and fill-in-the-blank (open cloze) questions. In addition, human-authored yes/no questions were also provided. All reading and test materials were provided in online courseware. The researchers measured students' engagement with the various questions during the semester, recording more than 60K interactions. The mean engagement for all question types was above 98%, i.e. the students used the automatically generated items as much as the human-authored items.

Steuer et al. (2022) evaluated the efficacy of AQG questions on college students' reading comprehension. They used a neural AQG system to generate full questions (interrogative sentences) for materials from college undergraduate textbooks (biology and anatomy), for chapters of about 1400–1700 words. The automatically generated questions were checked for readability (ungrammatical questions were discarded). The questions were provided as adjunct practice questions, and the students were asked to provide short written answers. In addition to the treatment group, the researchers also had a control group of students who read the same materials but without the questions (the control group could reread the materials instead of having questions). Students' comprehension of the materials was then tested with post-learning questions (human-authored). The researchers found that students who had the AQG questions performed better on the post-test measures than the control group, The authors concluded that automatically generated questions did contribute to student learning. Students in the treatment group were also asked whether they thought the adjunct questions were human-authored or automatically generated. Students considered half of all the questions to be human-authored and none of the questions were consistently recognized as AQG. The researchers concluded that students *"did not need a perfect question resembling a manually authored one to engage with the learning material actively."*

3.7 Summary

Evaluation of automatic question generation shares many similarities with evaluation methods in natural language generation. Intrinsic methods of evaluation strive to establish how good are generated materials (questions) by themselves. Intrinsic evaluations of AQG include human-rater based evaluations and automated evaluations. Human evaluations typically involve rating of generated questions on multi-point Likert scales, usually for the dimensions of fluency, grammatical correctness, semantic well-formedness, and contextual relevance. Another method of human evaluation is asking raters to distinguish between human-authored and machine-generated questions. Automated measures of AQG compare generated questions to reference materials (usually—human generated questions). Automated measures are typically fast, cheap, and can be used repeatedly. One of their disadvantages is that they may underestimate the quality of generated questions, because questions that are not similar to reference questions might still be good questions. On the other hand, similarity to reference materials may in some cases overestimate the quality, due to small but important differences. Extrinsic evaluations measure to what extent the generated questions are useful in the applications for which they were generated, for example how useful they are in the educational settings.

Classic Approaches to AQG from Text, Part 1: Syntax, Semantics and Discourse

4.1 Introduction

We present the classic approaches to automatic question generation from text in two parts. This chapter covers approaches that are based on linguistic analysis of text units. Template-based approaches are presented in the next chapter. While they are presented separately, those approaches do share some features, and some methods involve both templates and linguistic analytic components.

Linguistically oriented AQG systems emerged when the contemporary advances in the field of NLP presented quite robust tools for the analysis of text—syntactic parsers, semantic parsers, discourse parsers, named entity recognizers (NER) and tools for coreference resolution. Such tools provided explicit analytic structures, from which questions can be generated, again guided by linguistic insights. A standard classic pipeline for AQG from text often involved the following steps:

1. *Selection of important sentences (content selection).*
2. *Finding candidate targets in selected sentences.*
3. *Converting the sentence to interrogative form, focusing on the target expression.*

A different outline of the classic pipeline for AQG can sometimes be found. It involves the following steps:

1. The input text is segmented into tokens and sentences.
2. The text is analyzed with some parsers (syntactic and/or semantic).
3. Optionally some transformations are applied to the parsed structures, such as simplification and extraction of implied relations.
4. Questions are generated from the parse structures.

5. Optionally, generated questions are reranked, either for well-formedness (e.g. fluency) or for relevance to a specific purpose.

Such an outline does not contradict the three-step outline presented above; it just views the AQG pipeline from a different perspective. Tokenization and sentence segmentation are often used for content selection, while parse trees and other structures can also be useful in that stage. Finding good candidates, question-worthy phrases in selected materials, also operates over tokenized data and formal structures. Notably, both of these outlines represent only the basic schema of classic approaches; some proposed QG systems differ from those outlines in various ways. This chapter presents some select classic AQG systems, to not only demonstrate the classic approaches, but also to explicate what kinds of problems and issues they encountered.

4.2 AQG with Constituent Parse Trees

Syntax-based approaches to QG are probably the oldest ones in the research literature (Wolfe 1975). The initial attractiveness of syntax-based approaches stemmed from the notion of how to generate interrogative forms from declarative sentences, to which the contemporary linguistic theory provided an answer: via transformations over syntactic parse trees. With the availability of good constituent-structure parsing systems (towards the end of the 1990s), which could provide rather good parses for a variety of texts, the road was opened towards using constituent parse trees for general-purpose AQG. The common basic strategy was as follows: (1) parse sentences using a syntactic constituency parser; (2) simplify complex sentences, if desired, or avoid them; (3) identify target words/ phrases; (4) apply syntactic transformation rules to generate interrogative forms. Some representative systems for this approach are Ali et al. (2010), Kalady et al. (2010), Varga and Ha (2010).

A well-developed syntax-based AQG system was presented by Heilman (2011), Heilman and Smith (2009, 2010a, b). That system was an important milestone due to the sophistication of its design, and because many authors used it for many years as a comparison baseline in subsequent work. Heilman and Smith proposed to generate questions from syntactic analysis of sentences, specifically the sentence constituent structure, following the transformational approach. The system has three core stages. Stage 1 is focused on converting an input sentence into a canonical declarative sentence. This stage can also be used for simplifying the original sentence if it has complex structure. This stage is also used to extract implied relations from complex sentences. As a result, a single but complicated sentence can be transformed into a set of simpler declarative statements. For a detailed account of their extraction system see Heilman and Smith (2010c). Stage 2 involves the actual transformation of each simplified statement into a question form, using general transformation rules (see below). Since multiple questions can be generated

4.2 AQG with Constituent Parse Trees

even from a simple sentence, the system produces as output a set of possible questions. Such a set can be quite large if multiple statements are identified in stage 1. In Stage 3, the questions generated for the input sentence are ranked. The goal of ranking is to separate well-formed questions from ill-formed questions. The top ranked questions are then provided as the output.

Stage 3 of the system introduced an important aspect: overgeneration. Essentially, overgeneration of questions stems from the rich possibilities of generating various questions from a given input, looking at the different parts of the declarative statement. Without a clear external specification for focusing, i.e. what to ask about, an AQG system generates all the questions that it can. Overgeneration can also be used for regulating the quality (well-formedness) of generated questions. When multiple questions are generated for a given input, chances are that some of them might be ill-formed or just awkward. Some process can then be used to filter out the ill-formed questions and leave just the good ones. The overall effect then is that the system usually produces some good-quality questions. Heilman and Smith (2010a) used an ovegenerate-and-rank approach. The ranker component was trained using a supervised training approach. A logistic regression model was developed for question acceptability (acceptable/unacceptable) over a total of about 2800 manually annotated questions. The ranking model used a variety of features, including n-grams, counts of grammatical types (such as number of pronouns) and types of transformations involved in QG. The authors noted that ranking was effective: in the total evaluation data only 27% of the generated questions were acceptable, but in the top fifth of ranked questions, 52% were acceptable.

Many questions can be viewed as syntactic transformations of sentences in a text. For example, given a sentence *John went to the park*, one can easily transform it into *Who went to the park?* Indeed, the systematic correspondence of sentence structure between declarative and interrogative forms was a significant line of inquiry in transformational grammar (Ross 1967; Chomsky 1973). The apparent ease of such transformations was the inspiration for the early AQG systems. The correspondences between valid declarative and interrogative forms of English sentences can be described by sets of rules which define how to transform a declarative sentence into an interrogative one. For example, consider the transformation from a simple declarative sentence to a yes/no question *Did John go to a park?* Note how an auxiliary verb *did* is introduced and its position is moved to the beginning of the sentence.[1] In the Generative Grammar of the 1960s and 1970s, movement of constituents within the syntactic structure was considered a major aspect of sentence formation (and not only for questions).[2] Another class of transformations is *wh-movement*, which are used for describing the movement of constituents for the formation of wh-questions. For example, for the sentence *John is walking on the beach*, wh-movement of the

---

[1] This is an example of the Subject-Auxiliary Inversion (SAI) for question formation. For an overview see https://en.wikipedia.org/wiki/Subject%E2%80%93auxiliary_inversion.

[2] For a review of transformations for question formation in phrase structure theories, see chapter 9 in (Radford 1988), for a more modern treatment see chapter 4 in (Radford 2009).

beach constituent would result in *Where is John walking?*, with the focus of the question substituted with *where* and moved to the front of the sentence (so called *wh-fronting*). In linguistic research it has been shown that there are important constraints on wh-movement (Ross 1967) which greatly affect how grammatically-valid questions are formed.[3] One such phenomenon is known as *pied-piping*, where the extracted expression brings with it some other related constituents of a sentence. For example, starting with a sentence *John reads Mary's book*, and focusing on Mary, a question *Whose book John reads?* is grammatical, but *Whose John reads book?* is not well-formed; the word *book* should be transferred to the front of the sentence together with its modifier *Mary's*, that is converted to the interrogative *which*. Overall, it illustrates that designing systems for transformation of declarative sentences into interrogative sentences via sets of rules requires considerable familiarity with linguistic theory.

Khullar et al. (2018) presented a syntax-driven AQG system that focuses on explicit relative clauses for generating questions. The focus on relative clauses was specifically intended for handling some of the more complex constructions in English sentence structure. For example, in the sentence *The film director invited a composer who specializes in classical music*, the relative clause *who specializes in classical music* modifies the *composer* in the main clause. Such relative clauses use explicit relative pronouns, such as *who, whom, which, where, when, how, why, that*. Relative pronouns can be used to orient the AQG system around the clauses that might be dropped (not included in a question), and also to select the adequate pronouns for the question. For the above example, a question may be produced *Whom did the film director invite?*, but it should not be *What did the film director invite?* The selection of *whom* can be directly derived from appearance of *who* in the relative clause. The authors defined sets of syntax-based rules for handling explicit relative clauses. One set of rules concerned generating questions from the main clause, by checking what relative pronoun is used in the relative clause, and whether it can imply the correct wh-question word. Another set of rules applied to generating questions from the relative clause itself. This can be as simple as producing *Who specializes in classical music?* For conversion of clauses into adequate questions, proper handling of auxiliary and modal verbs is also required, including do-insertion (note the insertion of *did* in *Whom did the film director invite?*). An important part of their rule-based system was that relative clauses can be eliminated in order to simplify the resulting question. For a sentence like *Mary gave dark chocolates to Bart who works at Amazon which is the biggest online store* (an example of recursive embedding of relative clauses), the rule-based system could produce *Who works at Amazon?* instead of the bulky *Who works at Amazon which is the biggest online store?* For evaluation of their approach, the authors used 300 sentences with relative clauses from Wikipedia. Human evaluators rated each question on a 1–3-point scale (higher is better), for grammaticality, semantic correctness, and a 1–2 scale (no/yes) for fluency and uniqueness (how much the question differs from other

---

[3] Modern linguistic theory prefers constraint-based accounts to transformational accounts (Goldberg 2006; Müller 2018).

questions generated from the same sentence). This system achieved average scores of 2.89, 2.9, 1.85, and 1.8 on the respective dimensions, as compared to scores 2.56, 2.58, 1.3 and 1.1 for the Heilman and Smith system that was used as a baseline. This work demonstrated how some well-crafted rules can improve the quality of questions generated by a syntax-driven AQG system.

4.3 Semantic Roles and Question Generation

Semantic roles (also known in linguistics as *thematic relations*) are the roles that various components in a sentence have vis-a-vis the predicate (e.g. the main verb of the clause), the so-called *predicate-argument structure* (or simply argument structure). In linguistics, semantic roles arose as a major semantic account for sentence structure, as opposed to the syntax-oriented accounts (i.e. transformational and generative grammar).[4] Semantic roles[5] are an attractive approach to question generation, because semantic roles directly specify the structures in a sentence that reflect "Who did What to Whom, and How, When and Where?" (Palmer et al. 2005). Once semantic role parsers (**SRL**)[6] became available and showed reasonably good performance (Palmer et al. 2010), they were soon adopted for question generation purposes. Some of the AQG works in this line of research are Gates (2008), Mannem et al. (2010), Becker et al. (2012), Lindberg et al. (2013), Mazidi and Nielsen (2014a, 2015), Chali and Hasan (2015), Huang and He (2016), Flor and Riordan (2018).

The major roles from the PropBank are illustrated in Table 4.1, together with the corresponding potential questions that can be asked about sentence components that fill such roles. Given a sentence, an SRL parser identifies the specific components (usually phrases) and produces semantic role labels for them. Verbs in a sentence are considered as predicates. Semantic roles include the generalized core arguments of verbs—labeled A0, A1, etc.—and a set of modifiers such as location, time, and cause, etc., labeled AM. For example, an SRL parser may produce the following analysis:

[John $_{A0}$] gave [Mary $_{A2}$] [a book $_{A1}$] [for her birthday $_{AM-PNC}$]

From such analysis it can be rather straightforward to generate questions (and set aside answers) like *Who gave Mary a book for her birthday?* (John), *To whom did John give a book for her birthday?* (to Mary), and *Why did John give Mary a book?* (for her

---

[4] For a modern account of semantic roles in linguistics, see Williams (2015).
[5] There are different notions of semantic roles in computational linguistics, the most prominent being the abstracted semantic roles from the PropBank project (Palmer et al. 2005), and the event-specific frames from FrameNet project (Lönneker-Rodman and Barker 2009). The PropBank roles found wide application in AQG.
[6] Also called Semantic Role Labelers, hence the SRL acronym.

Table 4.1 Major semantic roles per PropBank 1.0 specification, with example sentences and some corresponding question words

Label	Role	Examples in sentences	Question words
A0	Proto-agent (often grammatical subject)	*John* broke the window	Who, what
A1	Proto-patient (often grammatical object)	John broke *the window* John greeted *the guests*	What, whom
A2	Instrument, attribute, benefactive, etc.	John hit the window *with a stick* Jon gave the book *to Mary*	With what, to whom, etc.
A3	Start point or state, amount	John sold the car *for $1000* John flew *from London* to Paris	From where, for what
A4	End point or state, amount	The seller raised the price *to $15* John flew from London *to Paris*	Where, to where
AM-LOC	Location	The dog is *in the yard* John mentioned it *in his letter*	Where
AM-DIR	Direction	The car turned *to the left*	Where
AM-TMP	Time	The letter arrived *today*	When
AM-CAU	Cause	The concert was canceled *because of the rain*	Why
AM-PNC	Purpose	Some extra energy is required *to carry the extra weight*	Why
AM-MNR	Manner	The prices were reduced *slowly*	How
AM-EXT	Extent (of amount or quantity)	We like this movie *a lot* The prices rose *by 2%*	How, how much
AM-DIS	Discourse	*Nevertheless*, we arrived safely	
AM-ADV	Adverbial (a catch-all class for various modifiers)	*Except for John*, everyone smiled	
AM-MOD	Modal verb	John *should* eat more fruit	
AM-NEG	Negation	They did *not* agree We *no longer* accept returns	

4.3 Semantic Roles and Question Generation

birthday). While this simple approach is effective and works in many cases, there are also many complications. First, SRL parsers do not always provide a correct parse for every sentence.[7] Even with correct parses, in many cases question generation from SRL requires additional considerations.

One of the considerations for AQG with SRL is handling of verbal groups in a sentence. In an English language clause, a verbal group consists of the main lexical verb and its related modifiers—negation, auxiliary verbs, and modals (Palmer 1987). A simple example of such handling is do-insertion, as shown above, where *"John gave..."* should be converted to *"To whom did John give...".* This can be more complicated in clauses like *John could have given a book to Mary*. Consider a sentence *They can fly from here to any country*, and the corresponding question *Where can they fly from here?* Note how the subject *they* needs to be inserted inside the verbal group *can fly*. The information for handling such cases can come from a POS tagger or a syntactic parser, as is done in many studies. But such information usually does not come from an SRL parser, so a combination of NLP tools is needed, and proper handling rules for verbal groups need to be implemented.

Another issue with SRL is that the choice of question words for a question is sometimes not quite simple. This is already partly illustrated in Table 4.1, as some roles have multiple wh-words, and often a combination of a wh-word with a preposition is required (e.g. *with what*). A required preposition is often already in the sentence, but it needs to be detected and handled. Without it, the generated question can be somewhat disfluent, e.g. *Whom did John give a book?* The issues can be even more complicated. Semantic role A4 typically goes with the question word *where*. For a sentence like *They can fly from here [(A4) to any country]*, we can produce a question *Where can they fly from here?*. However, for a similar sentence *Antarctica doesn't belong [(A4) to any country]*, we should not produce a 'where' question like *Where doesn't Antarctica belong?*, as it implies a totally different meaning. In another set of cases, the choice of the question word may depend on the intention of a question. For example, for the sentence *The bird sat on the branch*, both *Where did the bird sit?* and *On what did the bird sit?* are good questions; but which one is adequate depends on whether we are interested in the location or in the object.

An important issue in question generation is the decision on whether to use *who* or *what*. This often applies to the roles A0 (usually a subject), A2 (a direct object), and some other roles. For example, *John gave $500 to Mary* requires *to whom*, but *John gave $500 to charity* should use *to what*. An SRL analysis does not provide clues for this issue. Some such cases can be handled by checking the POS tag of the respective word/phrase (*Mary* would be tagged NNP, *charity* would be NN). However, in general, some module for determining the grammatical animacy of the word's referent is needed for proper handling of such cases and it might require some non-trivial resources (Flor and Riordan 2018). In some cases, the decision can be very complicated. Consider the following sentences, which could even appear in the same text

---

[7] Pradhan et al. (2022) cite an F1 score of 0.867 for a deep-learning-based SRL parser.

Table 4.2 Examples of subcategories of temporal expressions and corresponding questions (adapted from Flor and Riordan 2018)

	Type of time expression	SRL analysis	Question
1	Time point	[A0 Mary] called [AM-TMP on Monday]	When did Mary call?
2	Duration	[A0 Mary] called [AM-TMP for 6 hours]	For how long did Mary call?
3	Repetition	[A0 Mary] called [AM-TMP every day]	How often did Mary call?

(a) *The United Nations was established in 1945.*
(b) *The United Nations carried out several missions in Africa.*

To ask about the subject of the first sentence we use *what*: *What was established in 1945?* But for the second sentence we should use *who* and not *what*: *Who carried out several missions in Africa?* The same referent can be *who* or *what*, depending on the context.

Another issue for choosing the adequate question words may stem from the fact that SRL roles are in some cases too general. Consider AM-TMP for temporal arguments. It is not the case that everything tagged as AM-TMP can have a question with *when*. The tag AM-TMP does not distinguish between time points, durations, and sets (repetitive temporal specifications).[8] Time points are queried with *when*, durations are queried with *how long* or *for how long*, and repetitive temporal aspects are queried with *how often*. This is illustrated with examples in Table 4.2.

The subclassification of AM-TMP is not provided by SRL parsers. To adequately handle question generation for expressions tagged with AM-TMP, the subtype of temporal expression needs to be detected. Flor and Riordan (2018) described handling of temporal subtypes by utilizing prepositions in temporal expressions. This requires a processing module beyond the SRL parser.

Flor and Riordan (2018) presented a general purpose AQG system that utilized an SRL parser and a POS-tagger, as well as additional custom modules for handling some of the issues presented above. The system generated wh-questions and yes/no questions from SRL analyses. The system was evaluated on input of 171 sentences from Wikipedia articles and was compared to a contemporary neural AQG system (Du et al. 2017) on the same inputs. Evaluation used dimensions of grammatical correctness (score 1–5), semantics (score 1–5) and relevance (score 0–3). The SRL-based system managed to produce more questions (890) than the neural system (160) and achieved higher human ratings than the neural system; with average combined scores of 11.4 out of 13 (for yes/no questions) and 10.2 (for wh-questions) for the SRL-based system, compared to 8.0 out of 13 for the neural system.

---

[8] For temporal relations and nomenclature, see, Verhagen et al. (2010).

4.3 Semantic Roles and Question Generation

An SRL-based approach to question generation can be very useful for generating questions from sentences. The work on AQG with SRL has typically utilized contemporary SRL parsers that were developed for processing of verbal predicates and their arguments. This has left a gap for two aspects in question generation. One aspect is cross-sentence coverage—since classic SRL focuses on semantic relations within a sentence, it does not provide an analysis that could be used to generate questions across sentences. The second aspect is that predicates can also be expressed using other parts of speech, specifically nouns and adjectives. For example, for the phrase *sales promotion at the fair*, 'promotion' denotes an event, that has a theme/direct object (sales), and a location (at the fair), with corresponding potential questions *Promotion of what?* and *Where was the promotion?*. Annotation of nominal and other predicates and arguments has seen some research work since it was first introduced in the NomBank project (Meyers et al. 2004), and SRL parsers for non-verbal predicates are still an active research area (Orlando et al. 2023; Pradhan et al. 2022). However classic AQG systems have not utilized non-verbal SRL for question generation.[9]

Mazidi and Tarau (2016), Mazidi and Nielsen (2015) presented one of the most advanced AQG systems of the classic design. Their system incorporated three types of text processing: a constituency parser that provided the phrase structure of sentences and also provided POS-tags for words, a dependency parser that provided the functional grammatical roles of components in a sentence, and an SRL parser that provided PropBank-type semantic roles. For each sentence in a text, their system integrated the outputs of such analyses into a single data structure that allowed the AQG algorithms access to a variety of information. The SRL information was instrumental for defining which kinds of questions (and question words) were applicable to various components in a sentence. Functional grammatical roles were utilized to define which sentences to select for QG and which types of questions should be generated for them. This was an innovative step, because many previous AQG systems tried to produce all possible questions from a given sentence. Mazidi and Tarau focused their efforts on generating questions for university introductory-level textbooks, which are a type of expository texts. The authors defined patterns of typical sentence structure for expository text sentences. They quantified what are the most common sentence patterns in college textbooks. For example, the pattern *S-V-dobj* (subject, verb, and a direct object), which indicates a relation between two entities, occurred in 28% of the sentences in their sample; the pattern *S-V-pparg* (subject, verb, and prepositional argument), which often describes how/what/where aspects of an action that is conveyed by the verb, occurred in 17% of the sentences. Other patterns occurred less frequently. Note that while the patterns have linearly-composed labels (e.g. *S-V-dobj*), the components in the corresponding sentences do not have to appear in such order. This is one of the advantages of using dependency parses, as they allow to detect

---

[9] For an AQG approach that uses dependency syntax relations, see Afzal and Mitkov (2015). For an approach that learns transformation rules from enriched POS patterns, see Blšták and Rozinajová (2016, 2022).

and label grammatical roles in a sentence irrespective of their order in the sentence. The authors used such patterns for two purposes. First, the frequency of a pattern was used as an indicator of whether the pattern was question-worthy—sentences that correspond to infrequent patterns might be skipped in a QG process. Next, they used the patterns to define what kinds of questions should be produced from a pattern, *"so that generated questions will be meaningful and not trivial"*—i.e. not all possible questions that can be generated from a sentence of a given pattern are worth generating.

For implementation of such approach, the authors defined about 60 QG-oriented templates. A template involves a syntactic pattern (as above) that defines whether a sentence matches the template. A template then also includes some filters—rules that further define whether QG is applicable, and what type. Some of the possible question types can then be derived from the semantic roles of the sentence components. For example, for a sentence in the *S-V-pparg* pattern, a 'where' question might be derived (*…in the yard*) or a 'why' question (*…because of gravity pull*). A template can also specify questions that are not direct conversions of the declarative sentence or its parts. For example, for a sentence *Brain waves during REM sleep appear similar to brain waves during wakefulness*, which has an *S-V-acomp* pattern (adjectival complement that describes the subject), the following 'question' was produced: *Indicate characteristics of brain waves during REM sleep*. Note that *"Indicate characteristics of"* comes from the template, and such a question is applicable only for some types (patterns) of sentences. This kind of design feature comes from a designers' understanding of what this type of sentence is communicating.

To evaluate the system, they generated questions for 10 passages selected from science and humanities textbooks, with an average of 83 sentences per passage. For a baseline, they generated questions from the same data with the Heilman (2011) syntax-based AQG system. The baseline system generated on average 406 questions per passage, while Mazidi's system generated on average 50 questions. Top 20 questions for each text, from each system, were manually evaluated for quality by crowdsourced raters, on a 1–5 point scale (higher score is better). The questions from the baseline system had an average score of 2.9, the questions from Mazidi's system had an average score of 3.7, indicating much better overall quality.

4.4 Classic Cross-Sentence AQG

The classic AQG methods that rely on syntactic or semantic-roles analysis have a particular common shortcoming—they are sentence-oriented, utilizing analyses of a single sentence at a time. Such analyses do not provide information for generating questions that refer to relations that may span across sentences, for example inside a paragraph. To expand the classic AQG approaches beyond the sentence-boundary, several approaches were proposed. One approach focused on reference and anaphora resolution. Another

4.4 Classic Cross-Sentence AQG

approach looked at semantic relations between entities and events mentioned in different sentences. The third approach looked at discourse relations between sentences.

One of the most common relations across sentences is coreference, when the same entity is referred to in sentences of the same paragraph or document. Hasegawa et al. (2019) presented a study of question generation that focused on pronominal anaphora across sentences. Their use case was generation of Anaphora Reasoning Questions, questions that require a reader to reason about the reference of pronouns in a text. The outline of their system was as follows. First, within a text they search for a sentence that has a pronoun which refers to an entity in another sentence of the same text. Next, the sentence is transformed into a question, using a 'standard' sentence-oriented AQG system. If the question(s) still has a pronoun, the pronoun is replaced with its referent from the other sentence. This is illustrated with the following example.

S1: *When Andrew goes home after baseball, he likes to eat a snack.*

S2: *He eats carrots and bananas.*

S3: *Afterwards, Andrew finishes his homework.*

Q1: *Who likes to eat a snack?*

Q2a: *Who eats carrots and bananas?*

Q2b: *What does he eat?*

Q2c: *What does Andrew eat?*

Q3: *Who finishes his homework?*

The sentence S1 has two clauses, with the pronoun *he* in the main clause, which refers to *Andrew*. The question Q1 directly asks about the referent of *he*, which happens to be within the same sentence. For their study, the authors decided to exclude pronoun-oriented questions where the referent is mentioned within the same sentence (although even such questions might be useful for testing reading comprehension with beginning readers). Question Q2a was acceptable, because the answer to this question is not in the same sentence but is in the preceding sentence. Question Q2b was not acceptable, as it contains a pronoun, but once the pronoun *he* is replaced with its referent *Andrew* (Q2c), the question is acceptable—answering it requires reasoning across two sentences. A question like Q3 could be generated but would be discarded because the reference is within the same sentence.

To implement such an AQG system the authors used a coreference-resolution toolkit, and a syntax-based AQG system from Heilman (2011). Despite the simplicity of the examples above, such an approach can generate quite interesting and useful questions. For example, from the segment *"(S1) The inner series (corolla of petals) is, in general, white or brightly colored, and is more delicate in structure. (S2) It functions to attract insect or bird pollinators."* (from a botanical text), the system generated the following valid question: *What functions to attract insect or bird pollinators?* For evaluation, Hasegawa et al. used 57 articles with 200 questions generated by their system. The questions were manually evaluated for (a) grammatical correctness, (b) whether the answer could be found in the text, and (c) if the answer could be found, how many sentences were needed to answer the question. Of 200 questions, 115 were rated as grammatical, 68 had slight errors, and 17 had many errors. For answerability, 159 (79.5%) of the questions had an answer in the text. Sixty-three (31%) of the questions required more than one sentence for answering. The authors attributed the grammatical problems to problematic performance of the syntax-based AQG system, which struggled with complex sentences. Other errors stemmed from incorrect coreference resolution by the coreference-toolkit. The low number of inter-sentence questions may have resulted from the long complex sentences having mostly intra-sentence references.

Araki et al. (2016) presented another study of cross-sentence question generation. They worked with a corpus called ProcessBank (Berant et al. 2014). The corpus had 200 text segments (paragraphs) about biological processes, that were extracted from a high-school-level textbook on biology. The segments were annotated by human experts for entities, events, coreference between entities or events, and a set of semantic relations between events. Entities are typically expressed by noun-phrases, events are usually expressed by verbs (but also deverbal nominalizations). The semantic arguments of event verbs are typically the entities that are of interest in the text. The set of semantic labels for event arguments included Agent, Theme, Origin, Destination, and Location. Event relations used in annotation were Causes, Enablement, Temporal ordering (between events), Super (when one event subsumes the other), and Sameness of events, especially when one of them is expressed by a verb and the other by a noun phrase (e.g. proliferate/proliferation of). An example of such annotation is given below.

[A few tumor cells $_{(entityN1)}$] may [separate $_{(eventV1)}$] from [the original tumor $_{(entityN2)}$], [enter $_{(eventV2)}$] [blood vessels $_{(entityN3)}$] and [lymph vessels $_{(entityN4)}$], and [travel $_{(eventV3)}$] to [other parts of the body $_{(entityN5)}$]. [There $_{(entityN6)}$], [they $_{(entityN7)}$] may [proliferate $_{(eventV4)}$] and [form $_{(eventV5)}$] [a new tumor $_{(entityN8)}$].

Note that *they* (entity N7) is coreferential with *a few tumor cells* (entity N1), *there* (entity N6) is coreferential as a location with *other parts of the body* (entity N5). To generate questions that involve coreference, the QG algorithm needs to find sentences that have coreferential entities or events, and then proceed according to some templated patterns. For example, if the event in the second sentence is a verb, and the coreferential entity is the agent of the event, then a question can be formed along the pattern "*What + [event] + [complements of the event]?*". In our example: *What may proliferate and form a new tumor?* This is a suitable question because its answer is not in the same sentence. In the example above, the event *travel* (event V3) was annotated as "enabling" for event

4.4 Classic Cross-Sentence AQG

proliferate (event V4). From this, a question can be formed *What enables tumor cells to proliferate and form new tumors?* This can be achieved via a template like *"What enables + [agent] + [enabled event]?"* when the agents of the two events are coreferential and one of the events enables the other. The approach of Araki et al. tries to minimize transformations. It uses manually developed question templates and relies on reshuffling of components (phrases) according to predefined patterns over annotated relations. For evaluation, the authors had 200 questions generated by their system and rated the questions on grammatical correctness (scale 1–3, lower is better), and answer availability in the text (yes = 1/no = 2). The average grammatical correctness score for their questions was 1.46. The authors claimed that some grammatical problems stemmed from minor grammatical inficilities with verbs, such as *is uses* instead of *is used*, and handling of nominalizations. Average availability of the answer in text was about 1.4, probably because incorrectly formed questions were considered unanswerable.

One of the stated reasons for working on cross-sentence QG is that cross-sentence questions are supposed to be more difficult to answer as they require a reader to integrate information across sentences, possibly with some inference steps. To estimate the potential complexity of a question (in context), the authors suggested to count the number of inference steps that may be needed for a correct answer. They counted one point for each of the following potential steps: (a) event coreference and (b) entity coreference; within the original text and between the text and a question; (c) paraphrases in input text and in the question; (d) resolving negation, if present. This evaluation was applied only to questions that had an answer in the text. The average number of inference steps for the evaluated questions was 0.76, indicating that some inferencing was necessary, but not much. That result is a bit puzzling, since the QG algorithm was specifically geared to use coreference relations. It should be stressed that the study by Araki et al. used manually annotated entities and relations. If the same QG approach were to be attempted over free text that was automatically annotated with such relations (using technologies of the time), more errors would be expected.

In linguistic theory, **discourse relations** (also called *rhetorical relations* or *coherence relations*) are meaningful connections between propositions or segments of text (Taboada 2009). There are several different linguistic frameworks that attempt to describe, formalize and provide inventories of such relations.[10] One of the most influential approaches is the RST, Rhetorical Structure Theory (Taboada and Mann 2006; Mann and Thompson 1988). Another influential approach is the PDTB, the Penn Discourse Treebank (Prasad et al. 2008). All frameworks recognize that sometimes such relations can be expressed explicitly in text, via the use of discourse connectives (like *because* and *due to* to express

---

[10] For a recent short review of major discourse relations frameworks see Fu (2022).

Table 4.3 Examples of discourse connectors in texts (adapted from Agarwal et al. 2011)

Connection	Example
Intra-sentence	[$_{Arg1}$ Organisms inherit the characteristics of their parents] **because** [$_{Arg2}$ the cells of the offspring contain copies of the genes in their parents' cells.] Sample question: *Why organisms inherit the characteristics of their parents?*
Inter-sentence	[$_{Arg1}$ The scorers are directed by the hand signals of an umpire.] **For example**, [$_{Arg2}$ the umpire raises a forefinger to signal that the batsman is out ...] Sample question: *give an example where the scorers are directed by the hand signals of an umpire*
Intra-sentence	[$_{Arg1}$ Greek colonies were not politically controlled by their founding cities,] **although** [$_{Arg2}$ they often retained religious and commercial links with them] Sample question: *Were Greek colonies politically controlled by their founding cities while they retained religious and commercial links with them?*
Inter-sentence	[$_{Arg1}$ The rain poured all day. **As a result**, [$_{Arg2}$ the tent got really wet.] Sample question: *Why the tent got really wet?*

causality, *however* to express contrast, *for example* to introduce an example and elaborate), and sometimes the relations are implicit and are inferred from the text.[11] Discourse relations can connect short phrases and clauses within a sentence (intra-sentential), but many of them can also connect whole sentences or larger segments (inter-sentential). Overall, discourse relations contribute to the structuring of a text. The idea to base question generation around analysis of discourse relations, especially explicit relations, has been proposed by Prasad and Joshi (2008) who showed that causal relations annotated in the PDTB corpus can be a good source for why-questions.

Agarwal et al. (2011) presented a study for AQG over some explicit discourse connectives. The authors noted that not all discourse connectives are useful for question generation. For instance, the so-called conjunctive connectors, such as *and, or,* and *also,* are not quite conductive for producing a question. The authors focused on four subordinating conjunctions, *since, when, because* and *although,* and three adverbials, *for example, for instance* and *as a result.* Notably, all of them can be used for intra-sentence relations, but the adverbials can also be used for relations spanning across sentences. When such adverbials occur at the beginning of a sentence, they typically connect between something in a previous sentence and something in the sentence they are in. According to PDTB, most discourse connectors have two arguments (indexed simply as Arg1 and Arg2). Two examples of such relations are shown in Table 4.3.

---

[11] A basic example of implicit and explicit signaling of a discourse relation is the following one from Taboada (2009): Explicit: *Tom quit his job because he was tired of the long hours.* Implicit: *Tom quit his job. He was tired of the long hours.*

4.4 Classic Cross-Sentence AQG

Agarwal et al. noted that discourse connectors are conductive only for certain types of questions, typically targeting just one of their arguments. The connective *although* supports only yes/no questions about its arguments. The connectives *for example* and *for instance* can be used to ask to retell the example, but not for producing a wh-question. The connective *as a result* can be used to ask a why-question about whatever is in its Arg2 position, with the expected answer being whatever is in the Arg1 position. For generating questions, the authors devised the following algorithm. First, the selected discourse connectors are detected in text. Next, their arguments are identified. For intra-sentential connectives, such identification is done by using a constituent parse of the sentence. The connective *because* typically relates two clauses, and so the main verbs of those clauses can be used to identify the full phrases that are arguments of because. For inter-sentential connectives, the authors used only sentences where such connectives appeared at the beginning of the sentence, and assumed the prior sentence is Arg1 of the relation. Question formation depended on the specific connective and the type of question that it supports. The rules for such question formation are very specific and needed to be written for every connective separately. However, this study showed one of the earliest attempts for generating questions for cross-sentence information.

Desai et al. (2018) presented a study of AQG over a corpus of texts annotated with discourse relations as per the RST theory (Carlson et al. 2001). In RST, most relations are posited to have three components: a nucleus, a satellite, and a typed rhetorical relation between them. Both a nucleus and a satellite may reside within a sentence, but often they span over considerable segments of text, for example a sentence or more. Moreover, they can be nested, so that a sentence that is the satellite of one relation instance can be the nucleus of another relation instance. Typically, a nucleus sentence describes some state or event, and a satellite describes it farther, for example by providing an elaboration or a rebuttal, etc.

Desai et al. stated that designing an AQG system for all relations from RST theory was not feasible. They worked on several types of RST relations, which they regrouped into seven groups. The algorithm for question generation consisted of the following steps. In step 1, suitable discourse relations were collected from annotation and their spans were registered. In step 2, the algorithm identified, for each argument of a relation, what type of segment instantiates it (a phrase, a sentence, several sentences). Depending on the type of segment, some syntactic transformations were applied to convert the segment to interrogative form. In step 4, the actual question was formulated, according to the particular discourse relation.

The types of segments are presented in Table 4.4. Segments of type 0 and type 3 could be used in QG without modification. Segments of type 1 and 2 contain a main verb that might need to be adjusted for QG. Such adjustments moved the main verb to the beginning of the clause, adjusted its tense and handled auxiliary and modal components. It is notable that segment types in this study are not related to discourse relation types, rather the typing of segments served just for restructuring the segments for QG. This

Table 4.4 Segment types defined by Desai et al. (2018)

Type	Characteristics of segment	Example
Type 0	A group of many sentences	The cars are parked in a garage. They are protected from the rain
Type 1	One sentence, phrase, or a clause, not beginning with a main verb, but containing a verb	The cars are protected from the rain
Type 2	Phrase or clause beginning with a verb	Protected from the rain
Type 3	Phrase or clause without a verb	Protection from the rain

A segment is either a nucleus or a satellite of an annotated relation

generic treatment of segment types simplified the QG process, so that only a few rules were needed for transformations. To handle identification of components, the algorithm used a POS tagger, a dependency parser, and a morphological toolkit for handling verb inflections.

Generation of a question did depend on the type of discourse relation. Different types of relations are conductive to different types of questions. Moreover, the questions can be formed differently, depending on the type of segment that they handle. For this purpose, the authors defined a set of templates (essentially question-formation rules), as shown in Table 4.5. Note that some of the questions are not interrogative forms but rather requests to provide an answer or an explanation, and can be relevant in the context of a reading comprehension assessment.

The authors generated 3472 questions from the 385 annotated documents in the corpus and selected 140 questions for manual evaluation (20 questions per discourse relation type). The evaluation involved several dimensions. Three evaluation dimensions were binary (yes = 1/no = 0): grammatical correctness (the question is syntactically well-formed), semantic correctness (the question makes sense to a reader; non-grammatical questions were scored 0 on semantics), and superfluity of language (whether the question is too long—since the materials were not shortened or simplified). The discourse-relation-oriented questions received average scores of 0.94, 0.91 and 0.7 on those dimensions, indicating that they were mostly grammatical and made sense. Following the proposal from Araki et al. (2016), the questions were also evaluated for the number of inference steps that may be needed for a correct answer, an evaluation that may indicate the potential difficulty of a question. Evaluation assigned one point per question for the following three steps: resolution of coreference for entities, coreference for events, and detection of paraphrases. The sum of points per question was then divided by 3 (the max), to normalize it into the 0–1 range. The average score for inference steps across all questions was 0.43, indicating that the discourse-relation-oriented questions did invite some amount of inference.

Table 4.5 Templates for question formation, by discourse relation and type of segment involved (adapted from Desai et al. 2018)

Relation	Template for type0	Template for type1	Template for type2	Template for type3
Explanation	[Nucleus]. What evidence can be provided to support this claim?	Why [Nucleus]?	What [Nucleus]?	What caused [Nucleus]?
Background	[Nucleus]. Under what circumstances does this happen?	Under what circumstances [Nucleus]?	What circumstances [Nucleus]?	What circumstances led to [Nucleus]?
Solution	[Nucleus]. What is the solution to this problem?	What is the solution to [Nucleus]?	What solution [Nucleus]?	What is the solution to the problem of [Nucleus]?
Cause	[Satellite]. Explain the reason for this statement	Why [Satellite]?	What [Satellite]?	Explain the reason for [Satellite]?
Result	[Nucleus]. Explain the reason for this statement	Why [Nucleus]?	What [Nucleus]?	Explain the reason for [Nucleus]?
Condition	[Nucleus]. Under what conditions did this happen?	Under what conditions [Nucleus]?	What conditions [Nucleus]?	What conditions led to [Nucleus]?
Evaluation	[Nucleus]. What lets you evaluate this fact?	What lets you evaluate [Nucleus]?	What assessment [Nucleus]?	What evaluation can be given for [Nucleus]?

Note that Desai et al. conducted their study on a corpus of texts with manually annotated discourse relations. For farther research or for practical use (e.g. for educational purposes), it would be logical to utilize an automatic discourse-parsing toolkit. The main limitation of discourse-relations-oriented AQG approach is that discourse parsers are not yet quite accurate.[12]

4.5 Summary

The classic approaches to automatic question generation are based on strong linguistically motivated assumptions. They require the computation of explicit analytic structures from which question generation can proceed. Such analyses are supplied by POS taggers, syntactic parsers, semantic role labelers, NER systems, and discourse parsers. Building

---

[12] Despite recent advancements in automatic RST and PDTB parsing, the accuracy is still problematic, with F1 score of up to 0.535 for RST (Shen et al. 2022) and 0.53 for PDTB (Knaebel 2021).

AQG systems from such analyses requires good familiarity with the relevant type of linguistic analysis, understanding of the NLP analysis tools, and then crafting of rules for the extraction of relevant pieces from text and for generation of questions. Due to those factors, the classic AQG approaches are known as rule-based systems. Although designing rule-based AQG can be cumbersome, such systems have a distinct advantage. Their performance can be explicitly analyzed (by the researcher/developer) in every single case, thus providing complete transparency to the AQG process. If a generated question is not acceptable, one can trace as to whether the problem stems from inaccurate NLP analyses or from issues with the question generating rules. If necessary, rules can be added, removed, modified, or conditioned, thus allowing for focused incremental modification of AQG systems. A general limitation of such systems is that they are oriented around the structure of sentences and the structure of discourse. They can easily generate factoid questions but are less suitable for generating other kinds of questions.

Classic Approaches to AQG from Text, Part 2: Templates

5.1 Introduction

Many classic approaches to automated question generation have utilized templates in some form. The use of templates for AQG is not a single methodology, but rather a rich set of various approaches. It is sometimes listed as syntax driven, or rule-based, but such labels are not entirely correct. The template-based AQG approach flourished in the research literature from around 2006–2018, and often used rule-based and syntax-based components, such as sentence-structure parsers and SRL parsers.

Basic templates are lexical patterns with slots (placeholders) into which specific content can be inserted. For AQG, templates are generalized question patterns with slots. Some of the simplest such patterns are *What is X?*, *When did Y happen?*, *What is the significance of Z?* Once a slot is instantiated (i.e. filled with suitable content), a template yields a usable question (e.g. *What is hemodialysis?*). In such cases a question template is any predefined text with placeholders/slots to be replaced with content from the source text. In more sophisticated cases, templates may define patterns of syntactic and semantic requirements, specifying how a template can be chosen (matched to a text) and how a question would be generated.

The main issues in template-based AQG are: (1) how to produce templates; (2) how to match templates to context so as to produce adequate questions; (3) for what kinds of questions can template-based AQG be useful. In early research all templates were manually defined by researchers. Later research devised methods for automatic acquisition of patterns for templates form large data sets.

5.2 Simple Templates

Wang et al. (2008) described a study of template-based AQG for the medical domain. The focus of the study was generation of questions for estimating reading comprehension of medical concepts from 100 medical articles about causes, symptoms, and treatment of some medical conditions. Templates were generated manually by experts. For this study, the authors defined an extended template as a four-tuple that includes a pattern, required concepts, keywords and specification of an answer, as illustrated in the following example.

Question:	*What medications are used in <Disease>?*
Required entries (concepts):	*<Medicine> and <Disease>*
Keywords (for interpretation):	*Drug, medicine, effect, help, use, release, improve, suitable, effective*
Related answer:	*<Medicine> (whatever content that is resolved as 'Medicine' or 'Drug')*

The following excerpt is the base text:

Angiotensin converting enzyme (ACE) inhibitors or angiotensin receptor blocking (ARB) drugs are the drugs of choice in patients with heart failure, chronic kidney failure (in diabetics or non-diabetics), or heart attack (myocardial infarction) that weakens the heart muscle (systolic dysfunction).

In order to be matched to templates, the text needs to be annotated for medical concepts like this:

<Medicine>Angiotensin converting enzyme (ACE) inhibitors</Medicine> or <Medicine>angiotensin receptor blocking (ARB)</Medicine> drugs are the drugs of choice in patients with <Disease>heart failure</Disease>, <Disease>chronic kidney failure</Disease> (in diabetics or non-diabetics), or <Disease>heart attack (myocardial infarction)</Disease> that weakens the heart muscle (systolic dysfunction).

Then, anything annotated with *<Disease>* can serve in the *<Disease>* slot of the template. The phrases marked as *<Medicine>* can be the potential answers. Moreover, the presence of *<Medicine>* component(s) in the sentence is a prerequisite for activating this template, as *<Medicine>* is a required component in the template. After activation and instantiation, a possible question can be *What medications are used in chronic kidney failure?*, with the expected answer *angiotensin*.

Given a set of templates, questions for texts were generated automatically via the following process. First, texts were automatically parsed and annotated by a semantic parser

5.2 Simple Templates

MMTx (Meystre and Haug 2005), that uses the UMLS lexicon and UMLS metathesaurus.[1] This process annotates sentences with concepts like *<Medicine>*, *<Symptom>*, *<Disease>*, etc. The automated annotation provides the necessary domain knowledge and marks the text spans (or phrases) in a way that can facilitate template matching. The second step is template matching. Each template in a repository of templates is matched against the annotated concepts in each sentence. A match is declared if the sentence contains all required entities and at least one of the keywords specified in the template. Such matching improves the relevance of template to the content of the sentence. In addition, Wang et al., also briefly noted negative entities—concepts specified in a template, that if matched in a sentence trigger a rejection (don't use this template if this concept is mentioned).

With such simple approach, many different templates can be produced. An issue then arises—which templates are worth producing? Wang et al. (2008) describe some categories of questions/templates that they wanted to avoid. One category were templates for questions that can be interesting but not easy to answer. For example, a question *What is the article mainly about?* While such a question could be relevant for any article, extracting the potential correct answer was not simple (with the technologies of circa 2008), and since having an answer was a prerequisite for the task, such consideration disqualified templates for which answers were difficult to detect. Another category were questions that would be easy to answer but not interesting or relevant enough. Notably what is an 'interesting question' is usually task-specific. As stated by Wang et al., it is easy to extract person name, location, organization, and time from articles with the help of common NER tools. Thus, templates could be created with focus on who, where and when. However, such questions weren't relevant to the task that focused on medical concepts and relations between them.

Wang et al. also introduced an additional important aspect for AQG. Beyond generating individual questions, how questions are arranged together for use, what is known in educational settings as *test assembly*. Essentially, given an article or a set of articles, an assembly (to be used as a test for human readers) will include several questions. The issue is how those should be selected when multiple questions are available/generated, sometimes more than one per sentence. The selection criteria would usually be task specific. For their task, Wang et al. listed three criteria: variety, coverage, and overall limits. With regards to variety, a test shouldn't be full of the same question type, like *What is the symptom of <Disease>?*, and even if several such questions are included, for the sake of variety they should be about different instances of the general concept <Disease>. Differences in question form (syntax) can also be used for variety. With regards to coverage, Wang et al. cautioned against overloading questions on specific parts of the text,

---

[1] UMLS is the acronym of Unified Medical Language System, which is a compendium of controlled vocabularies and knowledge sources in the biomedical sciences. The UMLS (https://www.nlm.nih.gov/research/umls/index.html) is managed by the National Library of Medicine in the USA. See also https://en.wikipedia.org/wiki/Unified_Medical_Language_System.

for example no more than one question per sentence. If a sentence matched multiple templates, the templates/questions were ranked according to the weight formula and only one utilized. Finally, there can be a limit for the overall number of questions. This may require selecting which sentences are more question-worthy, and which questions should be asked from among those that can be generated. The requirements listed above are not part of the question generation process itself. In principle, given a set of texts and a set of templates, one could generate all the possible questions and proceed to evaluate their quality or adequacy. However, for practical applications, AQG algorithms and their results are often expected to provide support for task-specific question-selection. This is especially important for end-to-end systems that are expected to output a complete quiz form.

Mostow and Chen (2009) presented a template driven system for generating questions about mental states (beliefs and intentions) of characters in children's stories (as part of a reading tutor system). In that work, question templates were very generic question types; the templates were: *What did <character> <verb>?*, *Why/How did <character> <verb> <complement>?*, and *Why was/were <character> <past-participle>?* All the templates were manually constructed, specially designed for the specific domain of application— mental states of characters in children's stories. The relevant slots in templates provide simple specifications to be filled from a text. The slots define most of the content for the questions. The story-characters, verbs, participles, and complements come from the situation model of a given target text, which was inferred using several NLP tools, including an SRL parser, pronominal anaphora resolver and lists of mental-state verbs (e.g. believe. surprise, annoy, concern, etc.). Questions were generated only for the mental state verbs and were sentence-oriented. A morphological toolkit was used to adapt the tense/aspect of the verbs from a text to a question.

Evaluation of that QG system included examining the coverage and question quality. The authors used a corpus of 512 children's stories with a total of 14,727 sentences. This corpus had 1594 instances of mental state expressions. In a random sample of 100 such expressions, AQG was triggered in 83 cases (coverage of 83%). In total, the QG system generated 1537 questions; half of them were manually evaluated with a simple rating accept/reject (in the context of the story) and 71.3% were considered acceptable. Many of the ill-formed or otherwise unacceptable questions were the results of NLP tools errors or errors in inferring the situation model. For example, for the sentence *Mom likes flowers, they thought* the object of *thought* was misidentified as *flowers* rather than *Mom likes flowers*, and this led to the ill-formed question W*hy did they think flowers?* Errors in the situation model could also lead to unacceptable questions. Mostow and Chen provide the following example: for the sentence *He put his hands before his eyes as if he were trying to remember something*, the parsing was correct, but the situation model ignored the phrase *as if* and generated the counterfactual question *Why did he try to remember something?* The interesting aspect in this QG system is that the templates allow to generate questions

5.3 Automating the Acquisition of Templates

(such as 'why' questions) that go beyond the propositional content of single sentences—an answer might be elsewhere in the text or might be absent and would need to be inferred.

5.3 Automating the Acquisition of Templates

Zhao et al. (2011) presented one of the early approaches for automated acquisition of question templates. Their use case was rather non-standard: conversion of queries submitted to a search engine (Baidu) to questions that can be submitted to a community question answering (CQA) site. Their approach had two stages: template acquisition and question generation. For template acquisition they collected query-to-question pairs from the search engine query logs. Specifically, they were looking for events where users submitted a query (QR) and clicked (in search results) on a question (QS) from the archives of a large CQA website. Specifically, the relation might look like this:

(Imperial Palace) (ticket) ↔ How much is the ticket to the Imperial Palace?

If the original query terms are taken out from the question and replaced by slots, the following template is generated: *How much is <s1> to <s2>?* Note that such templates are often question frames with slots for entities. To constrain the acquisition process, Zhao et al. imposed the following constraints.

1. The query itself is not a question; its length is limited to maximum 3 words.
2. QS is a question and must come from the CQA site.
3. QR should be subsumed in QS, i.e. every word in QR must appear in QS. This constraint was designed so that questions are extensions of queries, but not deletions or transformations, to prevent considerable semantic drift for generated templates.

With this approach, different questions may lead to same templates. In their experiments, Zhao et al. utilized 15 million ⟨QR, QS⟩ pairs from query logs and generated about 547K templates. To improve the quality of templates, they then eliminated templates that were rarely instantiated, specifically templates that had less than 10 unique instantiations. After filtering, they had about 19K templates, each with 80 unique instantiations on average. They stated that most of the eliminated templates were long and complicated, and seemed not quite useful.

Another aspect of that research was that an initial query QR may be associated with several different questions QS and may lead to several templates. For example:

(Imperial Palace) (ticket) ↔ Is the ticket to the Imperial Palace expensive? ↔ Is the <s1> to <s2> expensive?

Given a large set of learned question templates, the question generation step can be viewed as retrieving and ranking suitable template candidates for a given new query, and instantiating the selected ones. Zhao et al. introduced a ranking function for candidate questions, that included two components: maximum likelihood estimation of a template given the query, and a fluency score for a question that is generated by instantiating the template with the current query. Given a query QR and all associated templates it can instantiate $\{T1, ..., Tn\}$, a maximum likelihood for query instantiating a template Ti is computed as conditional probability:

$$p(Ti|QR) = count(QR, Ti)/count(QR)$$

where $count(QR, Ti)$ is the number of all queries that instantiate the template Ti, and $count(QR)$ is the total number of queries.

The fluency score for a question (instantiated template) was computed by using a trigram language model trained on 15 million questions. In practice, the question generation system was more complicated, because the authors considered not only templates associated with the given query, but also expanded the query into a set of similar queries and added templates associated with those queries. Expansion to similar queries was done by ranking similarity of pre-stored queries to current query, using the cosine formula and *tf-idf* vectors.

Curto et al. (2011, 2012), Mendes et al. (2011) described the use of lexico-syntactic patterns for learning question templates and generating questions, also adding semantic information (named entities) to the patterns. Their use case was generation of factoid questions for text documents. The research involved two stages. First stage was acquisition of templates via pattern learning, the second stage was where the learned patterns are matched against a target document and the questions are generated. To learn patterns from sentences, they utilized syntactic components, specifically constituent phrase labels and POS tags (in Penn Treebank II notation). Given a question *Who sculpted the Statue of David?* and an answer *Michelangelo sculpted the Statue of David*, with the (collapsed) syntactic analyses $WHNP_0$-VBD_1-NP_2 and NP_0-VBD_1-NP_2, and the alignment (indicated by numeric indexes), so that NP_0 is actually the answer for $WHNP_0$. Essentially, the pattern can be viewed like this:

```
WHNP0[Who] VBD1[sculpted]     ↔     NP0{ANSWER} VBD1 NP2
NP2[the statue of David]?
```

Now, any sentence that matches the pattern NP_0-VBD_1-NP_2 can be converted into a question by rearranging the respective constituents into a sequence "__ VBD_1 NP_2?", and adding the lexical component of the $WHNP_0$ (*Who*). For example, the parsed sentence NP_0*[Botticelli]* VBD_1*[painted]* NP_2*[the Birth of Venus]* can be converted into *Who VBD_1[painted] NP_2[the Birth of Venus]?* Note that although this example looks very

5.3 Automating the Acquisition of Templates

much like a syntactic transformation. the idea behind this approach was to avoid manually writing syntactic rules for transforming declarative sentences into questions. Instead, transformation patterns can be learned from lexico-semantic patterns obtained from web (or corpus) data. For example, the pattern learning allows to associate with the above question template also additional declarative patterns, like NP_2-VBD_1-by-NP_0{ANSWER}. For a sentence like *One of my favorite pieces is NP_2[Moonlight Sonata] VBD_1[composed] by NP_0[Beethoven]* we can generate a question *Who composed the Moonlight Sonata?*

Learning of patterns was initialized with seeds, consisting of a question and its declarative answer sentence. Both were analyzed with a syntactic constituency parser. Correspondences between the parse trees were checked by lexical matches but indexed at the level of phrase structure nodes (e.g. VBD and NP). This already provides the first declarative pattern. For enrichment, additional patterns are then obtained from a search engine results in the following way. Different queries are built from the permutations of all the phrases of the declarative sentence, and a wild card * that allows for some diversity in search results. For example, "*Michelangelo * sculpted the statue of David*" and "*the Statue of David sculpted * Michelangelo*". If the search results include the snippet *the Statue of David sculpted by Michelangelo*, this can lead to the acquisition of the pattern NP_2-VBD_1-by-NP_0{ANSWER} (a passive form in subordinated clause). Thus, new declarative patterns are acquired for the template, by rewriting the search results at the level of phrase nodes in the constituent parse tree.

Curto et al. (2012) also introduced a distinction between strong, inflected, and weak patterns. This distinction relates to the desire to have considerable variability on the side of text matching patterns, so that for a given template (that corresponds to a question type), a variety of text patterns could trigger its activation (in other words, how useful this template is going to be). This is a typical issue with template-based approaches, because templates that can be triggered only in rare cases might not very useful. Strong patterns are patterns that instantiate all the lexical components from the seed question (except the wh-phrase).

One area where variations are expected are the inflections of the verbs in a sentence. Thus, Curto et al. introduced inflected patterns, created with inflected variants of the verb from the original seed. For example, from the seed *Michelangelo sculpted the Statue of David*, an inflected query can be "*Michelangelo * sculpting the statue of David*". This query may bring a sentence *Michelangelo finished sculpting the statue of David in 1504*, from which a pattern can be extracted (generalized): NP_0{ANSWER} [finished] VBG1 NP_2. Finally, weak patterns are patterns in which the original verb is omitted and only the noun phrases are used. For example, "*Statue of David * Michelangelo*", which can yield a phrase like *Statue of David by Michelangelo*, and lead to a pattern NP_2 [by] NP_0{ANSWER}.

In addition to pattern acquisition, Curto et al. also introduced pattern validation. Validation was used to filter out patterns that are too specific and won't be useful in many cases. For example, from the sentence *Statue of David: Michelangelo's Renaissance masterpiece was sculpted from 1501 to 1504*, a pattern might be acquired NP_2 [:]

$NP_0\{ANSWER\}$ *['s] [Renaissance] [masterpiece] [was] VBN_1*. Such a pattern is narrowly specific to mentions of renaissance masterpieces and would not be widely applicable to many texts. For validation of patterns, each seed question/answer pair was accompanied with a manually created validation pair that had the same parse pattern. For example, [*Who sculpted the Statue of David?; Michelangelo / Who invented penicillin?; Alexander Fleming*], both with the *WHNP VBD NP* pattern. Any pattern acquired from the "*Statue of David sculpted Michelangelo*" (e.g. NP_2 VBD_1 *[by]* $NP_0\{ANSWER\}$), would be validated with the "*penicillin invented Alexander Fleming*". Validation was defined as follows. The total number of search results that support the original set of components on the tested pattern was recorded, as well as the total number of search results that support the validation components with the same pattern. If the latter number is much lower than the former, then the associated generalized pattern is considered to be of low yield and is not admitted. Note that the admission/rejection threshold needs to be set manually, or by experimentation. Consider how the pattern NP_2 *[:]* $NP_0\{ANSWER\}$ *['s] [Renaissance] [masterpiece] [was]* VBN_1 would fare once instantiated with the penicillin example: "*penicillin: Alexander Fleming's Renaissance masterpiece was invented*". Such a query is unlikely to bring many results matching the sequence (even with gaps), and so the pattern may be rejected.

An additional important aspect of that research was the classification of seed answers into categories which essentially impose semantic types of questions. The authors used a two-layer taxonomy from Li and Roth (2002). The upper layer has six coarse-grained categories (Abbreviation, Entity, Description, Human, Location, Numeric), while the lower layer expands into fifty fine-grained categories (see Table 2.3). The taxonomy was based on WordNet hierarchy of nouns. Examples of assigned categories with seed pairs and syntactic patterns are:

Location:City—WHPP VBZ NP	["*In which city is the Wailing Wall?*; Jerusalem"/"*In which city is the Wembley Stadium?*; London"]
Human:Individual—WHNP VBD NP	["*Who sculpted the Statue of David?*; Michelangelo"/"*Who invented penicillin?*; Alexander Fleming"]

Given a set of templates, each one with a set of validated patterns, question generation for a text document involved computing a constituent syntactic parse for each sentence and then matching the template declarative patterns for both syntactic and lexical components, in sequence, but with gaps allowed. For example, the parsed sentence *IN[In] NP[November 1912] [NP]Kafka VBD[began] VBG[writing] NP[The Metamorphosis]* might be matched against a pattern [NP VBD VBG NP] that is associated with the question template [Human:Individual; WHNP VBG NP]. Moreover, the sentence might be matched in two ways:

5.3 Automating the Acquisition of Templates

```
NP VBD VBG     NP[November 1912]{ANSWER} VBD[began] VBG[writing]
NP:            NP[The Metamorphosis]
NP VBD VBG     NP[Kafka]{ANSWER} VBD[began] VBG[writing] NP[The
NP:            Metamorphosis]
```

The first match might be rejected because the potential answer *November 1912* does not match the question category, it is not a 'Human:Individual'. This kind of filter was implemented by associating each category with a set of high-level WordNet synsets. For example, 'Human:Individual' was connected with the synsets *person, individual, someone, somebody* and *mortal*. A potential answer identified in a sentence could be checked via WordNet noun hierarchy whether it is subsumed under one of those synsets, thus checking the applicability of the answer's semantic type. Note the tight dependence of the filter on the WordNet resource—if *Kafka* is not found under one of those synsets, a match would be invalidated and a question *Who wrote The Metamorphosis?* would not be generated.

Two additional filters were used in question generation. One filter discarded matches that had anaphoric references, thus preventing rather nonsensical questions like *What is it?*, *Where is there?* or *What is one?*. A more advanced system could, in principle, use anaphora resolution and substitute anaphoric references with their referents (though this could introduce new errors). A third type of filter implemented a plausibility check, just like the validation step during pattern acquisition. The matching components from the text would be arranged into a query and submitted to a search engine. If the amount of matching results was below threshold, the in-text match would be rejected, and a question would not be generated.

For evaluation of the template acquisition process, the authors manually created 139 question/answer seeds. They used the Google search engine and 16 top ranked snippets for each query. This generated 1348 accepted patterns (399 strong, 729 inflected and 220 weak) for 118 seed questions. The authors noted that some seeds did not lead to acquisition of patterns. Overall, the acquisition process depended on the algorithm of the search engine, and the popularity of component terms (queries about Leonardo da Vinci result in more patterns that queries about much less known artists). Two different types of evaluation for QG were used. One type of evaluation considered a holistic human impression of questions. Each question was manually judged and assigned to one of the following three categories. Plausible: if the question is well formulated at the lexical, syntactical, and semantic levels and makes sense in the context of the sentence that originated it. For example: *Who is the president of the Queen International Fan Club?* Implausible: if the question is not well formulated in lexical, syntactic, or semantic terms, or if it could not be inferred from the sentence that originated it. For example, questions like *Where was France invented?* and *Who is Linux?* Plausible-in-Context: for questions well formulated in lexical, syntactic, and semantic terms, but which contains pronouns or other references that can only be understood if the user is aware of the context of the question. For example: *Who lost his only son?* Questions were generated for 81 sentences (from informational texts). When all filters were applied, 29 questions were generated (which is a rather low yield), half of them were judged implausible. On a separate generation pass, only the semantic filter was used. This added 103 questions, of them 90 were judged as implausible. In another condition, questions were generated with no filters. There were 1820 additional questions, of them 500 were evaluated and 485 were judged as implausible. In a separate evaluation, questions were generated for 365 sentences from the Wikipedia article about Leonardo da Vinci. With all filters, the system generated 41 questions, of them 21 implausible (51%); without filters, the system generated 259 questions, of them 182 implausible (70%). Those results indicated that when all filters are used, the amount of generated questions is rather low, and even then only about half of them might be acceptable. When filters are not used (so called *loose matching*), more questions can be generated, but most of them are not acceptable (what is often called *high proportion of noise*).

5.4 Deeper Questions with Templates

In the examples described above, we have seen template-based AQG systems that were oriented towards factoid questions. In the next example, we will find a different kind of template-based system, one geared towards generating questions that go beyond facts directly expressed in a text.

Lindberg et al. (2013) noted that one limitation of the syntax- and semantics-based methods of QG is that they generate questions by rearranging the surface form of sentences, thus generating questions that are tightly related to the statements made in the text; they are focused on the facts that the text conveys. Those methods are not suited to generate deeper questions, which are still about the text, but go beyond the immediately expressed contents. Question templates offer the ability to ask questions that are not so tightly-coupled to the exact wording of the source text.

Lindberg et al. (2013) introduced a variant of template driven question generation. The application domain was rather standard—questions for informational articles, specifically for educational materials. The approach included two steps—template construction, and then application of templates to generation of questions. As described by the authors, template construction was done manually. This aspect allows the test developer to infuse human expertise into the process. The special technical aspect of the approach is in utilizing semantic constraints on slots and slot fillers of the templates. Most of the constraints are expressed with components of Semantic Role Labeling (SRL). The approach specifies that the texts (for which questions would be generated) should be processed with a POS-tagger, a lemmatizer, a NER system, and a semantic role labeler. In addition, a

5.4 Deeper Questions with Templates

Table 5.1 Examples of templates and questions, adapted from Lindberg et al. (2013)

Source text	As recently as 12,500 years ago, the Earth was in the midst of a glacial age referred to as the Last Ice Age
Template Question	How would you describe [A2—lp misc]? *How would you describe the Last Ice Age?*
Template Question	Summarize the influence of [A1—lp !comma !nv] on the environment *Summarize the influence of a glacial age on the environment*

morphological analyzer is needed for changing verb conjugations when converting text snippets to questions.

To get a gist of the approach, consider the examples of templates and questions in Table 5.1. The templates consist of up to three kinds of components. The (mandatory) free-text part is the actual question skeleton that is composed by the template author (e.g. a test developer). The slots to be filled are indicated with square brackets, and the constrains for filling the slots are specified within the slots. The ## symbols mark the end of textual part of the template, followed by optional specifications expressing constraints on how the template should be matched against a text. For example, the template *What caused [A2—lp !nv misc]? ## [A0 null]* specifies that the slot filler must be a text phrase that was analyzed as having semantic role A2, while the additional specification [A0 null] indicates that the template should activate only if the semantic role A0 (the agent) of the semantic frame is not explicitly present in the sentence.

Lindberg et al. (2013) provide a lengthy explanation as to why it is advantageous to specify slot filters and template match conditions in terms of semantic roles. Their argument is mostly contrasting with previous attempts at template design, which were defined in terms of syntactic constituents (and only sporadically with some semantic components, e.g., NER). They argue that semantic roles are much more succinct descriptions and allow to capture the relevant constraints in a more concise manner than constituent syntax. As they state, *"even the shallow semantics of SRL can identify the semantically interesting portions of a sentence, and these semantically-meaningful substrings can span a range of syntactic patterns."* For example, expressing causation within a sentence can use different syntactic components, but with SRL the relevant expressions would be consistently labeled with the role AM-CAU.

The template design approach of Lindberg et al. had some potential disadvantages. First the whole process of template constructions was fully manual. Moreover, the template writer needed to be closely familiar with the SRL theory and should have a good understanding of how SRL works, including for example problematic predicates like copulas, the verb 'have', and other aspects. In addition, the writer would need to have good knowledge of the additional components (e.g. NER tagger, morphological analyzer, POS-tagger) and the specific notations that are needed to handle those tools and their annotations. Another disadvantage was that the required technical expertise may stand in sharp contrast with the idea that this template system can harness the domain knowledge of educational experts; the problem being that subject-domain-experts are rarely also experts in computational linguistics and specifically SRL. Writing such templates is not a task that can be delegated to crowd-sourcing.

Liu et al. (2010, 2012, 2014) presented another kind of template-based AQG system, which they named G-asks. The system was designed for a very specific AQG task—support for college-level academic writing. In that type of activity, students are expected to critically read and analyze research literature, identify relevant information, integrate related work, and present their own arguments. While generic questions, like *Have you identified the research methods used in the literature reviewed?* can be useful in such contexts, the study aimed at generating content-specific reflection-triggering questions for student's essays. Specifically, researchers focused on generating questions in relation to citation sentences that students include in their essays. In that context, citation sentences are sentences that express the opinion of a cited author about some topic, or present the work of such an author. An example of a citation sentence is *Cannon (1927) challenged this view mentioning that physiological changes were not sufficient to discriminate emotions.* Some trigger questions that could be generated for that sentence are: *Why did Cannon challenge the view mentioning that physiological changes were not sufficient to discriminate emotions? What evidence is provided by Cannon to prove the opinion?* In this example, the questions are grounded in the source sentence, but go deeper than just the facts stated, i.e. they are not factoid questions. To support the deeper and task-focused nature of the required questions, Liu et al. adopted a template-based AQG, as templates allow them to inject the critical deeper aspects.

Some question templates from Liu et al. (2014) are presented in Table 5.2. Each template presents several thematically connected questions. Some questions in a template presented rules for integrating parts of a text (from an article), while the additional questions in the template provided scaffolding that should guide the readers' critical thinking about the information in the research paper. Templates were organized by categories. Those six categories reflect the types of citations that can be encountered in research papers, based on a taxonomy of conceptual citation categories (Lehnert et al. 1990).[2]

The system involved manually authored templates with specification of syntactic components that should relate to NLP processing of the texts on which AQG would be performed. The general design presumed over-generation of questions for a given text by applying all available templates, and then ranking the generated questions to select the best ones.

Processing of a target text involved several steps. Step 1 was designed to detect and extract citations sentences from essays. This was achieved by pattern matching with regular expressions. Then, a citation sentence would be simplified and converted to a standard form (active voice, if the original was in passive), by using the Tregex system (Levy and

---

[2] Lehnert's categories reflect the use of citations—to describe methods/aims/results of the cited work, opinions expressed in it, present the systems or applications, etc.

5.4 Deeper Questions with Templates

Table 5.2 Content categories and AQG templates from the study by Liu et al. (2012)

Rule	Category	Question template
1	Opinion	Why + *subject_auxiliary_inversion()*? What evidence is provided by + *subject* + to prove the opinion? Does any other scholar agree or disagree with + *subject* + ?
2	Aim	Why does + *subject* + conduct this study to + *predicate* + ? What is the research question formulated by + subject + ? What is + *subject* + s contribution to our understanding of the problem?
3	Result	*Subject_auxiliary_inversion()*? Is the analysis of the data accurate and relevant to the research question? How does it relate to your research question?
4	Method	In the study of + *subject* +, why + *subject_auxiliary_inversion()*? Which dataset does + *subject* + use for this experiment? Could the problem have been approached more effectively from another perspective?
5	System	In the study of + *subject* +, why + *subject_auxiliary_inversion()*? What are the strength and limitations of the system? Does it relate to your research question?
6	Application	Why + *subject_verb_inversion()*? Could the problem have been approached more effectively from another perspective? Does it relate to your research question?

Andrew 2006). Simplification involved splitting compound and complex sentences and removing some phrases such as appositives, non-restrictive relative clauses, and participial modifiers. In step 2, semantic and syntactic features were extracted from the citation sentence. Those included named entities (especially names of cited authors), syntactic parse features (such a subject, predicate, and object), sentiment words, negations, and other features. Using the extracted features, each citation was classified into one of the six citation categories (using a Naive Bayes statistical classifier). Step 3 was the step of question generation. Predefined templates corresponding to the citation category of the sentence were attempted. Each template seeks its relevant components in the analyzed simplified sentence: the subject, the main predicated (verb), and the rest of the constituents. Since the analyzed sentences are already in active voice from, only one syntactic transformation would be required to generate a question form (e.g. *Jones proposed...* → *Did Jones propose...?*).

Liu et al. (2014) illustrated the whole process with this citation sentence:

While it is shown that AES has inter-assessor correlations comparable to that of human assessors (Dikli 2006), many scholars are still highly critical of the validity and robustness of the approach (Britt et al. 2004).

The sentence is converted into two simpler sentences: (1) *It is shown that AES has inter-assessor correlations comparable to that of human assessors (Dikli 2006)* and (2) *Britt (2004) criticized the validity and robustness of the approach.* The first sentence is also converted from passive to active form: *Dikli showed that AES has inter-assessor correlations comparable to that of human assessors.* This sentence gets classified as a 'Result' category and that triggers the application of rule #3, producing the question: *Did Dikli show that AES has...?* That is supplemented from the template with: *Is the analysis of the data accurate and relevant to the research question?* The second original sentence is classified as 'Opinion' category, triggering template #1 and producing *Why did Britt criticize the validity...?*, supplemented with: *Does any other scholar agree or disagree with Britt?*

The whole system was evaluated on several levels, as it has several aspects that may lead to poor QG results. In addition to standard issues, like parse errors or NER tagger errors, one potential problem can be misidentification of the citation sentences. Liu et al. (2012) noted that on a controlled set of texts, citation extraction was rather good, with recall of 88% and precision 96%. Another problem was proper categorization of citation sentences. Indeed, Liu et al. (2012) commented that some citation sentence categories (such as 'System') are much more difficult to classify than others (classification of 'Result' reached as high as $F1 = 0.84$, while classification of 'System' citations had $F1 = 0.56$).

The system was evaluated on some technical aspects, processing 45 essays with 534 citations. Automated classification of citations into six categories had an average F-score of 0.7. The evaluation part of Liu et al. study also involved judging the quality of auto-generated questions. For 33 literature review essays written by PhD students in an academic course, G-asks generated 615 questions. In addition, questions were also written by student peers and by course supervisors (lecturers). Some generic questions, which were not specific to any essay, were also used in the study. Five quality measures were used: (1) This question is correctly written (grammar); (2) This question is clear (semantics and some grammar); (3) This question is appropriate to the context (relevance); (4) This question makes me reflect about what I have written (specific utility); (5) This is a useful question (specific utility). For each of those measures, evaluators provided a numeric score on a Likert scale, from 1 (strongly disagree) to 5 (strongly agree), with higher scores indicating better quality. The evaluators were the students who wrote the essays, so they were closely familiar with the subject matter and content of the essays. Citation-oriented questions generated by G-asks were rated on average 3.8, same or better scores than questions written by peers (3.77) or generic questions (3.73), and only lower than supervisor questions (4.4).

Labutov et al. (2015) described a research effort focused on generating high-level (deep) questions for general informational texts, such as Wikipedia articles. Their idea was that if the task is topically well-constrained, a large number of high-level question templates can be generated by human authors, even crowdsource workers without

5.4 Deeper Questions with Templates

educational or NLP background. For example, given the constrained topic 'Famous Person:Early life', a worker might pose a question that translates to a template *Who were the key influences on <Person> in their childhood?* Such a template can be right for the topic while also being high-level, in the sense that many relevant texts would not have the verbatim answers. Moreover, authoring of such a template might be accomplished even without reading any particular article.

To flesh out this idea the authors proposed the following considerations. If an informational text can be decomposed into intermediate-size topical sections, and if a section can be represented by some topical ontological labels, then questions templates could be authored for the ontological labels. The ontology needs to be general enough to cover a large variety of texts, but also precise enough to cover individual chunks of text. With a suitable ontology, the authoring task can be carried by crowdsourcing (which also adds a requirement that the ontology should be easily interpretable for crowd workers). With a sufficient number of templates, generating questions for a new text reduces to finding appropriate templates in a database. The process includes decomposing a text into sections, finding their ontological labels, retrieving label-matching templates from a database and then instantiating them against the text sections.

Labutov et al. proposed to use a two-layer ontology. Any potential topic for templates would carry a category-section tag consisting of two labels: a category label for the article, supplying a broad classification, and a section label for the specific section in the article text. On the assumption that Wikipedia provides a broad coverage of human knowledge, an ontology for Wikipedia articles could be a starting point for categories. The researchers decided to use eight top level categories: Person, Location, Event, Organization, Art, Science, Health, and Religion, which (at the time) covered 78% of Wikipedia articles. The section labels provide specificity to the broad topics, and are taken directly from existing section titles in Wikipedia articles (the article sections also provide a human-authored decomposition of the texts). A selection of frequent category-section combinations is illustrated in Table 5.3. Although many section titles would be specific to respective articles, the researchers found that the top 50 most frequent section titles cover up to 55% of the sections in articles for the broad categories they selected (e.g. many articles about Person would have an Early Life section), thus supporting the conjecture that substantial coverage of different texts is possible.

For the authoring task, the researchers chose the Person and Location categories, with 100 most frequent section titles per each (claiming coverage for over 50% of Wikipedia articles at the time). Crowd workers with adequate native English proficiency were recruited for authoring templates. Notably, for the template authoring task, workers were not asked to read an actual article. Instead, they were shown a prompt like in Fig. 5.1, asking them to pretend they have read an article in the given category, and to write a follow-up question for the imaginary section with the given section title. The workers were instructed to author deep questions and avoid factoid questions. The researchers have

Table 5.3 Categories and common section titles for Wikipedia articles (adapted from Labutov et al. 2015)

Person	Location	Organization	Art
Early life	History	History	Plot
Career	Geography	Geography	Reception
Personal life	Economy	Academics	History
Biography	Demographics	Demographics	Production
Science	Event	Health	Religion
Description	Background	History	Etymology
Taxonomy	Prelude	Causes	Iconography
History	Battle	Diagnosis	Worship
Distribution	Aftermath	Treatment	Mythology

shown that this strategy can be successful—the workers authored 995 question templates for that task, with good quality.

The evaluation effort did not work directly with templates, but rather with questions instantiated from the templates. For each of 100 category-section labels, four relevant article sections were randomly chosen. For each section, ten questions were instantiated from the category-section relevant templates. A different contingent of crowd workers were tasked with rating the questions with respect to the text sections, providing scores on three dimensions: Relevance (Does the article answer the question?): 1 (not relevant)—4 (relevant); Quality (Is this question well-written?) 1 (poor)—4 (excellent); and Scope (How long is the answer to this question?): 1 (single-sentence)—4 (paragraph). The mean relevance, quality and scope ratings were 2.3, 3.5 and 2.6 respectively. The 2.6 score for Scope indicates that many questions did indeed cover information across more than one sentence. The score 3.5 for Quality indicates that the authored question templates provided a solid support for grammatically well-structured questions. The score 2.3 for Relevance is a bit disappointing (lower than the scale midpoint of 2.5).

Labutov et al. also addressed two important issues: (a) how to provide category and section labels for texts that do not have such attributes; and (b) how to select question templates from the existing collection for new texts. The researchers cast category and section inference as text-classification problems, using logistic regression and *tf-idf* vectors as features, classifying articles into eight categories and classifying sections into 50

> You are reading an article about an important Person named X.
> You have just finished reading the Legacy section in this article.
>
> Your task: Write a follow-up test question about the Legacy section in this article about X.

Fig. 5.1 Worker's instructions for the question generation task for the category-section pair Person:Legacy (adapted from Labutov et al. 2015)

different section-labels (different ones for each category). Overall classification accuracy was 85% for categories and 95% for section titles. Category-section labels are important because human-authored question templates are essentially focused for those labels. Successful categorization showed that the category-section labeling approach can be extended and automated for new texts. The second issue, how to select question templates from the existing collection for new texts might seem trivial, since templates are already tagged by the category-section labels. The researchers found that retrieving existing templates for new texts, based on just the category-section labels, resulted in precision of 74% (in a separate evaluation), which means that despite labeling, the template-based questions are not always quite relevant for new texts. They implemented an additional classifier (using lexical features and word2vec vectors) for scoring the relevance of templates for text-sections and showed that it can improve the selection of templates for texts, up to 95% in some cases. They noted that even when the template label does not match the text-segment exactly, it can be still relevant, as for example a template labeled 'Person:Childhood' can be relevant for a text segment labeled 'Person:Early Life'. Selection of wrong templates, and thus generation of inadequate questions, can happen when the text/article category is incorrectly inferred, or when the section label is incorrect.

5.5 Summary

Templates are a powerful approach for automated question generation from text. They can integrate syntactic and semantic components. Templates can allow very precise targeting of questions for texts and avoid generating questions that are not essential to a specific task. They can be used to infuse expertise from test developers and instructors. They can facilitate asking questions that go beyond the basic statements in a text. Templates can also allow great flexibility—one might use simple templates in some cases and complex templates in other cases. Templates can also have disadvantages in that they can be quite complex and may require special NLP expertise for their creation and adjustment. Templates can be automatically learned from large datasets, but such templates may lack the flexibility and precision of manually crafted templates. Finally, if the number of templates in a project becomes very large, some form of prioritization of templates might be needed.

6 Neural AQG, Part 1: Early Models

6.1 Introduction

Since about 2018, classic methods for question generation were largely superseded in research by neural methods of question generation, following on the general success of deep learning approaches in NLP, and neural NLG in particular. In this chapter we introduce the first wave of neural QG models, built on encoder–decoder sequence-to-sequence architectures.

Wang et al. (2012) presented one of the earliest neural models for QG. They focused on the task of learning to generate questions from a collection of question answer pairs, obtained from a web forum. Specifically, they focused on the domain of Travel from the Yahoo Answers community. A notable point about this work is that it demonstrates the focus placed on association between question words and available answers. Wang et al. used a deep belief network (DBN)[1] to learn the associations of the words in the questions and the answers, based on their joint distributions in the datasets. This QG work focused on just five question types: what, when, where, who, why, and how. Their system learned to associate those question words with the declarative answers. It also learned to select (score) the most important content words in the answers, as associated with the question words. For training, the system used sets of about 4500 question–answer pairs. For question generation the system was given a declarative sentence; it first produced the most strongly associated question word, thus determining what type of question would be asked. In that work, the actual questions were generated from predefined templates (sequences with POS slots for content words, for example: *how + to + <verb> + <adj> + <noun>+?*). The automatically inferred most-highly-scored content words from the declarative sentence are then inserted into their slots in the template that is selected for

---

[1] The DBN used several stacked Restricted Boltzmann Machines (Hinton et al. 2006).

the question type. The word selection functioned as a content selection component in the system. Although the question formulation part of the system was rather simple and rule based, the system was an important precursor of later neural AQG, in that it learned to generate from the input (via associations) the most important components for question generation. Moreover, the selection of words in the input can be conceptually considered as some form of *learned attention*, while the transfer of those words to the output can be viewed as akin to a *copy mechanism* that would be introduced in later neural NLP systems.

The first wave of neural QG models utilized the seq2seq architecture with RNN networks. In the following section we present a brief overview of seq2seq networks. For a more technical introduction to seq2seq models in the context of natural language generation, see chapter 3 in Narayan and Gardent (2020).

6.2 RNN, LSTM and Seq2Seq Models

A recurrent neural network (RNN) is a type of neural network that is suited for processing sequential data. An RNN keeps a memory of prior recent inputs to influence processing of current input and produce a new output—the output of RNN depends on the prior elements in the sequence. This has obvious relevance to processing of natural language text (word sequences), because the order of words matters for expression of meaning. Like other types of neural networks, RNNs can have multiple layers of neurons, with a distinctive input layer and output layer. The state of each neuron and weights of connections are represented by real numbers and learning adjusts those numbers so that the set of activations at the input produces the desired set of activations at the output. Like other neural networks, RNNs can be trained with backpropagation and gradient descent, which gradually adjust the weights on the inter-neuron connections.

Basic RNNs are prone to losing information from the beginning of the sequences due to problems of signal propagation in the learning process, especially for long sequences (so called vanishing and exploding gradients). Several variations of the RNN architecture have been introduced, the most prominent being long-short term memory (LSTM, Hochreiter and Schmidhuber 1997) and gated recurrent unit (GRU, Cho et al. 2014). Both variants introduced architectures that function as gates and facilitate the flow of information in the network by learning to open, close or forget certain paths of activation. Another architectural variant are bidirectional recurrent neural networks (BRNN), and especially bidirectional LSTMs. Those typically include layers that process the input sequence from beginning to end, and layers that process the input in reverse, from end to beginning. A unidirectional RNN can only use the memory about previous inputs (words) in the sequence to make predictions about the current state. A bidirectional RNNs also can utilize data that is later in the sequence, to influence processing of a current element. For example, if the objective is to predict the word in a current position for a sequence *in the*

6.2 RNN, LSTM and Seq2Seq Models

new ___, the word *york* might be a good candidate; but knowing that the fuller sequence is *in the new ___ city*, can make *york* a much stronger candidate. For a survey of early RNN uses for language processing see De Mulder et al. (2015).

Early Sequence to Sequence (often abbreviated as **seq2seq**) models were a special class of RNN architectures that became the dominant architecture for language processing, and especially for NLG tasks, from 2014 till 2018. A typical seq2seq model has two components, an encoder and a decoder, each of them is an LSTM neural net (Sutskever et al. 2014), or GRU net (Cho et al. 2014). The core idea of seq2seq models is to learn to convert one kind of sequence (e.g., a sentence in one language) to another sequence (e.g., a translation of the sentence in another language). The basic approach for general sequence learning is to map the input sequence to a fixed-sized vector using an encoder network, and then to map the vector to the target sequence with a decoder network. The encoder of a seq2seq model encodes the input words one by one into a series of representations (activations of neural units, represented as real numbers, hence: a vector of real numbers). At each step of processing, the encoder uses two vectors—one vector represents the current state of the network (called *hidden state*), and one vector represents the current input word. The result of processing is a new hidden-state vector, which is used for processing the next word, etc. The decoder receives the set of such representation vectors (called *context vectors*) and decodes them one by one into a sequence which is then converted to words. At each step the encoder also uses two vectors: the context vector and the vector representing the previously decoded word.

The input words for LSTM need to be represented by vectors as well. Converting strings (words) into dense numeric representations (called *word embeddings*) has been the focus of another line of research in NLP, using learning over large corpora of raw text, and utilizing specialized recurrent architectures. Most commonly used word embeddings for early seq2seq models have been word2vec (Mikolov et al. 2013) and GloVe (Pennington et al. 2014).

Seq2Seq models are supervised models trained using Stochastic Gradient Descent (backpropagation) to minimize a predefined objective function over values. Such models require large amounts of training data per task (thousands of input–output examples and more). Overall, a seq2seq model is an end-to-end learning system. The notion of **end-to-end** learning refers to training a complex learning system (typically a deep neural network) as a whole, from input to output, without any intermediate explicit symbolic representations. Only the initial input and the final output are considered *observable*, whereas all internal intermediate states of a system are often called *hidden* or *latent*. The parts of a network that carry the hidden states are often referred to as *hidden units* or *hidden vectors*. For a theoretical discussion of such models see Glasmachers (2017). In practice, seq2seq models typically require some preprocessing before the neural model is applied. The preprocessing usually involves sentence boundary detection, tokenization, and conversion of words to vectors.

Conversion of output vectors to words can be done by looking up the closest (most similar) vectors in a predefined mapping of vectors and words (which is often called the *vocabulary* of the model). Seq2seq models typically use a predefined limited vocabulary, on the orders of 50–200 k words, and handling out of vocabulary words (and named entities) can be problematic. One solution for this is to use a mechanism that can indicate which pieces on the input should be copied to the output. Neural copying mechanism was proposed by Gulcehre et al. (2016) as well as Gu et al. (2016). Out-of-vocabulary words would be coded by a special token UNK on the input side and also kept in a shortlist. To prevent occurrence of UNK in the output, a special strategy is used—for the decoded UNK token at time step t, it is replaced in the output sequence with a corresponding token from the shortlist. During training, the neural mechanism learns when to use context for generating a next word, and when to point to the shortlist for copying a word from there.

After 2018, LSTM seq2seq models have been largely superseded by models with transformer architecture (Vaswani et al. 2017). The encoder and decoder components in transformers differ from LSTMs, but the general logic of converting the input text sequence into an output sequence is retained, and many transformer models are also considered as seq2seq encoder–decoder models. We discuss some of them in the next chapter.

6.3 Data Sets

Most of the early work on neural question generation was based on learning from datasets of question–answer pairs. A critical role at that time was played by the SQuAD dataset (Rajpurkar et al. 2016). The Stanford Question Answering Dataset (SQuAD) is a collection of question–answer pairs derived from Wikipedia articles. The dataset was developed for facilitating research on NLP systems for question answering, but it found a special use in AQG research as well. The first edition of SQuAD contained more than 100,000 question answer pairs. It was based on 536 English language Wikipedia articles. The articles were split into paragraphs and each paragraph was presented to vetted crowdworkers via Amazon Mechanical Turk. The workers were asked to write questions about information in the paragraphs presented to them, and highlight where the answer was contained in the paragraph. This resulted in a high-quality diverse collection of texts with questions and answers. The SQuAD dataset was subsequently used in many studies on automated question-answering, and on question generation, becoming probably the most widely-used dataset for those tasks.[2]

---

[2] SQuAD version 2.0 (Rajpurkar et al.) added 50,000 questions that were unanswerable from the texts, but looked similar to the answerable ones. That development was aimed at training question-answering models to avoid unanswerable questions.

Researchers, working mostly in the area of Question Answering, have developed many datasets of texts with questions and answers. Such datasets can also be used for training AQG systems, by using the questions as target materials for learning. Some of the QA datasets used in AQG research are MCTest (Richardson et al. 2013), MS MARCO (Nguyen et al. 2016), NewsQA (Trischler et al. 2017), TriviaQA (Joshi et al. 2017), TQA (Kembhavi et al. 2017), NarrativeQA (Kočiský et al. 2018), HotpotQA (Yang et al. 2018), QuAC (Choi et al. 2018); Natural Questions (Kwiatkowski et al. 2019), CoQA (Reddy et al. 2019), Forward Questions (Melly et al. 2020), MSQG (Liu et al. 2021), FairytaleQA (Xu et al. 2022). For a comprehensive survey of Question Answer datasets, see Rogers et al. (2023).

6.4 Seq2Seq Models for Neural Question Generation

Du et al. (2017) presented one of the first full end-to-end neural AQG system. They defined the QG task as follows: given an input sequence X (usually a sentence), the goal is to generate a natural question Y (which is also a sequence of words) related to the information in the input sequence. This is essentially a sequence-to-sequence learning task with an encoder–decoder architecture, which has become a staple of contemporary neural NLP models. The seq2seq neural QG system works by encoding the input sentence into a hidden representation vector, applying attention to the hidden representation, then passing it to the decoder that makes a prediction of the next output by optimizing the probability function. In probability terms the task was formulated as follows:

$$Y = \arg\max_{y} P(Y|X)$$

where $P(Y|X)$ is the conditional log-likelihood of the predicted word-sequence for question y, given the input word-sequence X. Following previous work on seq2seq models, the conditional in that equation was refactored into a product of word-level predictions:

$$P(Y|X) = \prod_{t=1}^{y} P(y_t|X, y_{<t})$$

where y_t is the output word at time-step t. Each new word in the output is conditioned on the whole of the input (X) and the words already produced in the output. The encoder used a bidirectional LSTM architecture with attention: the representation (vector) of each word was weighted by the average activations of all its context words. Input words were encoded using pretrained GloVe embeddings.

Du et al. investigated two related models for question generation. Their base model, a sentence-level model, was trained to generate one question from an input sentence. For this model, the QG decoder is fed only the representation of the encoder state of the input sentence. Note that the input sentence contains the answer to the corresponding question in the training materials, and the system learns to convert sentences to questions. The other model, paragraph level-model, takes into account the paragraph from which the input sentence is coming. Using a concatenation of the sentence encoder's output vector and the paragraph encoder's output vector. A large part of subsequent research on neural question generation adapted the seq2seq architecture as the standard (or baseline) architecture, while adding some variants and modifications.

To generate questions, the models were trained on SQuAD data of questions and answers. The authors split the SQuAD data question–answer pairs as follows: 70 K pairs for training, 10 K for development, and 11 K for the test set.[3] Two sets of evaluations were conducted. The automatic evaluations used the BLEU, METEOR and ROUGE metrics, to compare lexical overlap between the produced questions and the original human-produced questions for the same sentences. This kind of evaluation has become a standard practice for evaluating neural question generation systems. The results for Du et al. neural system are presented in Table 6.1. The attention-equipped system outperformed a vanilla seq2seq system, achieving higher results on all metrics. The authors also used the rule-based syntax-oriented AQG system from Heilman and Smith (2010a) as a baseline. The neural system had better performance on all metrics, although it could be noted that the rule-based system in that evaluation was not much worse, and performed better than the vanilla seq2seq. For the neural model, the inclusion of paragraph information did not lead to improved scores, it actually slightly decreased the scores. For another kind of evaluation, the authors selected 100 questions generated by their neural system and the same number of questions generated for the same input sentences by the rule-based system. Human evaluators were asked to score each question on a 1–5 scale (higher is better) on two aspects. One aspect, referred to as *naturalness*, concerned grammaticality and fluency of a question. The other aspect was called *difficulty* and was intended to measure "*the sentence-question syntactic divergence and the reasoning needed to answer the question*". The rule-based system achieved an average naturalness score of 2.95, and difficulty of 1.94, while the neural QG system had the scores 3.36 and 3.03 respectively. Moreover, since for each sentence there was one neural question and one rule-based question, the evaluators were asked which question was better. Neural questions were preferred in 38% of cases, the rule-based questions in 20% of cases, and the rest were ties. Those results were interpreted as indicating that the neural system generates better questions than the rule-based system.

The neural QG system from Du et al. was fed just the sentence text as input (after embedding to vectors), although in the SQuAD data each such sentence also had information about where in the sentence is the exact answer to the question. Since the answers were not indicated to the model, this kind of question generation is called **answer-unaware**. Typically, it learns to produce only one question from a sentence, conditioned

---

[3] This split has become influential as it was often reused, for the sake of comparability, in many subsequent studies. Note that the totality of this split is just 90% of whole 100 K SQuAD data, since 10% of SQuAD data was not released.

6.4 Seq2Seq Models for Neural Question Generation

Table 6.1 Results of automated evaluation measures for several seq2seq AQG systems using the SQuAD dataset

Authors	System	Dataset	BLEU-4	Meteor	Rouge L
Du et al. (2017)	H&S baseline	SQuAD[a]	11.18	15.95	30.98
	(syntax based):		4.26	9.88	29.75
	Vanilla seq2seq:		12.28	16.62	39.75
	+Attention,		11.86	16.28	39.37
	sentence-oriented:				
	With paragraph:				
Zhou et al. (2017)	NQG++	SQuAD[b]	13.29		
Du and Cardie (2018)	CorefNQG, seq2seq	SQuAD[a]	15.16	19.12	
Subramanian et al. (2018)	Answer-aware	SQuAD	10.4		
Zhao et al. (2018)	Sentence-level	SQuAD[a]	15.32	19.29	43.91
	Paragraph-level		16.38	20.25	44.48
Harrison and Walker (2018)	Sentence-level, answer-focused	SQuAD[a]	19.98	22.26	48.23
Zhang and Bansal (2019)	Baseline	SQuAD[a]	17.0	21.44	45.89
	With QPP	SQuAD[b]	18.25	22.62	46.45
	With QAP		18.12	22.52	46.45
	With QPP and QAP		18.37	22.65	46.68
	With QPP and QAP		**20.76**	**24.20**	**48.91**

[a] Indicates using dataset split introduced by Du et al. (2017)
[b] Indicates the split introduced by Zhou et al. (2017). QPP and QAP are explained in the text

on the input sequence. This contrasts with the **answer-aware** approach that we discuss next.

Zhou et al. (2017) also presented a seqs2seq neural system for question generation, trained and tested on the SQuAD dataset.[4] Their model had two special aspects: they incorporated lexical features into the model and made the model aware of where the answer is in the input sentence. The basic features were just the words of the input sentence (using pre-trained GloVe vectors.) The additional features are POS and NER tags of the words (obtained from the Stanford CoreNLP toolkit), and converted to vectors. The answer-awareness is the most distinctive aspect of this system. The answer target is that part (word or phrase) of the declarative sentence that serves as the answer to the given question, and for a QG process it is the target around which the question needs

---

[4] About 86 K sentence-question pairs used for training, about 9 K pairs used for development and 9 K for testing. This split differs from the one introduced by Du et al. (2017) and is also often used in research.

to be constructed.[5] Recall that in the SQuAD dataset, the answers to questions were specifically marked in the texts. Zhou et al. used the standard BIO positional tagging approach[6] to mark which words are the answers/targets. The BIO tags were converted to embedding vectors and this information was concatenated with word embeddings, and POS and NER vectors, to form the input vectors for QG. An obvious advantage of an answer-aware QG system is that it can produce a different question for the same sentence, if a different answer is marked on the input.

Another notable feature in Zhou et al. study was the use of a neural copying mechanism. Since LSTM networks typically operate with restricted vocabularies (pretrained embeddings), the occurrence of out-of-vocabulary (OOV) words (also names, etc.) in the input can hamper performance of seq2seq NLG systems. Vinyals et al. (2015), Gulcehre et al. (2016), and Gu et al. (2016) proposed *pointer neural architectures* that learn to point to one or more elements in the input and 'copy' those elements to the output. Zhou et al. incorporated a *pointer network* in the decoder of their neural QG model, with a copy-switch. When decoding a word at time *t*, the copy switch considers the current decoder state (words generated up to time *t*) and the context vector (from the encoder), and generates the probability of whether to generate a next word or copy it from the source sentence.

The neural QG system by Zhou et al. achieved a BLEU-4 score of 13.29 and outperformed several baseline approaches. Two hundred generated questions were also submitted to human evaluation. Evaluators were asked to rate (on a 1–2–3 scale, higher is better) whether a generated question matched the source sentence and the answer (i.e. whether it asked about the expected answer phrase). The average rating was 2.18, indicating that the overall quality was promising. An interesting aspect of neural generated questions is that they can sometimes involve paraphrases of phrases from the original sentence. In the following example, the phrase *a retaliatory attack on* was paraphrased in the question as *strike against*:

Source sentence:	In 1226, immediately after returning from the west, Genghis Khan began a retaliatory attack on the tanguts
Generated question:	*In which year did genghis khan strike against the tanguts?*

Subramanian et al. (2018) presented a set of studies related to neural question generation. Their neural QG system used a similar architecture—a seq2seq encoder–decoder system with a pointer network for OOV words. The system was answer-aware, but the

---

[5] For the pair [*John gave Mary a new book yesterday.*]—[*What did John give Mary?*], the target is *a new book*.

[6] BIO (or IOB) tagging (Ramshaw and Marcus 1995) is widely used in NLP for marking segments in word sequences. *B* stands for beginning, *I* for inside and *O* for outside. In the following example, *a new book* is focused (marked):

O:John O:gave O:Mary B:a I:new I:book O:yesterday.

method of integrating the answers differed from that described above. The input to the QG system was a whole short document and not just a single sentence. The encoder produced a separate hidden vector for the source sentence and a separate hidden vector for just the answer phrase (which was part of the text), and then concatenated those two hidden vectors. The decoder received such a vector and generated the output words for the question. The decoder used a vocabulary (lookup table for pretrained embeddings) of just 2000 most common words from the training data, so the system relied heavily on the copy mechanism. The system was trained on SQuAD data. In automated evaluation against the gold-questions from SQuAD, the QG system received a BLEU-4 score of 10.4. The authors noted that BLEU might not be an adequate measure in such cases, since a question for the same answer can be formulated in multiple ways. The authors also conducted a human evaluation. First, they trained their QG model on a larger dataset (three QA datasets, over 200,000 question–answer pairs in total). Then, 1300 generated questions were set for evaluation. Crowdworkers were asked to rate each question. One aspect was *fluency*, regardless of semantics, whether the question reads like normal English. 17.5% of the questions were rated disfluent, 22.7% were rated somewhat-fluent, and 59.8% were rated as fluent. This demonstrated that neural systems can produce quite plausible English outputs, as far as fluency is concerned. The other aspect was whether the question and the answer fit (whether the original answer is the correct answer for the question), with yes/no rating. The results were much worse for correctness, despite having the system trained on very large amounts of data, 64.4% of the generated questions were incorrect (not fitting the answer) and only 35.6% were considered correct.

The issue with semantic adequacy was quite pervasive for LSTM QG models. When using the neural QG system by Du et al. (2017), Flor and Riordan (2018), noted that *"the basic neural architecture of LSTM and attention already shows a surprising ability to produce readable questions, as indicated by reasonably high average grammaticality ratings (in human evaluation). At the same time, the neural system had difficulty producing semantically adequate and relevant questions."*

Du and Cardie (2018) revisited the issue of how a neural LSTM QG system can take contextual information into account. Du et al. (2017) compared a sentence-input model and a paragraph-input model and found that the sentence-input model was slightly better (see Table 6.1). In the 2018 study, they set out to improve the integration of coreference information for QG. Essentially, they were still feeding just a sentence to the QG model, but the sentence was modified to include the references of any pronouns appearing in it. For example, given a sentence *"They defeated the Arizona Cardinals"*, where the word *they* refers to *The Panthers* in some preceding context, the sentence for QG is modified to be *They the Panthers defeated the Arizona Cardinals*. This was done by using a coreference resolution system to identify pronominal anaphora, find referents and score them. In addition, the QG system was designed to be answer-aware, so the target answer was also identified in the input. For marking, an extended BIO schema was used, which marked the pronouns, their 'imported' antecedents, and the target answer. For example, the previous example was marked as follows (*pro* indicates the pronoun, *ant* indicates antecedent, *ans* indicates the target answer):

Words:	They	The	Panthers	Defeated	The	Arizona	Cardinals
Answer tags:	O	O	O	O	B_ANS	I_ANS	I_ANS
Coreference tags:	B_PRO	B_ANT	I_ANT	O	O	O	O

Word tokens were converted to vectors using pretrained embeddings. Tag tokens were converted to predesigned vectors, and weighted according to the score from the coreference toolkit. The input to the encoder consisted (for each word) of the concatenation of the word embedding, coreference tag embedding and answer tag embedding. The bidirectional encoder LSTM computed two hidden vectors from the input (forward and backward) and concatenated them for the final representation vector. The decoder LSTM received the sentence representation vector and generated output words (question) one by one, using attention and a pointer network (for dealing with OOV words). This, system, named CorefNQG, was trained on SQuAD data and achieved improved BLUE-4 and METEOR scores as compared to the system from Du et al. (2017) (see Table 6.1).

Zhao et al. (2018) introduced another encoder–decoder answer-aware QG system with LSTMs, attention and a copying mechanism in the decoder. They introduced two improvements. First, they wanted to have a better integration of information from the whole paragraph in the QG process. Second, they wanted to reduce the word-repetition rate in the output. To improve paragraph representation, they introduced the use of a gated self-attention in the decoder. The encoder still produces a hidden vector representation of the whole paragraph; however, it allows different words to influence this representation differently. For each new word in the sequence, the gated unit computes the sum of strengths of matching the vector of the current word with all other words in the sequence, and uses that to influence the hidden representation of the paragraph. This gated self-attention is learnable during training.

Word repetition in the output is a problem common to many encoder–decoder NLG systems with a copying mechanism. It is well-exemplified in the following generated question (from a paragraph about computational complexity): *What is an example of a circuit complexity in complexity complexity?* The word *complexity* occurred multiple times in the original text paragraph, gathering considerable strength in the paragraph representation, and the copying mechanism in the decoder tended to reproduce this word several times in the output. The repetition problem occurs in sentence-based neural QG, but it can be more pronounced for paragraph-based QG—a certain word might repeat a couple of times in a sentence, but it may repeat even more often in a whole paragraph. Since the copy mechanism takes into account the strength (influence) of all input words, the authors introduced a rather straight-forward solution: limit the influence of a repeating word to a certain maximum value so as to prevent excess influence, calling this a maxout pointer.

The authors were able to demonstrate that with a maxout pointer, the amount of word repetitions in generated questions dropped on average by a factor of 2 (as compared to using the standard copy mechanism).

6.5 Semantic Drift and Hallucinations

Neural text generation models can exhibit a fine level of fluency in produced outputs, but such models are also prone to generating hallucinated text (Perković et al. 2024; Ji et al. 2023; Zhou et al. 2021; Dušek et al. 2019). **Hallucinations** (also called *semantic drift, semantic noise, confabulations,* or *unfaithful content*) are factually incorrect statements, or words and phrases that are highly irrelevant or unrelated to the input context. Content hallucination by neural systems has been observed in a variety of NLG tasks, including abstractive summarization (Maynez et al. 2020), machine translation (Wang and Sennrich 2020; Martindale et al. 2019), image captioning (Rohrbach et al. 2018), dialog systems (Dziri et al. 2021), and question answering (Su et al. 2022). Both LSTM seq2seq models and pretrained models like transformers are prone to hallucinating content, though the pretrained models hallucinate somewhat less than task-trained seq2seq models (Maynez et al. 2020). Maynez et al. distinguish between intrinsic and extrinsic hallucinations. Intrinsic hallucinations are parts of the input document that are incorrectly combined or reused in the output, leading to content that is not semantically faithful to the original, or just simply incorrect. Extrinsic hallucinations are model-generated words and sequences that are not related to the input, or that cannot be verified relative to the input document; such content can often make the output look strange and incorrect or inadequate.

Hallucinations also appear in outputs of neural QG systems. Flor and Riordan (2018) used the neural sentence-level QG system by Du et al. (2017) and reported the following examples. Given an input sentence *Greater Helsinki has eight universities and six technology parks*, the neural QG system generated the question *How many universities does greater Strasbourg have?* In this case *Strasbourg* is the hallucinated component, as it does not relate to the original sentence (and not even to the original document which was about the city of Helsinki). For another sentence *But the real wonder is inside the volcano's crater itself*, the neural system generated the question *What is the real view of the planet?* The word *planet* here is totally hallucinated—the original document was about a volcano near Antarctica and did not mention any planets. Moreover, that neural QG system was not even fed with the rest of the document, the sole input was just the original sentence. As with many other cases of hallucination in neural NLG, the reason for producing such output is that the hallucinated parts have strong associative relations with the rest of the input, due to prior training of the system (Ji et al. 2023). Another example of semantic drift was presented by Zhang and Bansal (2019).

Source sentence: …during the age of enlightenment, philosophers such as John Locke advocated the principle in their writings, whereas others, such as Thomas Hobbes, strongly opposed it. Montesquieu was one of the foremost supporters of separating the legislature, the executive, and the judiciary…

Generated question: *Who opposed the principle of enlightenment?*

This example is more subtle, because there are no outstanding foreign components, all words in the question are related to the source text, and yet the meaning conveyed by the question is totally twisted, specifically the hallucinated notion *'principle of enlightenment'*.

The average amount of semantic noise in neural QG has not been quantified in published work, and though estimations exist for summarization (Maynez et al. 2020) and machine translation (Martindale et al. 2019), the amount of semantic noise would be specific to the any particular system and its training. Research work has shown that standard metrics used for automated evaluation of NLG, such as BLEU, ROUGE and BERTScore are not very effective for detecting the presence of hallucinations in the output; they also do not pinpoint which words in the output are wrong (Zhou et al. 2021). As stated by Reiter (2018b), *"researchers which rely soly or primarily on metrics such as BLEU for evaluation may not realise that their systems are generating completely unacceptable texts despite having reasonable BLEU scores."* Novel metrics and approaches to mitigation of hallucination in neural NLG are being actively investigated, and some promising approaches are listed in Ji et al. (2023). For neural QG, where generated questions are intended to be used by/for human audiences, the best recommendation is careful evaluation of generated questions by human experts, under specific instructions to look for unrelated content. Note the importance of specific instructions—the 'Strasbourg' example above was a perfectly grammatical and fluent output; it just was not properly semantically related to the input.

Zhang and Bansal (2019) proposed two methods to cut down on semantic drift. They used the same AQG architecture as Zhao et al. (2018)—an encoder–decoder system with LSTM and attention, and a copy mechanism with a maxout modification. Their first idea about reducing semantic drift was that during training the AQG system needs to learn to produce questions that are more semantically similar to the original questions. To implement this, they trained a separate neural system to recognize question paraphrases—this system was trained on a large dataset of questions. They then integrated the question paraphrase system with the AQG system in the following way: during AQG training, when the AQG system produces a question, the paraphrase module compares the produced question to the original question and provides that signal (as probability value) to the learning AQG system. The AQG system integrates that signal as a reward that biases it to produce questions that are semantically closer to the original. They called this approach QPP—query paraphrase probability. Their second approach to reducing semantic drift was based on the observation that a question with hallucinations often cannot be answered from the source text. To estimate the answerability of a generated question, they used a pretrained question-answering model. A newly generated question can be fed into a QA model with the source text, and the probability of getting a correct answer can be used as a signal (reward) to the AQG model. This approach was called QAP—question answering probability. The authors compared the performance of their baseline model and the performance of models equipped with QPP and QAP components. Overall, the QPP and QAP additions contribute to improved results on standard automated metrics (see Table 6.1). The improvements were statistically significant, albeit rather small. In addition, the authors conducted a small human evaluation: 300 pairs of questions generated for the same input by the baseline and the enhanced model were presented to human evaluators. In 160 cases the evaluators preferred the question form the enhanced model, in 131 cases they preferred the question from the baseline model, and 9 cases were ties. While those evaluation do demonstrate some success of the enhanced models, it is not clear to what extent it reduces semantic drift and hallucinations.

One of the approaches to reduce hallucinations uses Retrieval Augmented Generation (RAG). The basic idea of RAG is that output (text) generation should rely not only on the pretrained model, but also on some additional material than can influence the process and improve the output adequacy (Lewis et al. 2020). Given a task of generation, additional relevant materials can be supplied or retrieved (using a search component) to the model, to influence the generation process. It blends the pretrained language model with information retrieval (web search or document look-up). It can be used for reducing hallucinations, or for focusing the neural model on some specific content domain (Perković et al. 2024; Fan et al. 2024; Gao et al. 2024).

For a review of hallucination mitigation methods, see Ji et al. (2023). Two promising methods are notable in relation to AQG. One of the methods relates to detecting potential signals in the inner representations in the model, focusing on dynamic of pattens of activations (Snyder et al. 2024; Zhu et al. 2024). The other approach uses information retrieval and similarity: for each pair (input and generated output), an information retrieval query is executed for the input, and similarity is computed between the generated output and the most relevant retrieval results; relatively high dissimilarity may indicate hallucinations (Sadat et al. 2023).

6.6 Summary

Neural systems have taken over the AQG research and have become the standard approach to question generation. Their major appeal is in that question generation can be learned from data rather than engineered. The common approach for the first wave of neural AQG systems converged on using an encoder–decoder architecture with LSTM, and use pretrained embeddings for a predefined vocabulary (thousands of words). A copying mechanism (an additional LSTM) is typically added to the decoder to be able to handle out-of-vocabulary words in the input. Such models can provide surprisingly fluent and grammatical outputs (questions), and can sometimes include paraphrases in questions. Neural models can be answer-unaware or answer-aware (where the answer is specifically marked in the input). Some neural AQG systems can integrate spans of input larger than single sentences—i.e. paragraphs. A disadvantage of encoder–decode models is that they require very large datasets for training (tens of thousands of examples), and while the results can be impressive, it is not quite clear how much more training would be needed to improve the results dramatically. An additional problem is that evaluation of such models using automated metrics that compare the output questions to the original questions is problematic on two aspects. First it underestimates the paraphrasing aspect—questions can be asked in different ways. On the other hand, it overestimates the quality of output—overlap metrics are only an approximate measure for output quality. Unlike classic methods for AQG, neural methods have introduced a whole new type of error—hallucinated content or semantic drift in generated questions. Detecting and mitigating hallucinations, not only in AQG but in neural NLG in general, is a hot topic of ongoing research.

7 Neural AQG, Part 2: Transformers

7.1 Introduction

Transformer is a neural network architecture that uses the encoder-decoder framework, but without recurrence or convolution. In transformers, both the encoder and the decoder have multiple transformer blocks—feed-forward stacks/layers (six layers in the original paper, Vaswani et al. 2017). A key feature is that transformers use both attention and self-attention to jointly attend to information from different layers at different input and output positions. Attention was introduced in seq2seq models to allow the decoder to be influenced (guided) by the encoded representation of the preceding input (Bahdanau et al. 2014). In early LSTMs the decoder was influenced by a single vector that represented the whole preceding input, and with the introduction of attention, the decoder could be influenced by several representations from the input. In transformers, both the encoder and the decoder can attend to multiple vectors in different layers of the encoder (and the decoder layers can also attend to layers within the decoder). The attention mechanism allows any block in a transformer to be affected by a very long chunk of context (preceding context, or even subsequent context of the input), much larger than what was possible with LSTM models. In principle, the context can be enlarged by adding more attention units (and hardware processing capacity). The term **self-attention** relates to attention blocks that are within the same feed-forward module (encoder or decoder), processing the same input sequence. With self-attention, each element (vector) in a sequence of input elements is transformed as a weighted average with the weights of the rest of the sequence. This allows every element to be weighted according to its importance in the input sequence. Self-attention mechanism relates different positions of a single sequence to compute a weighted representation of the same sequence. Moreover, for any layer of input, several attention blocks can attend to it in parallel, with different connections; such an arrangement is termed *attention heads*. The output vectors of attention heads are concatenated, and the result becomes the input to a next layer of processing. The transformer architecture has become a de-facto standard for neural NLP processing since 2018[1], being the basis for Large Language Models (LLMs).

Unlike directional models (e.g. seq2seq), which read the text input sequentially (left-to-right or, technically, from beginning to end), a transformer's encoder reads the whole input sequence together (typically there are length limits, of course[2]). The whole input sequence is processed in parallel in the encoder blocks. This enables the model to learn contextual representations of any unit (e.g. word), influenced (via attention) by all the surrounding units (e.g. preceding and following words). Due to parallel processing, the information about the sequence of elements in the input can be lost. To preserve that information, transformers use positional encoding, i.e. the position of each input element is also encoded for the encoder (and, during pretraining—for the decoder).

A major advantage of transformer architecture is in its multilayered design, which can accommodate millions of learnable parameters (weights). Utilization of attention and self-attention allows those architectures to be trained on huge amounts of text during which time the models learn a variety of representations or some kind of knowledge about the natural language (on which they are trained, e.g. English) and also about statistical relations between entities that are represented in the training data. What exactly do such models learn in not quite clear,[3] but what is well-documented is that such pretrained knowledge allows such models to achieve state-of-the-art results on a variety of benchmarks that test NLP and NLG capabilities. The utility of such representations is often called **transfer learning**, as the knowledge gained during pretraining is useful (i.e. transferable) for performance on many other tasks (often called *downstream tasks*).

Although pretraining of transformer models is sometimes called unsupervised, it is in fact strictly supervised training, in the sense that correct targets are present during learning and systems learn to approximate those targets during training. The reason for calling it unsupervised is that the training datasets (text corpora) do not contain any additional labels, i.e. manual annotations, the targets are found withing the text. Such learning setting is also called *self-supervised*, since the supervision signal is included in the raw data.

---

[1] The transformer architecture was introduced by Vaswani et al. (2017). For a mathematical introduction to transformers, see Turner (2023). For a visual illustration, see Alammar (2018). For detailed analysis, see Tunstall et al. (2022) and Rothman (2021). For description of the Hugging Face library for working with transformers, see Wolf et al. (2020). For an in-depth discussion of large pretrained models and their implications, see the comprehensive paper by Bommasani et al. (2021). For a survey of transformer applications, see Patwardhan et al. (2023).

[2] Due to self-attention, the size of standard transformer's attention blocks is quadratic in input length. Subsequent research proposed a variety of ways to handle longer inputs with transformers, e.g. Kitaev et al. (2020), Beltagy et al. (2020).

[3] A variety of research papers have focused on uncovering what kind of information is learned by large neural language models. There have been studies focusing on lexical semantics (Vulić et al. 2020), morphology (Edmiston 2020; Hofmann et al. 2020), and syntax/grammar (Chi et al. 2020; Kulmizev et al. 2020; Hewitt and Manning 2019; Jawahar et al. 2019).

7.1 Introduction

Different systems use different pretraining tasks. One of the most common tasks is strict left-to-right (forward) language modeling, where the task is to predict the next word token given the preceding tokens, this is the standard task used in GPT (generative pre-trained transformers; Radford et al. 2019). Another target is to predict the whole next sentence or a larger chunk (Brown et al. 2020). A different learning task is the masked language modeling (MLM) objective. In this task some of the tokens in the sequence are randomly masked, and the objective is to correctly guess these masked words, given the context of the input sequence, utilizing not only the preceding but also the following words.[4] This objective was introduced by Devlin et al. (2019) for the BERT model. The BERT model uses only a multilayered transformer encoder (no decoder), which attends to bi-directional contexts during pretraining. The BERT model also used a next-sentence-prediction (NSP) objective. This is actually a discrimination objective (not sequence generation). For basic NSP, the model is fed with two sentences and has to decide (predict) whether the second sentence followed the first in the original text (shuffled sentences from the training text were used as foils). For a short survey of the variety of pretraining methods see Liu et al. (2020), for a more comprehensive analysis see Raffel et al. (2020).

Pretrained transformer-based large language models learn useful representations from massive datasets of text, and often achieve impressive result on NLP tasks. However, in many cases their capabilities need to be adjusted to the specific tasks. Such an adjustment is called **fine-tuning**. In practice in means additional supervised training of the pretrained model on a dataset (and labels or targets) for the specific task (such as text classification, summarization, translation, or question answering). Fine-tuning is simply training on new data, which changes some of the parameters in the pretrained model. However, the amount of data during fine-tuning is usually orders of magnitude smaller than the data used in pretraining. Hence, the changes in model parameters are relatively small, and the task-specific training is termed fine-tuning rather than training. On the other hand, the representation learned during pretraining are often useful for the task on which a model is fine-tuned.

Another important aspect of transformer-based large language models concerns their sizes, how their sizes are reflected in publications. Early models, such as the original BERT, were trained on English Wikipedia (about 2.5 billion words) and a corpus of 11K e-books (the Book Corpus, about 800 million words, Zhu et al. 2015). Later models were trained on much larger datasets, with many billions of words. However, the amount of training data is not the only aspect of model size. The other important aspect is the number of building blocks, which is reflected in the number of parameters (numeric values) that the model includes. The original BERT model came in two sizes: BERT-base and BERT-large. BERT-base had 12 layers, hidden layers had size 768, and used 12 attention heads, in total 110 million parameters. BERT-large had 24 layers, hidden layer vector size of 1024, and 16 attention heads, in total 340 million parameters. Larger models consistently

---
[4] This is very similar to the Cloze task in reading assessment.

achieve better performance on a variety of benchmarks for NLP tasks. The famous GPT-3 model had 175 billion parameters (Brown et al. 2020). Models are often reported in terms of their sizes (millions or billions of parameters), especially in publications that use pretrained models, while the size of the corpora they were pretrained on are typically mentioned only in the papers that introduce new models.[5]

7.2 Generating Questions with Transformers

Kriangchaivech and Wangperawong (2019) presented one of the earliest approaches for AQG with transformers. As an early approach, they did not use a pretrained model, but rather used a transformer architecture as a sophisticated encoder-decoder model to train an AQG model from scratch. They trained their model on the SQuAD dataset (Rajpurkar et al. 2016), using the SQuAD original training partition as the training set (about 80 K text-question–answer records) and the SQuAD dev partition as the test set (about 10 K records). The training regime used an inversion of SQuAD data. For each training instance, a whole text paragraph (rather than just the focal sentence) was concatenated with a special symbol (*) and then with the answer text of the question, while the supervised part was the original question (schematically: text + answer→ question). Note that this type of training belongs to the answer-aware type of AQG. It also allows to feed the model with the same text paragraph, but combined with an answer to a different question, so the model can be trained to produce different questions for the same text. In addition, the texts were considerably preprocessed before feeding into the Transformer model. The authors used a POS tagger and NER to detect a variety of named and numeric entities, such as companies, locations, organizations, and products. All such entities were replaced in the texts and in the answers (but not in the training questions) with generic class strings (e.g. any person name → PERSON). This was done to increase the chances for learning generalization. They also eliminated stop words from the questions and answers before feeding the materials to the transformer model. To generate embeddings, the authors used the pretrained model from BERT, with a vocabulary of 30,000 pieces.

To test the trained model performance, they measured how the model-generated questions differed from the original SQuAD questions in the test set. The evaluation metric was WER (word error rate)—essentially a Levenstein edit distance over word units that measures how many words (in the generated question) were omitted, inserted or correctly reproduced (as compared to the original test question). This kind of measure is suited to estimate how well the model can reproduce questions of the same kind that it encountered during training. A low WER score (e.g. 1 word) would indicate that the generated question is very similar to the original question, while a high WER score (e.g. 15) indicates that a generated question is considerably different from the original question. The authors

---

[5] For a systematic discussion of those issues, see Raffel et al. (2020).

7.2 Generating Questions with Transformers

stressed that this metric is not a direct measure of the quality of generated questions. Even with low WER, the different word could be one that changes the meaning of the whole question, while a question with high WER might be just a good but different question for the same text and answer. Still, they used WER as a proxy evaluation, since a good AQG model is supposed to reproduce many questions (such presupposition is intuitively appealing, but it is problematic). The authors stated that *"the questions generated were mostly grammatically correct and related to the topic of the context passage"* although no measures were presented to support this claim. Overall, 10,570 questions were generated for the test set and the WER distribution for those questions had a normal shape, with an average of 9.66 word errors, 88% of the questions had error rates between 6 and 20 words. This result may indicate that the model struggled to reproduce the SQuAD questions. The authors also noted that the average length of model-generated questions was 8 words, whereas the SQuAD questions have an average of 12 words per question, thus indicating that the model tended to produce questions of lower complexity. The authors also investigated the frequencies of the first words in generated questions, since the first words are often the asking words (e.g. what, how, who). The most common first word was *what*, both in the training set and in the model-generated data. Potentially, an imbalance of *what* in the training data could have led the model to prefer generating 'what' questions.

Chan and Fan (2019) provided one of the earliest investigations into using a pre-trained transformer model, i.e. BERT, for question generation. They used the BERT-base model (12 layers, 768 hidden dimensions, and 12 attention heads.) with a vocabulary of 30,522 words. They introduced three architectural variants. They also used the SQuAD 1.1 dataset, and so their work was also oriented around text–question–answer records. Their first model was a simple adaptation of BERT to QG (which they called BERT-QG). The input sequence to BERT was set as *([CLS]; C; [SEP]; A; [SEP])*, where C is the text sequence and A is the answer phrase, *CLS* and *SEP* are special tokens.. BERT was trained (fine-tuned) to maximize the probability of the words (comprising the question) in the output. The whole output sequence was generated at once. When the output was generated, the first generated *SEP* symbol was considered to be the end of the question. According to Chan and Fan, this model did not perform well when trained on SQuAD data, many outputs were not even readable sentences. According to the authors, the problem stemmed from that the later tokens produced in the output were not conditioned on the earlier produced tokens (of the question). Their second model called BERT-SQG produced the output question in a sequential manner, word by word. First, the same kind of input *([CLS]; C; [SEP]; A; [SEP] [MASK])* was fed to BERT. The model would produce one token at *MASK* position (initial word of the question), which was then concatenated to the input sequence and the sequence fed again to BERT. Each new output token would be concatenated to the input and processed in BERT. The process repeats until a *SEP* token is generated. This model was much more successful in AQG, but the authors noted two problems with the BERT-SQG model. First, the quality of generated questions (measured by BLEU scores) deteriorated when the input text was longer. Second, when an answer phrase appears multiple times in the context, there is ambiguity (for BERT) as for which one to use for generating questions, i.e. which part of the input is the context and which part is the answer. Thus, the authors introduced an additional model BERT-HLSQG. Instead of concatenating the answer phrase to the context paragraph, the answer phrase is specially marked in the context $C = [c_1; c_2; ... [HL]; a_1; ...; a_j; [HL]; ... c_j]$. Questions are then generated sequentially word by word as in the SQG model. The authors evaluated the models using SQuAD data and compared them to the previous leading AQG models, which were RNN-based neural models. Comparisons were conducted using sentence-level contexts (i.e. the context is just one sentence), and paragraph-level contexts. For paragraph contexts, the best RNN model had BLEU-4 score of 16.38. BERT-SQG achieved BLEU-4 score of 20.11 and BERT-HLSQG achieved 22.17.

UniLM (Dong et al. 2019) was one of the first transformer-based architectures developed to be able to perform a range of NLP tasks based on the same core pretrained model. Like BERT, UniLM includes an encoder stack that can be supplemented with output layers for tasks that require a limited set of outputs (NLU tasks, such as input classification). In addition, UniLM can also be configured with decoder components to make it suitable for NLG tasks. The model was pretrained on a range of different word prediction tasks (cloze tasks), with different ways of defining context. For a left-to-right unidirectional LM, the context of the to-be-predicted-word includes all the preceding words in the text snippet. For a right-to-left unidirectional LM, the context includes all the words following the target word. For a bidirectional LM, the context consists of both preceding and following words (like BERT). For training sequence-to-sequence generation, the input is two sentences, and the goal is to learn to generate words of the second sentence conditioned on the first sentence.[6] Different self-attention setups were used for the different tasks. The transformer components share parameters and thus learn representations that are jointly optimized for different tasks. Pretraining was done by mixing all the above tasks and learning over large corpora of text—the English Wikipedia (about 2.5 billion words) and a corpus of 11K books (the Book Corpus, about 800 million words, Zhu et al. 2015).

Once the model is pretrained, fine-tuning is used to adjust it for specific tasks. Indeed, several experiments were presented showing the UniLM capability to perform both NLU and NLG tasks. The NLU tasks included tasks from the General Language Understanding Evaluation (GLUE) benchmark (Wang et al. 2018a), including text-similarity estimation (for pairs of text snippets), linguistic acceptability (is the sentence plausible), sentiment analysis, paraphrase detection, and natural language inference (NLI). The NLG tasks included abstractive summarization of texts, Question Answering (generating answers), and generating questions for texts.

---

[6] Essentially, as in seq2seq models, generation of any next word is conditioned on the previous sentence and all the words of the second sentence that precede the current target word.

The QG aspect of UniLM was one of the early demonstrations of performing QG with a pretrained transformer model. UniLM was fine-tuned for the task of answer-aware question generation. Given an input passage and an answer span, the goal was to generate a question for the targeted answer. Such a task is posed as a sequence-to-sequence generation. For training, the full text and the answer are considered as one segment (and concatenated), while the question is the second segment, all separated with special delimiter tokens *[SOS] text + answer [EOS] question [EOS]*. The pretrained UniLM was fine-tuned on data of the SQuAD 1.1 dataset. It was evaluated with standard NLG metrics, BLEU-4, METEOR, and ROUGE-L, and outperformed several models that were based on older, non-transformer, seq2seq architectures. A more advanced version, UniLM-v2 (Bao et al. 2020) was also adapted for AQG and achieved slightly better results on the same metrics (see Table 7.2).

7.3 Question Generation with Large Transformer Models

Raffel et al. (2020) proposed to reframe all neural NLP tasks *"into a unified text-to-text-format where the input and output are always text strings."* Unlike UniLM, which allows encoder-only (BERT-like) configurations and encoder + decoder setups, the Text-To-Text Transfer Transformer (T5) model uses encoder + decoder for all NLP tasks. The text-to-text formulation is similar to the seq2seq formulation of earlier neural networks, but such similarity is limited—the T5 is built on top of massive multi-layered attention-based transformer architecture, while early seq2seq models were much shallower systems using the LSTM architecture. As we already noted, the transformer architecture allows to have a network pretrained on large collections of texts, and only then be fine-tuned for the specific NLP task. Since pretraining proved to be useful for many NLP tasks, the next logical move is to use the same pretrained model for many tasks. The text-to-text framework *"allows us to use the same model, loss function, and hyperparameters on any NLP task, including machine translation, document summarization, question answering, and classification tasks"* (Roberts and Raffel 2020).

Unlike UniLM, which was trained on data from English Wikipedia and a corpus of 11K e-books, T5 was trained on a much larger collection of text data—the Common Crawl web archive. Specifically, T5 was trained in 5 different sizes, from T5-small, base, and large (60, 220, and 770 million parameters respectively), and up to 3B and 11B (billions of parameters).[7] The pretrained T5 models were fine-tuned on several downstream tasks—sentence acceptability, sentiment analysis, text-snippets similarity estimation, natural language inference, sentence completion and question answering. It demonstrated

---

[7] Notably, many papers about LLMs report model sizes in terms of the number of parameters in the model, rather than the size of the corpus on which the model was pretrained. T5-base was pretrained on a corpus of 34 billion words.

superior performance relative to contemporary benchmarks on the relevant datasets. Question generation was not part of the study by Raffel et al. (2020), but several subsequent studies used T5 models for QG, and we describe them below.

Fung et al. (2020) used the T5-small model and fine-tuned it for the question generation task using the SQuAD 2.0 dataset. Their study was interesting in two respects: question focusing and evaluation. They used the T5-based AQG system for generating educational reading-comprehension questions, focusing specifically on wh-questions. As the T5 was trained as an answer-aware system, in order to generate questions for a text the user must specify the potential answers (question targets), specifically by marking the target spans via a graphical user interface. For a fully automated AQG, Fung et al. used a NER system to identify named entities in text and used them as question targets. They also carried out a survey study of their system with 15 teachers. One of the aspects of their survey asked participants about the overall quality of the auto-generated questions, on a 5-point Likert scale. While 46.7% were completely satisfied, 40% were satisfied, and 13% were not satisfied. The authors concluded that the quality of questions from the T5 AQG needed some improvement. They also noted that a NER system cannot help identifying potential targets for 'why' questions, since such questions are not about named entities.

Srihari et al. (2023) also utilized the T5-small pretrained model for question generation. To fine-tune the model, they used a sample of 50 examples from the SQuAD 2.0 dataset and 50 examples from a reference book on data science. QG training with T5 was answer-aware, i.e. the training examples specified the context (paragraph text), the target answer and its location in the text, and the question. For testing/generation only the text and the target answer are supplied. The size and nature of the test-set were not described; the reported evaluation results were BLEU-4 18.98, METEOR 25.22 and ROUGE-L 40.34. The authors reported the following issues with AQG: (a) some of the questions generated seem to extract phrases from context and present them in the form of a question; (b) some generated questions were not ending with a '?'; and (c) the last word in the question was often repeated. The authors noted that the AQG model produced predominantly identification-type questions, because 88% of the questions in SQuAD are such questions.

Qi et al. (2020) presented yet another transformer-based general NLP architecture, ProphetNet. Unlike the standard transformer architectures, which predict the next one token at each step, ProphetNet was designed to predict the next n tokens simultaneously, using a n-stream self-attention mechanism. ProphetNet (with a setting of $n = 2$) was pretrained on English Wikipedia and an 11K e-book corpus. It was fine-tuned for QG using the SQuAD 1.1 dataset. The AQG performance was assessed using the common automated metrics (see Table 7.2), it outperformed LSTM based models and achieved results slightly better than UniLM (which was pretrained on the same data). Wu et al. (2022) used ProphetNet and enhanced it with attention on the location of the answer in the text paragraph, and with syntactic information (using Stanford NLP toolkit for dependency parsing) merged into the neural architecture. The enhanced model achieved slight improvement on the SQuAD QG data.

Xiao et al. (2020) presented another variation of a transformer-based architecture. Their ERNIE-GEN system was based on a multi-layer transformer with an encoder and a decoder. A special aspect of ERNIE-GEN is the use of two different generation flows. The word-by-word module generates text by using context and predicting one word at a time. The span-by-span generation module generates multi-token sequences, as an approximation for semantically-complete spans (i.e. language expressions). The two modules operate in parallel, and their outputs were integrated via an additional attention module. The system was pretrained on the English Wikipedia and the Book Corpus. It was fine-tuned for several NLG tasks, including abstractive summarization, generative question answering, and AQG. For AQG, the system was fine-tuned on the SQuAD dataset, using two different train-dev splits. The system slightly outperformed previous transformer-based systems on the AQG task, as measured by the standard automated evaluation metrics (see Table 7.2).

Lopez et al. (2020, 2021) utilized the pretrained GPT-2 model for question generation. They fine-tuned and tested it on the SQuAD dataset. Their results (with the standard automated metrics) were lower than other transformer-based AQG systems (see Table 7.2). An important aspect of their study was their investigation on how the length of the text paragraph (context and the answer) influences the quality of QG. They also noted some frequent QG failures. A peculiar aspect—some generated questions seem to be simply phrases from the paragraph context, returned with phrase order reversed, what they call context-copying (see examples in Table 7.1). In some cases, the last words of the generated question keeps on repeating. They attributed this behavior to *"attention mechanism is not working properly in pinpointing important context words, which leads to the model being confused in generating the next token."* In other cases, the system seems to be copying too much context into the question, sometimes reaching the generation length limit resulting in a premature cut. The authors considered that the system has learned the context-copying strategy because of the composition of the SQuAD dataset. About 88% of questions in the training set are identification questions (who/what/when/where), which typically involve some context copying. They claim that diversifying the style of questions in the training set might alleviate this problem. However, this highlights the tendency of large language models to learn any statistical relations in the data, even spurious ones.

Varanasi et al. (2020) introduced a transformer-based version of a copying mechanism. The idea is that during QG, some words can be generated while some words can be copied from the input context paragraph. Their implementation uses a transformer encoder-decoder architecture where the encoder and decoder share the weights model (which reduces the model size and overall training time). The copying mechanism is implemented via cross attentions between source and target words in every layer of the transformer. For each new token position in the output, the system computes the probability of generating a word (from a fixed vocabulary), or copying a word from the input.

Table 7.1 Examples of failed generations from Lopez et al. (2020)

	Context	Generated question	Note
1	Teaching may be carried out informally, within the family, which is called homeschooling, or in the wider community. Formal teaching may be carried out by paid professionals. Such professionals enjoy a status in some societies on a par with physicians, lawyers, engineers, and accountants (Chartered or CPA)	What is a profession of the profession of the profession of the profession of the profession of the profession of the profession of the profession of the profession of the profession of the profession	'Endless' repetition
2	In 1900, the Los Angeles Times defined southern California as including"the seven counties of Los Angeles, San Bernardino, Orange, Riverside, San Diego, Ventura and Santa Barbara." In 1999, the Times added a newer county Imperial to that list	Which newspaper in the United States defined Southern California as including the seven counties of Los Angeles, San Bernardino, Orange, Riverside, San Diego, Ventura and Sant	The generated question was cut prematurely. The list of counties should have been omitted

Table 7.2 Results of automated evaluation measures for several transformer-based QG systems

Authors	System	Dataset	BLEU-4	Meteor	Rouge L
Dong et al. (2019)	UniLM transformer (trained on EW + BkC)	SQuAD[a]	22.12	25.06	51.07
		SQuAD[b]	23.75	25.61	52.04
	UniLM-v2	SQuAD[a]	24.43	26.34	51.97
		SQuAD[b]	26.29	27.16	53.22
Chan and Fan (2019)	BERT-QG	SQuAD[a]	6.10	16.80	41.01
		SQuAD[b]	4.08	14.18	37.94
	BERT_SQG	SQuAD[a]	20.11	23.88	48.12
		SQuAD[b]	21.04	24.25	48.23
	BERT_HLSQG	SQuAD[a]	20.33	23.88	48.23
		SQuAD[b]	22.17	24.80	49.68
Qi et al. (2020)	ProphetNet (trained on EW + BkC)	SQuAD[a]	23.91	26.6	52.26
		SQuAD[b]	25.8	27.54	53.65
Wu et al. (2022)	ProphetNet enhanced	SQuAD[a]	24.37	26.26	52.77
		SQuAD[b]	26.30	27.25	53.87
Xiao et al. (2020)	ERNIE-GEN (trained on EW + BkC)	SQuAD[a]	25.4	26.92	52.84
		SQuAD[b]	**26.95**	27.57	**53.77**
Lopez et al. (2021)	GPT-2 small, 124 M parameters	SQuAD[b]	8.21	21.11	44.27
Varanasi et al. (2020)	CopyBERT	SQuAD[a]	21.17	23.48	49.91
	SpanBERT + copying	SQuAD[a]	22.71	24.28	51.6
Srihari et al. (2023)	T5 small	SQuAD	18.98	25.22	40.34
Murakhovs'ka et al. (2022)	Baseline T5-base	SQuAD	23.74	43.63	49.81
	MixQG on T5-base	9 QA datasets	23.53	43.83	50.05
	MixQG on T5-large	9 QA datasets	24.42	45.07	50.99
	MixQG on T5-3B	9 QA datasets	25.42	**45.75**	51.85

When using the SQuAD dataset. [a]Indicates using dataset split introduced by Du et al. (2017), [b]indicates the split introduced by Zhou et al. (2017). EW is English Wikipedia, BkC is Book Corpus.

Their model achieved results comparable to the other contemporary transformer models (see Table 7.2), although they claimed that their model trains much faster than other models.

Murakhovs'ka et al. (2022) presented a study that advanced transformer-based AQG in two directions. First, they trained a model on several QA datasets, instead of a single one, and second, they trained to generate different and varied kinds of questions. One direction of their research was to demonstrate the improvement of AQG results by training on a larger set of data. They used nine published QA datasets, including SQuAD 1.1, and used the training subsets from those to train their model, MixQG, on answer-aware question generation. They used the pretrained T5 models (T5-base, 220 million parameters, and T5-3B, 2.8 billion parameters) for this exercise. They also used T5-base to train on just the SQuAD 1.1 data. Their training subset of SQuAD data had about 86K training examples, whereas the combined (mixed) dataset had 560K training examples, which is 6.5 times larger. They evaluated the AQG models on the validation subset of SQuAD data, using standard NLG metrics. The results are presented in Table 7.2. The T5-base model trained on just the SQuAD data obtained a ROUGE-L score of 49.82, which is comparable to other transformer-based models when trained on the same dataset. MixQG that used T5-base and trained on the combined dataset obtained a Rouge-L score of 50.05. That was an obvious improvement, but given that the new training set was more than six times larger, the improvement was notably small. MixQG that used the T5-3B model and trained on the combined dataset obtained a Rouge-L score of 51.85. Again, it demonstrates that using a larger model improves the results. But the improvement was rather small. Using a more than 10-times larger pretrained model and training on more than 6 times more QG examples resulted in very small improvement on the standard metrics. Even on the novel BERTscore metric (score range 0–1), the differences are rather small: 0.5568 for T5-base trained on just SQuAD data, 0.5566 for MixQG with T5-base, and 0.5789 for MixQG with T5-3B. It seems that using larger pretrained models and utilizing more QG training data helps improve results on standard metrics, but at a very slow rate of improvement.

Murakhovs'ka et al. (2022) also conducted a human evaluation of generated questions. To facilitate the answer-aware nature of the QG process, they designed the following scenario. Teachers recruited for the experiment were given several select Wikipedia texts to produce quizzes (on various subjects). The teachers had to select (highlight) the target answer in the text, and then an AQG system would generate a question for that text with the target answer. The teachers had to indicate whether the question was acceptable, or indicate a reason for rejection—the question being off-target, disfluent, or the question being unsuitable in the given context. They collected 3164 human-rated samples, with seven different transformer-based AQG models generating the questions. Among all models, the MixQG model had the best acceptance rate (68.4%), while for the next best model (trained just on SQuAD data) acceptance rate was only 58.4%.

7.4 Summary

Transformer architectures are designed to handle and abstract sequential data by using multiple layers with attention. They have achieved great success in NLP, including various NLG tasks. Transformers have also shown improved performance on AQG tasks, as compared to LSTM-based networks. One advantage of transformers is that they typically are pretrained on large datasets of text. thus, acquiring considerable 'knowledge' about language regularities that can be transferred to specific tasks. In that sense they became *foundation models* (Bommasani et al. 2021). On top of which specific NLP tasks, like question generation, can be implemented. Such specialization, typically called fine tuning, allows to utilize the pretrained capabilities for generating quite fluent questions from texts. Even with fine-tuning, transformer-based AQG system require large amounts of training data. This is alleviated, to some extent, by proliferation of large question–answer datasets.

Transformer AQG models do have disadvantages. Like other neural models, they sometimes produce hallucinated content. The type of questions they produce strongly depends on the type of questions in the training materials. That means that tuning to produce only specific types of questions or improving performance for only certain types of questions might be difficult. The standard solution is then to retrain (finetune) a model on different data, or continue finetuning on the specific type of questions (which may require procuring more of the special data).

Content Selection for AQG

8.1 Introduction

The notion of content selection refers to a seemingly simple issue—which parts of a text are question-worthy. Many rule-based and neural question-generation methods presume that a target answer has been preselected in a text. But how do we select a target answer, the focus of the question? In educational settings, a typical reading passage for school reading assignments may consist of a hundred to couple of thousand words. Wikipedia and news articles also contain from tens to a few hundred sentences. Other textual materials, like book chapters or instruction manuals, can be even longer. How should an automated system be set up to select content for questions?

Even a simple declarative sentence with just a subject and a direct object, such as *John bought a book* allows at least two obvious questions: *Who bought a book?* and *What did John buy?* More complex sentences contain multiple statements, which all could be the focus of question formation. Consider the sentence *Organic farmers keep the soil healthy by feeding it natural fertilizers.* The core of this sentence is *Organic farmers keep the soil healthy.* It can support the question *Who keeps the soil healthy?*, while *What do organic farmers keep healthy?* is possible but would be quite awkward. Yet there are more possibilities: *What kind of farmers keep the soil healthy?*, and also the yes/no form *Do organic farmers keep the soil healthy?* The original sentence also includes the idea that organic farmers feed the soil with natural fertilizers. This idea could be extracted and could form the basis for additional questions, like *Who feeds the soil with natural fertilizers?*, *What do organic farmers feed the soil (with)?*, and even *What is fed natural fertilizers?* Another question could be *How is the soil kept healthy?*, and an involved question could be *What does feeding natural fertilizers do for the soil?*. These examples demonstrate the potential richness of text that needs to be considered by an AQG process.

One of the answers to content selection issue is very simple—the AQG system should not select any content, rather it is the task of the user of such a system to point out what to ask about. Such a solution can be implemented with a graphical user interface that displays the text, and a user can select the question-worthy material, often by highlighting the chosen text span on the screen. Once a user selects the focal span, an AQG system can generate questions about this part of the text and provide them to the user for accept/reject/edit or other operations. This kind of interactive QG is certainly a viable solution for certain cases, especially when tight control over question foci is required, for example in some educational test-development scenarios or producing quizzes for specific content.

A radically different approach to content selection is that an AQG system should try to generate questions about every possible aspect in the given text.[1] An early example of such an approach was presented by Heilman and Smith (2010a). Their AQG system worked in two steps. First, all kinds of potential questions were generated form the given text. Next, a ranking algorithm was used to sort the questions, and only a top-ranked set of questions would be produced at the final output. Although part of their motivation was to sort out poorly-formulated questions, the general idea is also that an AQG system produces many questions for even a single text document. Another example of massive generation was presented by Flor and Riordan (2018), where an SRL-based AQG system generated 890 questions from 165 sentences, that is on average 5.4 questions per sentence. That was done by allowing the AQG system to generate a question about every instantiated semantic role from every predicate (main verb) in a sentence. The intent of such efforts was to demonstrate how specific AQG algorithms can generate abundant outputs (and to evaluate the quality of generated questions). For practical applications, overgeneration of questions may seem unreasonable, but this approach can have some benefits. It can present an AQG user with plenty of questions to choose from. Moreover, it can sometimes generate unexpected or unusual questions, or pose questions about less prominent parts of text that might be neglected in user-initiated content selection scenarios. In a different perspective, the AQG overgeneration approach might be seen as an approach that shifts the content selection stage from before actual AQG to after the generation step. Instead of selecting content for questions, the users might want to consider selecting from among the generated questions.

The research literature on AQG has a variety of proposals for question-worthy content selection. A common assumption is that some form of automated preselection of

---

[1] Exhaustively generating all possible questions that relate to a given text segment is technically possible with various AQG systems. However, the utility of such an approach depends on the purpose of question generation. If we need questions to train some ML-based system, exhaustive generation might be useful. When questions are generated for use by test developers, teachers, or students, overgeneration might not be useful as the large quantity can overwhelm the users, and many of the questions might not be suitable for the task (Madnani et al. 2019). Still, exhaustive generation might be useful in some cases, for example when a user wants to find an unusual or surprising question for a given textual material.

content for AQG would be useful or even necessary for AQG systems. One useful distinction among the many methods is a distinction between approaches that address sentence selection—which sentences in a text are worthy of question generation (Agarwal and Mannem 2011), and approaches that focus directly on potential answers and do not consider sentence selection as an explicit step in the process (Subramanian et al. 2018).

8.2 Selection of Sentences

Huang and He (2016) described an AQG system that was intended to generate questions for reading comprehension assessments for English second language low and intermediate proficiency level students. They used seven reading passages of length 250–400 words. To select representative sentences for AQG they used three criteria: keyness, completeness and independence. *Keyness* considers the importance of the term in a text. When no background corpus of relevant texts is available, the most frequent words in a text (excluding stop words) may be considered as its key words. From this, sentence importance can be inferred: *"a sentence containing denser frequent words is likely to contain more of the important meaning of the text."* Thus, sentence keyness was computed as sum of the frequencies of the sentence words in the whole text, divided by the number of words in the sentence. The criterion of completeness emphasized that different paragraphs in the text must be represented in the selection of sentences, proportionally to the number of sentences in each paragraph. The criterion of independence reflected a desire to select sentences that are not closely related in their meanings, so as to cover different aspects of content in a text. For this purpose, words were represented as LSA vectors, using a pretrained semantic space. Sentence vectors were computed as averages from vectors of constituent words. Semantic similarity between sentences was computed as cosine values between the respective vectors. The combined selection algorithm worked on a list of all sentences from a passage that were sorted by keyness. Sentences were selected by higher keyness values, with two constraints: a candidate sentence was excluded if its paragraph had already met the quota, or if its meaning was too similar to one of the already-selected sentences (using a threshold similarity value). Sentence selection by this algorithm was compared to sentences selected from the same texts by three trained educators. The results indicated that the algorithm worked better (its selections were closer to human selections) than a plausible baseline that selected just the first sentence in each paragraph.

Das and Majumder (2017) presented a simple rule-based approach to identifying question-worthy material. Their study is illustrative as they aimed at generating factual questions (answerable from the text). The goal of questions was not accessing reading comprehension, but just the content knowledge retained by learners after reading passages of text (Wikipedia articles). They set to generate Open Cloze (gap-filling) items, which means just finding potential phrases to blank out. The selected sentences with the blanks can then be presented to learners after reading the text. The QG task was framed as a classic two-step process: (1) identify informative sentences (sentence selection); (2) identify phrases that would be blanked out and serve as answer-keys (answer-key selection). To simplify matters, the authors decided to avoid complex syntactic structures, and avoid sentences with coordination or subordination. Thus, their sentence selection process used a combination of filters: a filter to eliminate sentences with complicated structures, and a filter to select sentences with suitable content. The elimination filter utilized dependency parse of each sentence, checking for certain patterns that indicate complex sentences (presence of multiple grammatical subjects, as indicated by dependency relations *nsubj* and *nsubjpass*). An additional filter was used to refine the set of selected sentences. This filter used patterns of POS tags, such as having at least two separate NNP/NNPS sequences (i.e. seeking to have sentences with some named entities), and not having any RB/RBR/RBS (adverb) tag sequences (eliminate complicated descriptions).

One idea for sentence selection is that question-worthy are those sentences that are most important in a text, sentences that are most informative or carry the most important concepts. A very simple approach to selecting sentences in a text for QG is to assume that the sentences that would be most important for a good summary of a text would also be the most likely important for questioning. In many cases this can be a reasonable assumption, and it can lead to quite efficient selection of content within a text, especially when more specific requirements for content selection are not available. In such cases, using an automatic extractive summarization system[2] for content selection can be a useful and efficient approach.

Narendra et al. (2013) applied an extractive summarizer for selecting informative sentences and chose the top 10% of the ranked sentences from the summarizer to generate questions. Becker et al. (2012) stated: *"we make use of our own implementation of SumBasic (Nenkova et al. 2006), a simple but competitive document summarization algorithm motivated by the assumption that sentences containing the article's most frequently occurring words are the most important. We thus use the SumBasic score for each sentence to order them as candidates for question construction."* Many extractive summarizers inherently use sentence ranking 'under the hood'. Therefore, sentence ranking can be utilized directly for sentence-importance ranking in AQG. Lovenia et al. (2018) tested several such approaches for QG, in particular the TextRank algorithm and also LSA vectors. Both approaches assume that most important sentences in a text are those that are most strongly semantically related to the rest of the text. TextRank (Mihalcea and Tarau 2004) is a graph-based algorithm that computes how much semantic similarity support a sentence (or a chunk) gets from other sentences. LSA (or other vector-based models) can calculate

---

[2] Extractive summarization techniques try to identify and extract the most important segments from texts. This stands in contrast to the so-called abstractive techniques, which create 'hidden' representations of text contents and then generate the summaries from such representations, typically using deep learning methods (Giarelis et al. 2023).

the average cosine between the vector of a given sentence and vectors of all other sentences in text. The resulting summed scores can be used to rank the sentences and pick the top subset of sentences as the best candidates for QG. The technical complexity of such approaches may vary. For example, the original TextRank requires morphological analysis to be able to match inflected variants of the same lemma, whereas vector-based approaches do not need a separate syntactic and morphological analyses.

Adamson et al. (2013) have worked on a quite different problem. Instead of focusing on factoid questions, the object of their research was generation of *"deeper, more subjective questions drawn from a text"*, questions that might be more suitable for group discussion and deep engagement with a text. Moreover, unlike much other AQG research that works with informational texts, Adamson et al. were interested in literary texts. Specifically, they worked with the story *Animal Farm* by George Orwell. Their approach to content selection was as follows. Instead of generating questions from the original text, they generated questions from the summary of the original text. Note that this approach is quite suitable for longer literary texts, especially for conceptually deeper questions that need to relate to the more prominent aspects of the long story (such an approach might not be suitable in other cases). They worked with a summary professionally prepared by educators. Even the summary was quite long, and so the authors evaluated several approaches to selecting sentences from the summary for AQG. One approach used cosine similarity between sentences. They computed similarity between each sentence of the summary and the sentence preceding it. Sentences with high similarity to the immediate predecessor sentence were interpreted as marking an important concept, and were selected for question generation. Another approach was to use a measure of sentence uniqueness, computed as average *tf-idf* scores for all words in a sentence. They used the original long story as the 'corpus' for the IDF measure. Here the logic was that summary sentences with rare words (relative to the source text) *"may contain new ideas that are not literally present in the original"*, which might be useful for generating discussion-stimulating questions. The third approach to sentence selection was considered as 'topical'. The words and sentences of the original story were arranged into a word-sentence co-occurrence matrix which was then reduced to a 5-dimensional LSA space. Each dimension was then considered as a latent topic. Sentences from the summary were then encoded into such vectors.[3] Summary sentences were selected with the highest weight in each of the topic dimensions, i.e. five sets of candidate sentences, representing such latent topics. The authors did not evaluate sentence selection directly. They used the syntax-driven AQG system by Heilman and Smith (2010a, b, c), with some modifications, to generate all possible questions from selected sentences in each condition. They picked top 50 questions (as ranked internally by the AQG system) from each condition for human evaluation. As a baseline, the authors selected 50 questions generated from sentences randomly selected in the original story. Four teachers judged all the generated questions on six evaluation dimensions (with a 7-point scale for each dimension): (1) the question lends itself to multiple answers; (2)

---

[3] Presumably by averaging vectors of their constituent words.

answering this question could engage a student's personal values or perspective; (3) the question would be valuable for stimulating discussion among students; (4) the question touches upon important themes from the story; (5) the question is comprehensible; (6) the question is grammatical. Such evaluation mixes content selection with AQG quality, although the first four aspects are more related to content selection. The cosine and the topic-based selection methods led to the higher-rated questions in all of evaluation aspects 1–4, scoring statistically significantly higher than the other approaches. The authors noted that although the questions from summary sentences selected by the cosine method and the topical method had similar evaluation scores, the questions were quite different. The cosine method stressed repeating elements in the summary, including the main protagonists and major abstractions in the summary. The latent-topical selection method promoted contents that echoed the latent topics of the original text, including some chronological aspects of the original story.

Chen et al. (2019) conducted an extensive study on sentence selection methods for AQG, with three groups of methods. One set of strategies focused on sentence informativeness. One basic method in this group defines importance by length—the longest sentences in a text contain a large amount of information and might potentially be the most important ones. A concept-rich method assumes that most important sentences are those that contain the largest number of entities. A variant of that method measures informativeness of a sentence by the number of entity types in a sentence (concept-type-richness). While such methods might seem quite simplistic, their simplicity might be useful is some situations. A second group of methods adopts the notions of difficulty and novelty. One assumption is that the most question-worthy sentences in a text are those that are the most difficult. Difficulty can be estimated by using some proxy indicators; Chen et al. used the Flesch Reading Ease Score as difficulty indicator.[4] A different assumption is that question worthy sentences are those that contain relatively novel materials. Chen et al. implemented this by calculating, for each sentence, the number of words that never appeared in previous sentences in a document. The third group of strategies utilizes some methods for estimating relative importance of sentences in a text, methods that were borrowed from document summarization approaches. A simple strategy is to assume that the first sentence in a document might present the gist of the document and thus could be the most important one. A well-established method for summarization is to compute a graph of inter-sentence relatedness for all sentences of a document and score sentences by their degree of semantic relatedness to other sentences in the text. Chen et al. used LexRank (Erkan and Radev 2004), which is one of the most widely used graph-based methods for computing salience. Another method for scoring sentence importance is by considering a trade-off between importance and redundancy—an important sentence is related to many other sentences, but it does not convey the same information as other sentences.

---

[4] The Flesch Reading Ease (FRE) uses proportions of word counts and syllable counts as indicators of difficulty. It was developed for text passages, not single sentences. See https://en.wikipedia.org/wiki/Flesch%E2%80%93Kincaid_readability_tests.

8.2 Selection of Sentences

An interesting part of Chen et al. study was that they measured how much those proposed general strategies reflect selection of sentences for questions in several datasets of texts with human-produced questions. They used four datasets, of them two from educational settings, in order to evaluate the utility of sentence selection strategies on different types of texts. TriviaQA (Joshi et al. 2017) contains questions from trivia quizzes for which answers are found in Wikipedia articles. MCTest contains short stories and questions for young children. RACE (Lai et al. 2017) includes reading comprehension articles for English language learning, with assessment questions. LearningQ (Chen et al. 2018) contains complex educational articles on a variety of topics (for adult students), with some instructor-designed questions. Those datasets contain, on average, 200, 19, 19, and 43 sentences per text.

Chen et al. devised the following methodology for evaluation. They used the different methods to select question-worthy sentences from the texts in the datasets. They used a neural AQG system trained on SQuAD (the system by Du et al. 2017) and generated questions from the selected sentences (for each dataset separately). They then compared the generated questions to the human-authored questions from each dataset, using BLEU and ROUGE-L metrics. The idea of this evaluation was to find which sentence selection strategies produce questions that are most similar to human-authored questions. Overall, LexRank was consistently among the best selection methods for all datasets. Importance-based strategies were found to be more effective than informativeness-based methods (Longest, Concept count) and difficulty-based and novelty-based methods. However, the evaluation results also indicated that different methods are suited differently for different texts and contents. The selection method that prefers early sentences in a text was effective for Wikipedia articles (since Wikipedia articles tend to contain the most important information in the first sentence). A strategy that prioritizes the longest sentences was quite effective for children's stories, and also for texts for English language learners. A strategy that focuses on sentences that contain novel information was effective for educational articles for adults.

Du and Cardie (2017) proposed a neural method for learning to select question-worthy sentences in a text. They used the SQuAD dataset that includes Wikipedia articles with human-authored questions and with the answers manually marked in the text sentences. Sentences that contained answers were considered question-worthy, while all other sentences as non-worthy. To learn a binary classifier over sentences, they used a bidirectional LSTM network. Words were encoded using GloVe embeddings and sentence vectors were derived from word embeddings using convolution layers. Several models were compared. One model learned binary classification while being fed each sentence separately, while another model learned a sequence of yes/no decisions over a sequence of encoded sentences from a paragraph of text. Training, validation, and testing used SQuAD data in a split of 80, 10 and 10% respectively. Evaluation used precision, recall and F1 measures. The trained models achieved precision of about 74%, recall of about 86–89%, and F1 scores of about 0.80. They out-performed feature-rich bag-of-words models trained via logistic regression, which achieved comparable recall, but lower precision (about 69%) and thus lower F1 of about 0.79. Overall, this work demonstrates that it is possible to learn to identify question-worthy sentences. However, this requires a large number of ground-truth labels of question-worthy sentences (tens of thousands). Obtaining such labels is a long, laborious, and usually costly process. Furthermore, the proposed deep neural network was only validated in short paragraphs instead of the whole article. Du and Cardic (2017) also noted that *"because of the variability of human choice in generating questions, it is the case that many sentences labeled as negative examples might actually contain concepts worth asking a question about."* In other words, what the model learned from the large corpus is not unique and the learned sentence-selection preferences might not be optimal in other circumstances.

Mahdavi et al. (2020) presented a study of sentence selection for QG, and a neural QG system that used the sentence selection model. The core of their proposal was to use machine learning to learn sentence selection from relevant prior data. They extracted features of sentences in the training data and trained a binary classifier based on the extracted features. They defined two types of features for each sentence: features coming from the sentence itself, and features about the context of the sentence in the larger text. Sentence-internal features included the numbers of verbs, nouns, adjectives, adverbs, and connector words (all those obtained from a POS-tagger analysis), sentence length and the ratio of stop words. Context-based features included several groups. One feature was *tf-idf* score: token frequency was counted within the sentence and *IDF* was computed over the whole text; average *tf-idf* from all words in the sentence was used as a feature, assumed to reflect the importance of the sentence in the text. The other group of context features were sentence-importance ranks, as provided by several different text-summarization methods, TextRank (Mihalcea and Tarau 2004), SumBasic (Nenkova et al. 2006), and LexRank (Erkan and Radev 2004). A Random Forest classifier was trained with a variety of those features. Mahdavi et al. used two different datasets for training and evaluation of sentence selection. One dataset was SQuAD, with about 70 K questions in the training partition (same splits as Du et al. 2017). The feature-based trained model achieved F1 score of 0.69 on the test set, as compared to human selection of sentences, while LexRank (not trained) had F1 of 0.59. The other dataset was Car Manuals, which had 4672 question–answer instances created by human annotators from two car manuals, with 80/10/10% split for training, development, and testing. There, the feature-based model achieved F1 score of 0.71, while LexRank got 0.53. Those results demonstrate that it is possible to learn from data a set of QG-oriented sentence-selection preferences, to some considerable extent.

8.3 Keyphrase Selection

Instead of selecting question-worthy sentences from a text, many researchers proposed to focus directly on the words or phrases that can serve as potential answers and thus be the targets for questions. Automatic extraction of key terms and keyphrases from text is an old and prolific area of research in computational linguistics, with applications in many areas, such as information retrieval, text summarization, topic analysis, and sentiment analysis (Xie et al. 2023; Garg 2021; Alami Merrouni et al. 2020). The basic idea is to automatically recognize the most important words and phrases in a document, or in a set of texts.

In an early study, Becker et al. (2012) posed the focusing problem for AQG as a two-step process: (1) given a text for QG, one needs to decide which sentences to use for QG, and (2) for each selected sentence—what part of the sentence the question should address. They proposed to select sentences based on sentence importance, as identified by an automated summarization tool. For step 2, selecting which part of a sentence a question should address, they suggested to let a system learn the preferences from human annotators. They used a set of sentences from Wikipedia articles and generated a varied set of gaps (including single words and larger phrases). Those gaps and their corresponding fillers were presented to human annotators, to rank them as potential question targets on a 3-point scale (Good, OK, Bad). The scores where then collapsed to just good/not-good (good versus the rest) and averaged across raters. The resulting set of about 1800 sentences with scored target phrases was used to learn (via logistic regression) to mimic human preferences for target selection. For a selected sentence, multiple gap locations (target phrases) can be considered, and a statistically trained model would then rank them. A variety of features were utilized for the learning model, including token counts (length of target phrase), POS tags, features derived from constituent parse trees, features from SRL analysis of sentences, and features derived from NER analysis (e.g., person, location, organization). Sentence length and the number of word tokens in the target were used, following a heuristic that targets with too many words might be too difficult to answer. Since the model learns to score/rank the candidate targets, the results were presented as a ROC curve.[5] For a threshold set at 0.5, the true positive rate was 0.83 and the false positive rate was 0.19. This demonstrated that human-annotator preferences for keyphrase selection for questions can be successfully learned using a rich set of linguistic features. The authors also noted that the ranking approach allows tuning the classifier to different scenarios. For a strict scenario, setting the acceptance threshold higher, less targets can be accepted, but most of them would be considered adequate. In a more relaxed scenario, setting the threshold lower may allow a more varied set phrases as candidate QG targets, though many of them might be less preferable.

Subramanian et al. (2018) presented a neural system that learns to perform both keyphrase selection and question generation as a two-stage system. Each component was

---

[5] See ROC at https://en.wikipedia.org/wiki/Receiver_operating_characteristic.

trained separately. The keyphrase detection model learns to select keyphrases from the distribution of the human-selected answer phrases in the SQuAD dataset (using about 70K training examples). Specifically, keyphrase selection was posed as supervised learning to maximize the probability of potential answers conditioned on the text document. The learning model was implemented as a pointer network (Vinyals et al. 2015), which is essentially a bidirectional LSTM with attention, that learns to point to a sequence of elements in the input (and thus selects those elements) and copy those elements to the output. The trained model was evaluated on the test set, comparing to the true answer keyphrases; it achieved precision of 44.8%, recall of 38.7%, and F1 score of 0.404. The model was compared to a baseline that takes as potential keyphrase targets all entities that are identified in the text by an extended NER system. The authors noted that about 50% of the question answers in SQuAD are entities [Table 2 in Rajpurkar et al. (2016)], including dates, persons, locations, numeric entities (e.g. *12, five*) and other entities (e.g. *ABC Sports*). The NER-based algorithm for target keyphrase selection achieved precision of just 29.5%, recall of 54.7%, and F1 score of 0.347. The authors also used the NewsQA question–answer dataset (Trischler et al. 2017) to test how well the learned model transfers to a different type of texts (news articles). On this data, the neural model achieved precision of 46.7%, recall of 42.7%, and F1 score of 0.435. The entity-based method achieved precision of 12.5%, recall of 47.9% and F1 score of 0.183. The higher levels of recall for the entity-based method on both datasets indicate that indeed human workers tended to ask questions about various entities. The neural learning model was able to learn, to some extent, the preferences of crowdworkers regarding the question targets.

Wang et al. (2019) also presented neural models that learn to select keyphrases from input sentences. They presented two different variants of keyphrase selection. The simple variant (which they call *local extraction*, EL) was quite similar to the keyphrase selection model from Subramanian et al. (2018). It consisted of a pointer network (implemented as bidirectional LSTM with attention in the decoder) that learns to select text spans from the input as keyphrases. For supervised learning they used the SQuAD dataset with sentence + question + answer as data instances (with a split of about 60K instances for training, 10K for validation and 11K for testing). In evaluation of keyphrase selection, this trained model achieved an F1 score of 0.386 (which is comparable to 0.404 from the work of Subramanian et al.). For a baseline comparison they used a NER system to extract just named entities as keyphrases. On the test set, the NER baseline achieved an F1 score of 0.173 (which is comparable to 0.183 F1 score for the entity-based approach from Subramanian et al. study1). The second model presented by Wang et al. was much more involved. First, they presented a neural question generator that takes as input sentences with keyphrases selected by the EL model. The question generation model included an encoder with bidirectional LSTM, and a decoder LSTM with attention. The novel aspect in Wang et al. study was a multi-agent *message passing* (MP) module. The representation of the input sentence from the EL module and the representation of the corresponding generated question from the QG module are fed to the MP module. The MP module is

8.3 Keyphrase Selection

similar to EL, it uses a pointer network to learn to extract the keyphrase from the sentence, however, unlike EL, the MP module uses the question representation in this process. The newly extracted keyphrase is again fed to the question generation. Such passing of messages between the MP and the QG module continues for several iterations. The model trained with MP extraction achieved F1 score of 0.467, an obvious improvement over the simpler EL model. It seems that refining the keyphrases by re-matching them with corresponding generated questions can improve the keyphrase extraction.

Willis et al. (2019) proposed two other methods for learning extraction of keyphrases for QG. One approach, KPE-Class, trained a neural classifier for keyphrase selection. The data was again taken form the SQuAD dataset. All text data was preprocessed with a POS tagger and a NER system. Words, POS tags and NER tags were converted to embeddings (pretrained GloVe vectors were used for words, and special vectors for the tags). The neural classifier used all those inputs to learn a binary classification (yes/no keyword) for each input word. The other approach, called KPE-Gen, used a neural model to learn to generate keyphrases. As input, for each word token, the system took the concatenation of the word embedding, the POS tag embedding and the NER tag embedding, A bidirectional LSTM encoder was used to obtain a hidden representation of the inputs. A self-attention layer was also used. The result was fed into an LSTM decoder, which learned to generate the keyphrases (using the true answers/keyphrases as the supervision signal). In this way, keyphrases are not extracted but rather generated from the input. Both KPE-Class and KPE-Gen were trained on the training subset of SQuAD. For a baseline comparison, all entities detected by a NER system (dates, persons, organizations and locations) were used as keyphrases.

Unlike previous work, Willis et al. presented an important twist for their evaluation. They rightfully pointed out that the questions in the SQuAD dataset were produced by crowdworkers and not by expert teachers. Therefore, they argued, the questions in SQuAD might not have special pedagogical value. The authors selected 60 passages (Wikipedia articles) from the SQuAD data and asked professional teachers to construct questions for the passages. For each text passage, the teacher experts were instructed to imagine *"that they were teaching a class and were assigning the text passage to be read. The participants were asked to identify the most important information in the passage, and generate 2– 5 questions to test whether a student had correctly read and understood that important information in the passage."* The questions had to have keyphrases in text as answers, just as in the SQuAD dataset. The adjudicated set of most agreed keyphrases over the 60 passages (about 300 in total) was then considered as gold keyphrases produced by educational experts. The original keyphrases from SQuAD, for those 60 passages, were considered as produced by novices.

The three keyphrase extraction methods were applied on the 60 articles and their results were evaluated against the two gold standards, results are presented in Table 8.1. Both learning-based selection methods outperform the NER baseline in both novices' and teachers' comparisons. It seems that to some extent learning models can learn the

Table 8.1 Evaluation results for keyphrase detection methods from Willis et al. (2019)

Evaluation	SQuAD (novices) data				Teachers' data			
Model	EM	Precision	Recall	F1	EM	Precision	Recall	F1
NER baseline	26.38	28.79	15.30	19.98	26.31	30.21	27.11	28.58
KPE-Class	20.66	29.71	21.02	24.62	17.67	25.84	22.43	24.01
KPE-Gen	36.50	37.81	32.94	35.21	29.91	33.58	28.10	30.59

EM is percentage of exact matches

keyphrase/target-answer selection from data. Willis et al. noted that the NER baseline method performed better as compared to teachers' preferences than in comparison to novices' preferences. Teachers were focusing more on named entities. The learning models performed better when evaluated on novices' data than when evaluated on teachers' data. This might reflect the fact that the models were trained on the SQuAD (novices') data, and thus learned to better reflect the questioning preferences of that group. If that is the case, it may cast a cautionary light on the endeavor of machine-learning the questioning preferences—if preferences change, or a different set of preferences is required, the learning materials would need to be reannotated (a costly and time-consuming process) to enable learning the different set of preferences.

The studies mentioned above show that it is possible to use general importance considerations when selecting sentences or keyphrases for QG. At the very basic level, it can be fruitfully assumed that named entities are valuable targets for questions, and thus base content selection on just those. Using text-summarization methodologies can also be instrumental for obtaining importance indicators when selecting content for questions.

Finally, there is a variety of methods to learn content selection directly from data. The learning methods for content selection require large amounts of ground-truth labels (thousands or tens of thousands) on question-worthy materials in corpora of texts. Obtaining such labels for specific use cases might be a rather complex endeavor. Yet different kinds of texts, or different contexts of use, may require rather different preferences on context selection, making preferences learned from data less useful when transfer to a different context is needed (Horbach et al. 2020).

Some researchers have noted that the generic content-selection approaches presented above do not reflect any particular pedagogical considerations. To the extent that educational settings are probably the most important area of application for AQG, it makes sense to consider some pedagogically motivated considerations for selection of question-worthy segments in texts.

8.4 Specific Content Selections

Ai et al. (2015) describe an AQG system for language learners. They proposed to focus question generation around the mentions of relations between entities, because such relations might be salient enough as stimuli for reading comprehension exercises. Their system relied on relation-extraction (RE) systems that extract patterns such as *married(person1, person2)* from large corpora of text. The extraction systems extract entities (such as people, organizations, locations) using a NER system, and detect relations using lexico-syntactic patterns such as:

marriage relation:

- *person1 tied the knot with person2.*
- *person1 and person2 were married.*

Ai et al. (2015) utilized a set of predefined patterns from previous research. Once instances of such patterns are recognized in the target text, the sentences that contain them can be selected for question generation. Ai et al. (2015) noted that recognition of relations and entities in text can be noisy and human supervision is needed for checking the quality and relevance of extracted instances.[6] For AQG, such an approach allows to define a set of task-specific relations that need to be identified in a text as question worthy contents. This can be also useful for domain specific QG where questions need to be focused around particular kinds of contents.

Steuer et al. (2021) proposed to focus on one particular type of pedagogically-relevant contents—definitional sentences. Their work was concerned with AQG for textbooks used in higher education, i.e. college/university entry level books. In such context, they pointed out that textbook contents may include a large amount of concept definitions, specifically for concepts that are most important in the relevant content areas. Thus, a viable and educationally-relevant content-selection approach for AQG can be to select sentences that contain concept definitions. This study deserves some elaboration not only due to its content selection approach, but also for its evaluation component.

First, the authors made the assumption that the most important concepts in a textbook are likely to be reflected in a back-of-the-book index. Next, sentences in the book that contained instances (keywords and keyphrases) from such a list were selected as candidate sentences. The next stage required a method of detecting just those sentences that contained definitions. The authors noted that detecting definitions in text is not a simple task. They opted to use a deep learning system that was trained on a large corpus of definitions from the science domain, and achieved an F1 score of 0.78 on that task. The

---

[6] Relation extraction continues to be an active and prolific research area, for recent reviews see Zhao et al. (2023) and Han et al. (2020).

authors wanted to prefer precision over recall, to reduce the amount of less relevant materials selected. They used a ROC plot (of system performance on another subset of data) to tune the threshold of definition detection acceptance. They noted that even with such filtering, the definition detection system still supplied an ample amount of question-worthy sentences from the books.

Having set the sentence-selection method, the authors needed to set the target-answer selection within selected sentences. This was particularly motivated by the following educational consideration: the authors wanted to use an answer-aware AQG system, so that for example answers to questions could be highlighted for the students in the text. Moreover, they wanted to select pedagogically meaningful answers, i.e. concepts that may have educational value. As the inputs sentences contain concept definitions, it reasonable to prefer that *"the answer candidates should describe the definiteness' characteristics or should ask for the definiendum itself."* Although the authors could have used just the keyphrases (which were used in early filtering, and thus were present in the sentences), they opted to consider a more sophisticated methodology for selecting target-answers in sentences. While most of the defined concept are nouns or noun phrases, the authors pointed out that adjectival and adverbial clauses and prepositional phrases are also often important components in definitions. For example, in the sentence *The cell wall is a rigid covering that protects the cell, provides structural support, and gives shape to the cell*, the core definition is that "*cell wall is a rigid covering*", but the relative clause provides important information about the functions of the cell wall. Thus, the authors ran dependency parsing over definitional sentences and extracted target-answers by using patterns over dependency trees, with a fallback to using just the direct objects of verbs. Notably development of such patterns is still a manual task that needs linguistic expertise. Given definitional sentences and selected target answers, the next step was question generation. The authors used the deep-learning pretrained transformer system UniLM (Dong et al. 2019) that had been fine-tuned for answer-aware question generation.

For the AQG experiment, the authors used six undergraduate textbooks from different academic domains: anatomy, biology, chemistry, physics, psychology and sociology (three chapters from each book, in total 325 sections). They ran the sentence selection, answer selection and AQG on that data and obtained about 868 questions. They selected 150 questions (25 per book) for human evaluation. The goal of the evaluation was to estimate the educational value of the generated questions, or as authors called it *linguistic and pedagogical appropriateness*. That is a wide and valuable spectrum of evaluation, because it spans from mere grammatical correctness to the actual educational usefulness, which is rarely evaluated in AQG research. Three experienced educational experts were asked to evaluate the questions (in context of the respective sections), every expert evaluated all 150 questions. The evaluation effort followed the scheme from Horbach et al. (2020), with nine evaluation items per question. The evaluation dimensions were: whether the question was (1) understandable (y/n), (2) domain-related (y/n), (3) grammatical (y/n), (4) clear (yes/more-or-less/no), (5) in need of rephrasing (y/n), (6) answerable (y/n),

8.4 Specific Content Selections

(7) what information was needed for answering,[7] (8) central to the topic of the textbook segment (y/n), (9) would the evaluator use the question for instruction (yes/maybe/no). Notably the evaluation scheme is hierarchical, if the evaluator marked 'no' for dimensions 1, 4, or 6, the question would not be evaluated further. The inter-annotator agreement in this study was rather low, which the authors attributed to the fact that evaluators were not experts in every one of the six different subject domains. Agreement was 0.81 for understandability. 0.74 for domain relatedness, 0.70 for grammaticality, and below 0.7 for all other dimensions; notably about 0.4 for *information-needed* and for *would-use-the-question*. This underscores the need to have domain-relevant experts for evaluating the educational aspects of generated questions—while linguistic aspects of a question require just good command of the language, other aspects require both educational and subject-matter-specific expertise. As for results of evaluation, 83% of the questions were considered understandable, 73% were grammatical, 64% were considered as clear and 17% more-or-less clear (so overall quite good linguistic quality); 78% were related to the text, 72% considered as answerable from the text (39% answerable from one location and 26% from multiple places), 57% of the questions were considered central to the topic. As for the *'would-use'* dimension, 41% of the questions were marked 'yes', and 25% 'maybe'. Some of the problems with the AQG pipeline in this study were: accuracy of definition detection; erroneous dependency parses, which led to selecting inappropriate target answers; and infelicities of the neural AQG model, which sometimes generated flawed or even nonsensical questions (e.g. *Where do ATP molecules move the ATP molecules to?*). The authors did not provide a separate evaluation of their content selection strategy, i.e. focus on definitional sentences, and thus we have only indirect evidence for its success. Given that 66% of the evaluated questions were rated as yes/maybe educationally useful, the overall content selection strategy may be considered as quite valid and noteworthy.

The idea that definitional sentences have special educational value has already been utilized in AQG before. Gates et al. (2011) proposed syntactically driven AQG for some restricted types of definitional sentences intended for second and third-grade students that are learning new words/concepts (very unlike the undergraduate textbooks data described above). While definitions can be expressed in a variety of grammatical forms, the Gates et al. study worked with a particular format that *"gives a context for the word in the definition and it states the definition in a complete sentence"*. For example: *A steak is a large flat piece of meat., If you abandon something or someone, you leave them and never go back.* In that study the sentences were already preselected by educators and the goal of NLP work was extracting the target answers that would be used for questions. The extraction was defined with lexico-syntactic patterns over automatically derived constituent parse trees. For example, the pattern "(SBAR (S (NP (PRP you)) (VP (VP x)..." could match definitions of new verbs—whatever matches the x would be the candidate answer (e.g.

---

[7] Describing what a student might need for answering the question: (a) one position in the text, (b) different positions in the text, (c) text and some external knowledge, (d) external knowledge only, or (e) feelings and beliefs of the reader.

leave them in the example definition above). The Gates et al. study was concerned with generating gap-filling exercises, so no full interrogative sentence generation was on the agenda. The extracted target answers were evaluated by educators, with 77 out of 91 deemed acceptable (85%). That study demonstrates an early attempt for automated answer selection over a particular type of sentences.

A very different proposal for content selection for AQG was investigated by Stasaski et al. (2021). They proposed to focus on cause-and-effect relations expressed in text, because such relations are considered to be of special educational importance, for example in reading comprehension. The general schema of their approach was twofold. They utilized an NLP system for detecting cause-and-effect relations expressed in sentences; the system can also extract the cause and effect mentions. Then, either the cause or the effect phrase can serve as a target answer for QG. They then used a transformer-based AQG system that takes as input a sentence and a target answer and generates a question.

Cause-effect relations can be expressed in a variety of ways in text. A cause and the related effect can be contained in one sentence, or they can relate across multiple, usually adjacent, sentences. English has variety of expressions that indicate cause-effect relations, which can be categorized (Altenberg 1984): adverbial connectors (*so, hence, therefore*), prepositional connectors (*because of, on account of*), clause-subordinating connectors (*because, as, since*), and clause-integrated linkers (*that's why, the result was*). Some examples are shown in Table 8.2.

To extract causal relations from text, Stasaski et al. adapted the system from Cao et al. (2016), which uses pattern matching over defined syntactic patterns. The patterns utilize lexical components (the terms used to express causal relations), additional function

Table 8.2 Examples of causal relationships from different syntactic categories, with causes bolded, effects italicized, and causal link words underlined

Type	Example
Adverbial	**Different energy levels in the cloud have different numbers of orbitals.** Therefore, *different energy levels have different maximum numbers of electrons*
Prepositional	The *shape of sharks teeth differ* according to **their diet**. Species that feed on mollusks and crustaceans have dense flattened teeth for crushing, those that feed on fish have needle-like teeth for gripping, and those that feed on larger prey, such as mammals, have pointed lower teeth for gripping and triangular upper teeth with serrated edges for cutting
Subordination	Because **the coffee particles lost some of their kinetic energy to the spoon particles**, *the coffee particles started to move more slowly*
Clause-integration	**The stars outer layers spread out and cool**. The result is *a larger star that is cooler on the surface, and red in color*. Eventually a red giant burns up all of the helium in its core

Examples are from the TQA dataset, adapted from Stasaski et al. (2021)

8.4 Specific Content Selections

words, and the positions of cause-and-effect components. For example, a pattern *[&C (,/;/./–) (&AND) as a (&ADJ) result (,) &R]* indicates that a phrase *as a result*, with a possible intervening adjective *(&ADJ)*, signals a cause-effect relation, where the effect/result phrase *&R* would follow the result word, (with an optional comma), while the term expressing the cause *&C* precedes them with some optional punctuation marks *(,/;/./–)* and additional optional words *(&AND)*. While Cao et al. have defined multiple patterns for extraction, Stasaski et al. noticed that some causal linking phrases (such as *as*, *so*, and *since*) can be ambiguous and lead to lower causal detection accuracy than more direct phrases like *because*. Therefore, to increase detection accuracy, they recommended dropping the low accuracy patterns.

For their experiments, Stasaski et al. used passages from the SQuAD 2.0 dataset (Rajpurkar et al. 2018) and from the Textbook Question Answering (TQA) dataset (Kembhavi et al. 2017). The latter includes passages from Life Science, Earth Science and Physical Science textbooks. Since causal relations can span across sentences, Stasaski et al. extracted sequences of 2 to 3 sentences from their texts, avoiding crossing paragraph boundaries. To evaluate their adjusted causal extraction system, the authors sampled 100 passages from TQA and 100 from SQuAD. The system achieved precision of 83% on TQA data and 79% on SQuAD data. This demonstrates that quite high-levels of accuracy of detection for cause-effect relations in text can be achieved over academic and other informational texts.

For question generation, Stasaski et al. used ProphetNet (Qi et al. 2020), a large pre-trained transformer-based system that was fine-tuned for AQG using the SQuAD 1.1 dataset. The system is supplied with a context and a target answer from the context, and generates a question. Since cause-and-effect relations involve two components—the cause and the effect—the same context can be used to generate two questions: once feeding the cause as the answer (leading to a cause question), and once feeding the effect as the answer (and leading to an effect question).

Using a heuristic search for 'why' questions, Stasaski et al. have found that only about 1.3% of the questions in the SQuAD 1.1 dataset are causal questions. Thus, although ProphetNet was fine-tuned on SQuAD data, it might not have had enough training for causal questions. To alleviate this, the authors produced an additional fine-tuning dataset. They used their cause-effect detector to extract causal text snippets from SQuAD and TQA passages. Then they used this data to generate questions with a syntax-driven AQG system Syn-QG (Dhole and Manning 2020). The resulting 3800 causal questions were used to farther fine-tune the ProphetNet AQG model towards cause-and-effect questions. This is a notable instance of fine-tuning a neural AQG model with examples generated by a rule-based AQG model.

To evaluate the overall question-generation performance, the authors devised three different approaches. In one approach, they measured how many words from the cause/effect phrases were included (present) in the respective question. In the second effort, they conducted human evaluation for a subset of generated questions. In the third approach, they used an automated question-answering system to answer the generated questions with the original text passages.

For the word-presence evaluation the authors claimed that a question which assesses understanding of cause/effect relationship should include a direct mention of the cause or the effect. Thus, a question that asks about the cause of something should retain the words that describe the effect, and a question that asks about an effect should retain the cause phrase. Since the original phrasings are available (from the detection tool), the presence of relevant words can be computed automatically, thus enabling an automatic evaluation metric, which the authors called *Cause/Effect Presence metric*. It is computed as proportion of the relevant words from the cause/effect phrase that are present in the question (a recall measure). Table 8.3 shows the results of this evaluation. For the base AQG system the proportions are rather low (0.55 and 0.37), it seems the AQG system fails to include many relevant words in the questions, although the results are better for data from academic texts than for data from SQuAD (Wikipedia articles). When an additionally-finetuned AQG model is used, the proportions become higher. It is not clear with this metric how close to 1.0 the results need to be to consider them as acceptable for practical use, but overall, the achievement seems to be very promising. Another issue with this evaluation is that the assumption about word presence is reasonable, unless some form of paraphrase is involved. Since neural AQG systems can sometimes produce paraphrases in their output, it may be unclear how much presence of original words should be expected and whether lower numbers indicate bad questions or just presence of paraphrases. The authors also conducted a human evaluation of generated questions. They used just those 162 segments that were first verified to have cause-effect content. The corresponding 1620 questions generated by the base neural AQG model were evaluated by crowdworkers, who were asked to mark whether the question is (1) ill-formed or ungrammatical, (2) whether the question is causal (y/n), and (3) whether the predefined target keyphrase correctly answers the question. Only 22 questions (1.4%) were marked as ill-formed. Overall, the evaluators marked 91% of the questions as causal, and 90% as matching the intended answer. This can be taken as an indicator that the model "*is able to reliably generate questions which are correct for the intended answer and are valid cause-and-effect questions*".

Table 8.3 Cause/effect presence metric results for automatically generated questions, from Stasaski et al. (2021)

Model	TQA dataset			SQuAD dataset		
	Causes questions	Effects questions	Total	Causes questions	Effects questions	Total
Base	0.52	0.57	0.55	0.32	0.42	0.37
With fine-tuning	0.71	0.72	0.72	0.54	0.57	0.56

The third evaluation approach involved using an automatic Question Answering system to answer the generated questions. The logic of such evaluation is as follows: If the AQG model produces ill-formed or incorrect questions, then the QA model will be less likely to produce the correct answers. Since the correct answers are known in advance, the accuracy of the QA system in answering the questions can be measured automatically. The QA success rate then can be taken as indicative of questions quality. The authors used a pretrained transformer-based fine-tuned QA model with "good credentials" (F1 score of 0.93 on the SQuAD 2.0 test set). This QA model achieved an F1 score of about 0.20 on the questions generated by the base AQG model. The same QA model achieved F1 score of about 0.52 on questions generated by the fine-tuned AQG model. This is again a solid indication that more training on cause-effect questions is helpful for the neural AQG system. However, the overall performance of the strong QA system on auto-generated cause/effect questions was rather disappointing even for questions from the fine-tuned AQG variant—F1 of just 0.52. That might have been due to a problem with the QA system—due to low prevalence of cause-effect questions in the SQuAD dataset, the QA system might not have been well-trained on such questions. Or it might be a genuine indication that the auto-generated cause-effect questions were not of good quality, which would stand contrary to the human evaluation for a subset of the questions. This case illustrates that the indirect evaluation of AQG via QA can be problematic and difficult to interpret. Despite some indeterminacy with the evaluation, the study by Stasaski et al. (2021) demonstrated that focusing on cause-and-effect relations expressed in informational texts can be a viable content selection approach for AQG.

8.5 Summary

Content selection refers to picking sections of the source text for which questions should be generated, i.e. what parts of the text are worth asking a question about. Overall, there have been two types of approaches in content selection. On the one hand there are approaches that rely on some generic estimates of importance for sections of texts. A very simple approach is to assume that named entities in texts are often a good target for questions. Other approaches utilize methods from text summarization to find the most important sections in texts. Some approaches focus on selection of potentially important sentences. They might still need to consider which phrases in a selected sentences to ask about (or generate many questions, for various parts). Other approaches use a variety of methods to directly focus on the most important keywords in a text, which can then be used as the target answers for AQG systems. Another direction within this family of approaches is to learn the selection preferences automatically from annotated or pre-existing data. Both classical machine learning and deep learning approaches have been shown to be able to learn questioning preferences, to some extent, albeit they require considerable amounts of training materials (thousands to tens of thousands of examples).

Another family of selection approaches looks to select segments that have some a priori special value. In the educational domain, such value can be assigned, for example, to sentences that carry definitions of concepts, or segments that describe cause and effect relations. Ultimately content selection depends on the type of texts being used, on the type of questions that need to be generated, and on the goals of the particular AQG project.

Question Generation from Ontologies and Knowledge Bases

9.1 Introduction

As the interest in question generation from texts grew in the first decade of the century, there was a parallel strong interest in AQG systems that utilize formal methods of knowledge representation, i.e. knowledge bases and ontologies. The research on AQG from knowledge bases focused on issues like: how can questions be generated from knowledge bases and ontologies; how multiple-choice items can be generated and what properties can be supported for them.

9.2 Ontologies

In order to describe this line of research, we need to provide some background information about ontologies. An ontology is a structured description of a domain, a concrete conceptual model of a relevant part of the world (Gruber 1995). Ontologies are a form of knowledge representation and thus can be used as components for building intelligent applications.

Ontologies typically list: (a) the types of objects (entities) that are postulated for the domain and also might list specific instances of such objects; and (b) the types of relationships that connect entities. Ontologies may also list constraints on the ways that entities and relationships can be combined. As such, ontologies provide a machine-readable form for describing the semantics of a specific domain—knowledge representation that can be manipulated by formal methods. While entities are the basic building blocks of ontologies, they can represent many things: specific objects (also called *individuals*, or *instances*), classes (also called *types*, or *concepts*), entity relationships (or *properties*), and also *data properties* (*metadata*). Object or class properties can be represented as relations between instance and class entities and property entities. For example (from Al-Yahya 2014): a 'library' ontology may contain the classes 'book' and 'journal' and the relations 'has_author' and 'has_publication_date.' It may also state that 'book' and 'journal' are types of 'publication'. An ontology may define certain constraints, such as 'a book must have at least one author.' For individual objects, the ontology may contain information such as 'A Tale of Two Cities is a Book', possibly represented as *isA(ATaleOfTwoCities, Book)*, and that its author is Charles Dickens—*hasAuthor(ATaleOfTwoCities, CharlesDickens)*.

The Resource Description Framework (RDF) proposed by the World Wide Web Consortium (W3C) is a data model and has become a widely adopted standard for designing and expressing ontologies. Ontologies that rely on entities and relations can be viewed as graphs, where entities are nodes and relations are arcs. RDF is a directed graph composed of triple-component statements. An RDF graph statement is represented by: (1) a node for the subject, (2) an arc that goes from a subject to an object for the predicate, and (3) a node for the object. Knowledge graphs such as DBpedia, Freebase, or Wikidata, always contain a taxonomic backbone that allows the arrangement and structuring of various concepts in accordance with hyponym-hypernym ("class-subclass") relationship (Nikishina et al. 2022).

Table 9.1 presents a simple example of triples in the domain of Anatomy and Physiology. Each of the three parts of the statement can be identified by a URI.[1] For example, the simple statement that *Bob knows John* can be represented as:

http://example.name#BobSmith12

http://xmlns.com/foaf/0.1/knows

http://example.name#JohnDoe34

where the URIs for Bob and John represent very specific individuals, while the URI for *knows* refers to the concept of 'know' in the ontology of interpersonal relations (FOAF ontology[2]), which is quite a specific notion of knowing (e.g. versus knowing a language or knowing a fact). From a language perspective, this aspect can facilitate disambiguation—indeed generation and encoding of ontologies requires considerable disambiguation from knowledge expressed in a natural language like English. Since knowledge represented in ontologies is often intended to be manipulated by semantic reasoner systems,[3] disambiguation of entities and relations is often very useful.

The RDF data model has expressive power to represent complex situations, relationships, and other things of interest, while also being appropriately abstract, and is thus

---

[1] See https://en.wikipedia.org/wiki/Semantic_triple.
[2] See https://en.wikipedia.org/wiki/FOAF.
[3] Software applications that can infer logical consequences from asserted facts or axioms.

9.2 Ontologies

Table 9.1 Examples of knowledge triples in the domain of anatomy and physiology

Subject	Predicate	Object
Capillaries	Carry	Oxygen
Cardiac muscles	Perform	Contractions
Dendrites	Transmit	Electrical impulses
Heart	Is a	Organ
Heart	Belongs to	Circulatory system
Cardiac muscles	Are part of	Heart

used as a basis for formal languages for knowledge representation, such as Web Ontology Language (OWL).[4] For detailed descriptions of Semantic Web Ontology Languages, see Horrocks (2008, 2013) and Antoniou et al. (2005).

While there exists a variety of syntax notations and data serialization formats for RDF, RDF triples may be stored in a type of database called a *triplestore*. Modern triplestores can support millions of triples, and they usually support SPARQL, which is a standard query language for RDF graphs.[5] However encoded, ontology axioms provide facts about a subject domain, and thus can be directly utilized to generate questions about the given domain.

Note that not every ontology might include instances. For example, an ontology about human anatomy and physiology might encode only generic knowledge, so no instances would be expected there. On the other hand, an ontology about history, or a tourism area, might include quite a lot of specific instances (for example—Paris the city, or even particular neighborhoods or buildings there).

As noted by Horrocks (2013), "*an ontology is an engineering artifact, usually a 'conceptual model' of (some aspect of) the world*", and thus it can be used as a tool. Even prior to the advent of the Semantic Web, ontologies were used for interoperability and systematization of knowledge (i.e. formalized knowledge representation), for example for research activities, such as the Gene Ontology project.[6] On the Semantic Web, ontologies are used to support information exchange in distributed environments, including search engines, e-commerce, multi-agent systems, etc. Ontologies are usually developed by groups of experts. They provide systematically organized, machine-readable factual knowledge about many domains of interest. In 2023, the NCBO BioPortal[7] listed over 1000 ontologies just in the biomedical domain. The Linked Open Vocabularies project[8] lists over 800 domain specific ontologies, including geography, travel, transport, society,

---

[4] See https://en.wikipedia.org/wiki/Web_Ontology_Language.
[5] See https://en.wikipedia.org/wiki/SPARQL.
[6] See https://en.wikipedia.org/wiki/Gene_Ontology.
[7] See https://bioportal.bioontology.org.
[8] See https://lov.linkeddata.es/dataset/lov.

business, government, etc. Given the proliferation of such curated resources, their utility for learning and assessment has not been overlooked. Sicilia and Garcia Barriocanal (2005) noted the convergence of two concepts: *learning objects* and ontologies. A learning object is any piece of content (usually in a digital format) that can be reused in various educational contexts. Ontologies can be used to express learning objects in a formalized way, as representation of the content and as metadata for learning objects. Knight et al. (2006) described the utility of ontologies for technology-enabled environments, including discovery of resources, and automated production of educational materials.

9.3 Question Generation with Ontologies

The interest in using ontologies for learning and education has naturally led to the interest in automatically generating quizzes and knowledge assessments directly from ontologies. The structured and well-defined domain knowledge in ontologies can be used for the assessment of student knowledge and skills (Cubric and Tosic 2011). Of particular interest is automated generation of multiple-choice questions (MCQs); especially since they are automatically gradable, can be utilized in computer-based environments, such as intelligent tutor systems, and can provide students with immediate feedback.

Holohan et al. (2005) describe one of the earliest implementations of ontology-based AQG. Their system, OntAWare, included software tools for courseware authors, including content authoring, management and delivery. The system used RDF-based ontologies for content representation, and could generate learning objects, such as lesson plans, content slides, and content questions. They emphasized the use of explicit class-relations in ontologies (class-subclass and class-instance) for AQG. This allows to generate questions of the type *Which of the following items is (or is not) an example of the concept X?*, for example *Which of the following is an organ?—dendrite, capillary, heart*. This is possible when an assertion that *heart-ISA-organ* is explicitly stated in an ontology, while none of the other entities in this example are marked as belonging to the class 'organ', and so may be safely presumed to be valid distractors.

There are some important observations about this early system. First it is notable how the ontology-based approach is conductive to generating multiple-choice questions, where entities will appear in the roles of item key and distractors. Second, it exemplifies the reliance on the *closed-word assumption* for generation of valid distractors. In formal knowledge representation this assumption says that what is not currently known to be true, is presumed false. Thus, entities in an ontology that are not explicitly stated to be of a certain class, and for which it cannot be deduced (basing on the facts in the ontology and using logic rules via semantic reasoners) that they are of that certain class, it can be presumed they are not instances/subclasses of that class and thus can be used as valid distractors. The closed-world assumption can be utilized beyond class-relations. Any assertion that is not in the given ontology, and which cannot be proven as true based

9.3 Question Generation with Ontologies

on assertions available in the ontology can be presumed false and thus can be used for distractors in MCQ. For example, starting with an ontology assertion *capillaries carry oxygen*, the entity *capillaries* can be removed, thus becoming the potential key, and we retain ___ *carry oxygen*. Then, the goal for the AQG system is to find any other entities in the ontology for which it is neither explicitly stated nor can be proved that they 'carry oxygen', and such entities can be candidate distractors for the MCQ. On the other hand, by changing the selection procedure, other types of MCQ items can be produced. For example, selecting multiple asserted or derived (true) statements can be used for creating *odd-one-out* or *all-of-the-above* item types.

If an ontology is quite large, and especially if it covers multiple domains of knowledge, many entities can be found that could be potential distractors. For example, in a large ontology, it might be found that *whiskey, Napoleon Bonaparte*, and *malaria*, do not carry oxygen, which makes them valid as potential distractors for an MCQ *Which of the following carries oxygen?* However, they are not very attractive distractors, and except for maybe *malaria* they are not even from the relevant content domain. This illustrates how aspects of relevance play a role in ontology-based AQG. For ontology-based generation of MCQs, restriction of distractor selection to the relevant domain is a basic technique to promote relevance. Such restriction also reduces the amount of computation (less entities to consider). However, this presumes that every entity and assertion in an ontology is marked for its content domain. For most ontologies, such marking is not present in the subject-predicate-object triples, but would be carried in the metadata. However, since metadata can be coded in RDF triples as well, distinguishing between content records and service/metadata records is necessary.

Bühmann et al. (2015) and Al-Yahya (2011) have demonstrated that in addition to MCQs, it is also possible to generate Yes/No questions and Cloze items from ontologies. Cloze items can be generated by simply choosing a triple (statement) and blanking one of the components, usually the subject or the object, for example *capillaries carry oxygen* can produce ___ *carry oxygen* and *capillaries carry* ___. Blanking of the predicate is also possible, for example *capillaries* ___ *oxygen*.

Yes/No questions for which the answer is 'true' can be based simply on the assertions in the ontology. For example, for the triple (*subj:capillaries, predicate:carry, obj:oxygen*), a simple question could be *Please select: 'capillaries carry oxygen'—true or false?* In such case, the stem of the question *Please select: ___—true or false?* can be based on a predefined template, while the true statement is generated from a record in the ontology. Generating a false statement requires some more processing—it requires producing a distractor that would provide a false statement. Note that the core of the false statement would still be obtained from the ontology—a true statement that would be converted into a false statement. A triple can be selected from the ontology, then a subject or object would be removed (e.g. ___ *carry oxygen*), and substituted with some other entity from the ontology (e.g. *dendrites*). This generates a new triple. The new triple would be checked in the ontology to verify that it is not true, and if that is confirmed, the new false statement (*dendrites carry oxygen*) can be used for a false Yes/No question.

The system described by Bühmann et al. (2015) demonstrated automated generation of an additional type of questions—what they called *Jeopardy questions*.[9] Such questions are also MCQs, but they can describe an entity without naming the entity itself. The stem of the question contains a description of the entity, but the entity's exact name is one of the response options. A simplified example of such a question can be as follows: *Which book by Leo Tolstoy describes events occurring during Napoleonic Wars?—(a) Anna Karenina; (b) War and Peace; (c) Vanity Fair*. The difference from typical MCQs is in the amount of detail that may go into the entity description in the item stem. Moreover, some of the features might be shared by the key and the distractor entities, though only the key would have all the features stated in the stem. In the example above, (a) and (b) are by Tolstoy, (b) and (c) have content related to Napoleonic Wars; but only (b) fits the question. The composition of such a question depends on the ability to retrieve from the ontology distractors that share some common features with the key entity.

Generating questions from an ontology can provide a degree of control to the system user. Since the relations between entities are explicitly represented in the RDF triple, an AQG system can be equipped with selection mechanisms allowing a user (e.g. instructor or test developer) to state what kind of relations they want to be included in the generated questions. For example, users might be able to specify to have questions based on class-inclusion (e.g. *Which of the following is an organ?*, or properties of entities, *Which of the following is part of the heart?*. Depending on the information available or inferable from an ontology, sophisticated filtering can be used to restrict or guide the content selection for AQG from ontologies.

Ben Abacha et al. (2016) presented a study on question generation from an ontology, where the goal of questions was ontology validation, which is quite a different use than educational applications. Specifically, their focus was on discovery of erroneous statements (records, propositions, facts) that can be included in ontologies during ontology population, especially for ontologies built automatically from textual documents. The general idea was to generate questions from the ontology, submit them to domain experts and use their feedback about the contents of the ontology. A special constraint was that content-domain experts should not face complex formal descriptions; the questions should be natural and fluent. The researches worked on a biomedical ontology involving information about diseases and treatments. In the one part of their study the researchers sought to generate yes/no questions about certain types of statements in the ontology, for example relations between classes and subclasses, instances and classes, and relations between concepts (e.g., *administrated for*), etc. They used a template-based AQG approach where they defined patterns for questions with slots that could be automatically filled with concepts and relations from the ontology. For example, the following pattern is a template for questions about drug doses administrated to patients with a particular disease: "*Is DOSE*

---

[9] Named after the famous TV game show, see https://en.wikipedia.org/wiki/Jeopardy!.

of DRUG well suited for PATIENTS having DISEASE?". It has 4 variables which are also class labels that constrain the instantiation (matching to ontology statements). The pattern could be automatically adjusted—for example the main verb in the pattern could be adjusted to singular/plural depending on the part-of-speech of the direct object, as determined by a syntactic parser. Such patterns are defined manually and strongly depend on the developer's acquaintance with the content of the ontology. It can allow very high precision for question formulation as well as flexibility of design, at the expense of being a rather slow and complex process.

Question generation from ontologies need not be restricted to using only curated established ontologies. Olney et al. (2012) described question generation from concept maps, which are organized as triples of *concept + predicate + concept*. Alsubait et al. (2016) reported on successful experiments with AQG for two ontologies that were created within a couple of days by university instructors for computer-science courses. Al-Yahya (2011) described AQG with several ontologies, including one created especially for an 8th grade history unit.

Generation of questions from ontologies has four core aspects.

(a) How to select content and frame the question from elements in ontology.
(b) How to generate distractors (incorrect answer options) for the question.
(c) How to control the difficulty level of generated questions.
(d) How to ensure that a question is fluent and grammatically correct.

9.4 Language Aspects

There are some language aspects that need adjustments even with this simple methodology. In our example of *capillaries carry oxygen*, the predicate is *carry*, as it matches the plural subject *capillaries*. If a synthetic false statement is generated with a different entity, like *anemia*, which is singular, a subject-verb agreement needs to be adjusted to prevent an awkward statement like *anemia carry oxygen*. This is a very simple example, but it illustrates that linguistic postprocessing is often required to produce grammatically well-formed questions from ontology content.

The study by Bühmann et al. (2015) used ontologies where knowledge is encoded in RDF triples. The AQG system used separate architecture layers—a data layer and an NLG layer. The base data layer accommodated a knowledge base composed of RDF triples (which can be a very large knowledge base, e.g. the DBPedia). The data layer can be queried to retrieve a subset of the knowledge triples, which pertain to a certain domain that a user is interested in (for example human blood circulatory system, or more specifically, RDF triples about veins and arteries.) Note how user input (selection of domain of interest) can be used for focusing the system. The selected set can be broad or constrained, depending on user preferences/selections. For example, additional subsets of RDF triples (i.e. knowledge statements) can be retrieved by expansion from entities in the already-retrieved subset. The resulting subset of RDF triples can be viewed as a graph (because its entities are interrelated), and it serves as a basis from which questions are generated. The NLG layer included two components—a verbalizer and a realizer. The verbalizer produced words and a sentence parse tree, it used syntactic and semantic rules for composition. The realizer took the parse tree as input and generated a question form in natural language.

One of the hidden tasks in ontology-based AQG is verbalization of entities/concepts. Most basically this means choosing natural language words or expressions for entities or relations selected from an ontology. The need for verbalization depends on the way that entities are encoded in the ontology. If entities and relations are encoded 'transparently', e.g. *capillaries* for capillaries, then the need for description selection is minimal. However, entities in ontologies are often encoded in ways that cannot be directly used in questions (or other natural language outputs). For example, individuals might be encoded like http://example.name#BobSmith12, and it would be up to a verbalizer component to convert it to *Bob* or *Bob Smith*.

Verbalization is not an issue unique to AQG. As noted by Konstas and Lapata (2013), verbalization, or concept-to-text generation is the task of automatically producing textual output from non-linguistic input, e.g. from ontology records. The task is especially important for ontologies that use complex standards-compliant formal languages for content representation, such as OWL. Verbalization tools are used to translate ontology records (e.g., OWL RDF statements) to natural language expressions. Originally such tools were developed for the benefit of domain experts, presenting sections of an ontology in natural language for easier reading and verification, but more advanced systems can generate multi-sentence texts for end-users (Androutsopoulos et al. 2013). One of the issues with entity verbalization form ontology is generating very compact descriptions of individuals and concepts and removing redundancy (Venugopal and Sreenivasa Kumar 2019).

Another aspect in verbalization is expressing relations (predicates). For example, an ontology might have a relation 'has_height', which might be verbalized as *has a height of...*. A relation 'has_part' might be verbalized in different ways, sometimes simply as *has* or *have*—depending on context, but sometimes as *includes* or *consists of*, etc. Moreover, it can be verbalized *is part of* when the focus is on the part and not on the whole. After verbalization, a realization component might also be responsible for selecting and adjusting syntactic structures. For example, from a relation (*subj:capillaries, predicate:carry, obj:oxygen*), a question might be formulated as *Oxygen is carried by which of the following:....?*, which requires passivization of the original predicate.

A variety of tools can be used for verbalization and final question realization, including ad-hoc rules, templates, or full-fledged NLG toolkits. Verbalization depends on the way entities are encoded in the given ontology, so a verbalizer component might need to be ontology-specific and might need domain-dependent resources. Question realization is concerned with well-formedness of the language generation and can be assisted with general NLG. Bühmann et al. (2015) have utilized the SimpleNLG toolkit[10] for question realization, reporting strong evaluation results for verbalization—average question fluency of 4.46 on a six-point scale.

Reddy et al. (2017) presented a neural model that learned to generate questions from a large knowledge graph. Their goal was generating large quantities of question–answer pairs for training of QA models. They formulated the AQG task as a sequence-to-sequence generation problem, and used an LSTM network with attention to generate questions. The basic idea was that the input to the network is an ordered set (a sequence) of words that should be included in the questions (but not the answer words), and the output should be a sequence of words that constitutes the question. In such case, an important aspect is how the input sequence is obtained from a knowledge graph. In fact, the authors designed their system with two modules. One module extracts candidate words from the knowledge graph, and the other module is an LSTM network that learns to generate questions. For extraction from knowledge graph, the authors defined the setting as follows. The knowledge graph consists of records (assertions), each of them being a triple of subject, predicate, and object, for example (*subj:London, pred:Capital, obj:United Kingdom*). Moreover, typically the subjects of a predicate belong to a defined subject type (domain). For example, for the predicate 'Capital', any valid subject is a 'City'. Similarly, the objects of a given predicate belong to specific object type (or range). For 'Capital', the objects are countries. With this, for any record in the knowledge graph, the authors define a 5-tuple that includes the subject, the domain, the predicate, the object and the range. Note that each of them must be represented with a natural language word or a phrase. For example, the 5-tuple would be (*s:London, d:City, p:Capital, o:United Kingdom, r:Country*). From any such tuple, at least two questions can be produced. One question focuses on the subject *What is the capital city of United Kingdom?*, using the domain, the predicate, and the object (*Capital, City, United Kingdom*), and keeping the answer, *London*, aside. Another question could be *London is the capital city of which country?*, using (*London, City, Capital, Country*) and leaving aside the answer, *United Kingdom*. The authors defined two rules for selecting how words from a 5-tuple are selected for producing a question. Both rules require uniqueness. The Unique Forward Relation rule stated that a subject and predicate from a tuple can be selected only if the subject-predicate combination is unique in the knowledge base (e.g. London is capital of only one country). Similarly, the Unique Reverse Relation stated that a predicate and an object from a tuple can be selected only if the predicate-object combination is unique in the knowledge base (e.g. United Kingdom has only one capital). Those rules were designed to ensure that there is a unique answer to a potential question. This requirement is not absolutely necessary and was specific to that study. In principle, one might want to generate questions that have multiple answers in a knowledge base, such as *What is located in London?* (with multiple sites and famous buildings listed in a knowledge base).

---

[10] See https://github.com/simplenlg/simplenlg.

Given the words selected from a 5-tuple from the knowledge graph, an encoder-decoder neural system was used to generate a question. The words were taken in order (sequence) and encoded into fixed size embedding vectors. The encoder (a bidirectional RNN with a hidden layer) took the sequence of embeddings and produced an encoded hidden state vector for the whole sequence. An LSTM decoder with attention was used to decode the hidden state into a sequence of vectors, which were in turn converted to words. The length of the output sequence may be different from the length of the input. To train the overall model, the authors used a dataset of one million human-produced questions.[11] To simulate input words, the authors parsed each question and used the extracted nouns, verbs and adjectives as input.

An interesting twist was used for the sequence of words from a knowledge graph tuple. Although the words were treated as a sequence, in fact every permutation of the given set of words was attempted as a separate input sequence, and an output question with the highest probability of generation across all permutations was selected as the generated question. This approach was used only after the model was trained—i.e. with the test data. The authors evaluated the neural AQG approach against two baselines. One baseline approach used templates for AQG. The other approach used phrase-based statistical machine translation trained on the same training data (treating conversion from a sequence of words to a question as a monolingual translation task). For the evaluation, 5000 question instances from WikiAnswers were used as test set. The authors computed BLEU scores comparing the generated questions vs the original questions. The template-based system achieved a BLEU score of 20.58, the translation-based model had BLEU score of 50.90, and the neural AQG system had BLEU score of 50.14. In addition, a human evaluation was conducted, with 700 generated questions from each system. Raters scored each question on a 1–4 scale (higher is better), with respect to well-formedness of the question. Among the questions generated by the template-based approach, 28.57% got a top score of 4. For the translation-based method, 44.29% of the questions got a top score. For the neural AQG system, 60.13% got a top score. Those results suggest that the neural AQG system produces more fluent questions than the baseline systems. Note that the above evaluations did not use a knowledge graph, but rather words extracted from questions. The authors conducted two additional evaluations. In one evaluation they used an actual knowledge graph (Freebase) and extracted 5-tuples for a variety of entities, then retained 485 sets of inputs. Questions were generated from those inputs using the neural AQG system and were manually evaluated. Evaluators were asked whether the generated question and the set-aside answer were together correct. 33.61% of the question–answer pairs were rated as correct. Examples of question and answers related to France are presented in Table 9.2.

In another evaluation, Reddy et al. (2017) set to check whether auto-generated questions with answers can improve the performance of an existing QA system that answers

---

[11] From the WikiAnswers dataset, which has 20 M questions. http://knowitall.cs.washington.edu/oqa/data/wikianswers.

Table 9.2 Sample inputs, generated questions, and answers, from Reddy et al. (2017)

Words for question	Generated question	Answer	Is correct?
IOC code France	What is the IOC code for France?	Fr	Yes
Capital France	What is the capital of France?	Paris	Yes
Location lake Annecy	What is the location of lake Annecy?	France	Yes
Albin Haller country	Is Albin Haller a country?	France	No

questions posed to curated knowledge bases (Berant et al. 2013). The QA system used 3778 human-produced QA pairs for baseline training. Reddy et al. investigated what happens if the base QA training set is enlarged using 7556 more human-produced QA pairs, or with same amount of QA pairs produced with the neural AQG model. All three variants were tested (for question answering) on the same test set of 2032 questions. The systems achieved the following F1 scores: base system: 39.9%; the system augmented with more human-produced data: 43.6%; the augmentation with AQG-produced data: 42.1%, which was quite close to the improvement from human-produced data. Thus, the authors concluded that AQG-produced data can be fruitfully utilized for training knowledge-base-oriented QA systems.[12]

9.5 Selection of Distractors

For educational use, items generated from ontologies and knowledge bases are very often (but not exclusively) multiple-choice items, with a key and several distractors. Selection of distractors is one of the most important components in ontology- or KB-driven AQG. Generally, any entity in an ontology can be selected as a potential distractor. For example, Žitko et al. (2009) mention random selection of entities from within the ontology to serve as distractors. However, selecting plausible distractors can facilitate the quality of generated questions and ensuring plausibility is an important aspect of AQG. This is sometimes called pedagogical appropriateness—an item with implausible distractors would be too easy and would not have value for student testing and learning (Alsubait et al. 2016). Note that plausibility of distractors is always relative to the other components of a question, specifically relative to the core assertion that is used as the backbone of a question. Papasalouros et al. (2008) described some of the basic strategies for ontology-based generation of plausible distractors for AQG. They presented three families of strategies: those based on is-a relations between instances and classes, those based on is-a relations between classes (class-subclass), those based on other relations (so called *property-based*). Essentially, for is-a relations to any class/concept A, plausible distractors can be obtained by considering instances or concepts that belong to superclasses of A or to siblings of A

---

[12] Serban et al. (2016) presented another study of neural AQG for improving QA training.

in the class hierarchy (but are verified not to belong to the class A itself)—such candidates might be semantically close to the key and thus plausible distractors. For an MCQ *Which of the following carry oxygen?—capillaries, ...*, the word *veins* might be a plausible distractor because it belongs to the same superclass 'blood vessels' that capillaries belong to. The concept 'anemia' can be automatically ruled as a poor distractor for this MCQ because anemia is not a blood vessel or even a tissue or organ.

The notion of distractor plausibility is closely related to the notion of item difficulty. An MCQ for which all distractors are very implausible would be very easy to solve. It might even be claimed that plausibility and difficulty are different parts of the same scale. Up to some level, distractors can be implausible and thus too easy; at some point distractors can be plausible, and way beyond that they can be difficult to distinguish from the correct answer. Mitkov et al. (2009) have demonstrated that plausibility of distractors and overall item difficulty can be estimated by measuring semantic similarity of distractors to the key of the item. The more similar are the distractors to the key, the more knowledge one needs to discriminate between them and select the correct option (Alsubait et al. 2014, 2016).

In the examples presented above, the core of a question is typically based on a single assertion from an ontology. Venugopal and Sreenivasa Kumar (2015, 2018) demonstrated how a question core can be based on a combination from several assertions, leading to generation of more complex questions. They describe methods where the core proposition of a question can be (a) composed from more than one record in an ontology, and (b) might represents facts that are not explicitly encoded in an ontology but can be logically derived. They called the first approach pattern-based and illustrated it with an example from an ontology of movies. An ontology might represent the facts that Birdman is a movie, that it was directed by someone named Alejandro Iñárritu, and its release date was August 27, 2014. There are three assertions, and they might be encoded in something like this:

Movie(Birdman)

isDirectedBy(Birdman, Iñárritu)

hasReleaseDate(Birdman, "Aug 27 2014")

or in RDF-like format:

subject: http://example.name#Birdman33

predicate: is-a

object: http://movies_ontology/movie

subject: http://example.name#AlejandroGonzálezIñárritu

9.5 Selection of Distractors

predicate: directed

object: http://example.name#Birdman33

subject: http://example.name#Birdman33

predicate: releasedOn

object: http://example.time/date#20140827

This information can be used to generate a question like *Which movie was directed by Iñárritu and released on August 27, 2014?* It could also support questions like: *Who directed the movie Birdman that was released on August 27, 2014?* or *When was the movie Birdman, directed by Iñárritu, released?*

Stasaski and Hearst (2017) explored the generation of multiple-choice questions from an ontology, for educational use. Specifically, they worked with an ontology of K-12[13] Biology concepts, an expert-produced ontology which had 1260 unique concepts (nodes) and 227 unique relationship types, with a total of 3873 node-relationship-node triples. Instead of simple questions that use a single node-relation-node triple as a core, the researchers set to use the graph structure of the ontology to create complex and challenging questions that link multiple concepts, since such questions can have educational value.[14] For example, the concept 'water' might be involved in the following records: (subj:*salt, pred:DissolvesIn, obj:water*), (*subj:water, pred:HasProperty, obj:cohesion*), (*subj:water, pred:InputTo, obj:evaporation*). From those records, a complex question can be constructed as *What dissolves salt, has cohesion, and is an input to evaporation?*, with the answer *water*. To generate such questions, an algorithm starts with a randomly chosen concept (like 'water') and finds k records in the ontology in which such concept participates (with k initially set to 3). Thus, starting with the correct answer node, n0, it is connected to three other nodes n1, n2, and n3, via relationships r1, r2, and r3 respectively, i.e. n0–r1–n1, n0–r2–n2, and n0–r3–n3. To generate the actual question, the researchers used some simple rules to convert relations into language expressions. For example, if a concept C was in the object position of a triple, and the relation was HasProcess, the verbalization rule was to convert this to *has a process called C*, with variable C substituted with the label of the concept. When a relation was a Characteristic (attribute), the conversion depended on the part of speech of the C concept: if it were a noun, the verbalization would be *has C* (e.g. *has wings*); if it were an adjective, the verbalization would be *is C* (e.g. *is solid*).

To generate distractors, the researchers tried seven different selection methods. Note that distractors in this case are also concepts from the ontology. Five of the methods

---

[13] As per terminology used in the USA, K-12 means kindergarten to 12th grade of school.
[14] For practice studies, asking students which concept relates several stated different features may promote conceptual integration and memory for that information.

used the ontology structure for distractor selection, by selecting concepts/nodes that are somehow related to the concepts in the question via relations in the ontology. In a method called One Matching Relationship, a distractor *d* can be chosen if the ontology has a triple d–r1–n1. In a method called Two Matching Relationships, a distractor d can be chosen if the ontology has a triple d–r1–n1 and a triple d–r2–n2, so a distractor shares two features with the correct concept. In a method called One Matching and One New Relationship, a distractor *d* can be chosen if the ontology has a triple d–r1–n1 (a matching relation) and a triple d–r4–n2, with $r4 \neq r2$ (a new relation). In a method called Two New Relationships, a distractor d can be chosen if the ontology has a triple d–r4–n1 and a triple d–r5–n2, with $r4 \neq r1$ and $r5 \neq r2$. The fifth method for distractor selection chose a distractor from ontology nodes by using graph similarity and picking nodes most similar to the answer concept. Two nodes are considered as similar to the extent that they link to the same other nodes (shared neighbors) and use the same relation types in their connections. The sixth method for distractor selection, Correct Answer Embeddings, chose distractors by vector similarity. All nodes (labels) in the ontology were converted to embedding vectors (using word2vec), and similarity was computed as vector cosine value. Distractors were chosen as concepts most similar to the correct answer. The seventh method, called Question Component Embeddings, also used vector similarity, but distractors were selected as having maximum similarity to nodes n1, n2 or n3, which were components in the question.

Twenty auto-generated questions and their distractors were evaluated by an experienced school-teacher; with questions rated on a 1–7 scale, and distractors rated on a 1–5 scale (higher is better). The questions average rating was only 2.25. The low scores were mostly due to problematic wording of the questions, stressing the need for a more sophisticated verbalization approach. One example of such slightly problematic question from that study: *What is driven by electrical field, has example aromatic molecules in air, and is defined as from higher concentration? (the answer is diffusion)*. In the evaluation, the average scores for distractors, by selection method, were: Two Matching Relationships: 2.37; One Matching, One New Relationship: 2.78; Two New Relationships: 2.03; One Matching Relationship: 2.07; Node Structure 2.63; Correct Answer Embedding: 2.10; Question Component Embedding: 1.60. Distractors selected with the help of ontology relations were rated higher than distractors selected by using vector similarity of concept labels. Some distractors were rather implausible. For the question *What eats mice, eats deer, and is a type of predator? (with the answer mountain lion)*, a distractor *vole* was chosen because voles eat mice and are predators. However, voles are too small to eat deer, so the distractor was implausible for that question. The authors suggested that "*more formal reasoning and real world knowledge coupled with the ontology information*" would be needed to prevent such distractors being chosen.

9.6 Summary

Ontologies, knowledge bases, and knowledge graphs, implement formal methods of knowledge representation, oriented for select semantic aspects of knowledge and represent them is structured ways. Automatic generation of questions from ontologies utilizes such accumulated knowledge and is especially useful in technical domains. Ontologies and formal knowledge bases from technical fields can be utilized for educational uses, generating quizzes for testing student knowledge in those areas. Since concepts and relations between concepts in knowledge bases are rigorously typed, this aspect allows for selecting the kinds of concepts and relations that are used for questions.

Ontologies are very useful for generating multiple-choice questions, since selection of distractors can utilize the same semantic formal organization that is used for generating the question stem. Sophisticated questions and distractors can be generated by integrating multiple assertions from a knowledge base. In addition, due to the formal methods of knowledge representation, AQG from such resources can utilize methods and tools of formal (truth-preserving) reasoning, for generating more complex questions.

Generation of questions from formal representations involves an aspect of verbalization, translating the formal concepts into a fluent output. Early ontology-based AQG systems used rule-based and statistical NLP tools for linguistic realization. Later systems utilized neural network architectures.

Question Generation with Large Language Models and Generative AI

10.1 Introduction

As the transformer family of models for deep learning became the leading type of neural architecture, researchers have noted the significant advantage that pretraining provides. Learning (pretraining) performance of transformer models scales as a power law with the amount of training data and model parameters (Kaplan et al. 2020). Hence, there began a race for training larger and larger language models. GPT-2 (Radford et al. 2019) was trained on about 8 million text documents and the model variants had between 117 million and 1.5 billion parameters. Google's T5 model (Raffel et al. 2020) scaled up to 11 billion parameters. The GPT-3 family of models (Brown et al. 2020) has up to 175 billion parameters. GPT-4 is estimated to have up to about 1.8 trillion parameters (Schreiner 2023). Other contemporary large language model families include LLaMA (Touvron et al. 2023), Gemma/Gemini (Gemma Team 2024), Mistral (Jiang et al. 2023) and many others. Zhao et al. (2023) present a comprehensive multi-faceted review of large language models. Note a terminological distinction between LLM—large language models, and PLM—pretrained language models. The former emphasizes the model size, while the latter emphasizes the pretrained aspect.

One definition for a **large language model** (LLM) is *"a computational model capable of language generation or other natural language processing tasks"*.[1] A notable component in such definition are the generative capabilities. The sequence-to-sequence processing model in deep learning provides a natural path for generation of various outputs, viewing the input as a **prompt**, and aiming for the output to be a fluent and relevant text. As noted by Radford et al. (2019), Raffel et al. (2020), and by See et al. (2019), language models begin to show capability for generating coherent texts without any explicit supervision

---

[1] See https://en.wikipedia.org/wiki/Large_language_model. For a broad account with historical aspects, see Mitchell (2024).

when trained on a very-large-scale data, with typical tasks being summarization, question answering and machine translation. And, as noted by Raffel et al., almost any NLP task (and not only NLG) can be posed as sequence-to-sequence task for a neural generative model. Generative AI systems based on those principles can respond to queries/prompts and can create answers, stories, images, videos, music, and programming code. Obviously, question generation is also one of such generation tasks.

Neural generative language models, given a query/prompt, decompose it into parts (tokens and word fragments), vectorize them and then compute a probability distribution for generating a plausible next token (from the models' vocabulary), given the processed input. For the next token, the probability is computed taking the input into account, but also the just generated previous token. Such process is iterated, appending the newly generated tokens to the original prompt, and using this new context to select a next token (Kirchenbauer et al. 2023; Narayan and Gardent 2020). Transformer architectures allow long distance lexical relations in text to influence selection of the next word in sequence (expanding from 2 to 4 K tokens for some models circa 2019 to more than 50 K tokens just a few years later).

Beyond massive pretraining, researchers distinguish three broad task-learning models for LLMs—zero-shot learning, few-shot learning, and fine-tuning. Zero-shot learning is not a training procedure. This notion describes situations where pretrained LLMs can rather successfully respond to requests (queries/prompts) on new tasks without special explicit training. Few-shot learning describes the cases where providing a few task-specific training examples allows to significantly improve the model performance on such a task (or content area). Fine-tuning (which we encountered in Chap. 7) is a case were some considerable amount of training data is used to modify the model parameters so as to improve the model's performance on the given task(s), and the task-specific training data is often human-labeled.

The notion of hallucination refers to generating factually wrong, inaccurate, or fictitious information that deviates from what might be expected as factually adequate. While the problem of hallucinations was already evident in the early deep learning models that used LSTM architectures, hallucinations continue to be a major problem in outputs of transformer models, and also in the recent very large models (Perković et al. 2024; Ji et al. 2023). In addition, LLMs trained on web-scale content tend to have problematic outputs with generation of inappropriate language (toxicity or offensiveness) and various kinds of cultural bias (Gallegos et al. 2024; Bender et al. 2021). Those aspects are important for evaluating questions generated with LLMs, especially when QG is intended for educational uses.

In addition to prompting an LLM to generate some plausible and fluent textual outputs, it turned out that LLMs can also be trained to follow task instructions. For instruction training, researchers use datasets with human-written task instructions and examples of desired outputs. With some considerable amount of training (significant fine-tuning), pretrained LLMs exhibit a behavior of following the task instructions for given new prompts.

One of the seminal examples of this was GPT-Instruct (Ouyang et al. 2022). Which led to the ChatGPT with capabilities to follow instructions. Notably, instruction training involves different objectives than just language modeling; instruction tuning typically uses reinforcement learning. Many recent LLMs are now released pretrained for 'understanding' and performing in accordance with user instructions (Lou et al. 2024; Jiang et al. 2023; Zhao et al. 2023).

Those developments have led to emergence of **prompt engineering**, a process of designing instructions/commands/queries, in plain language, that can effectively describe a task to LLMs (White et al. 2023). Prompting an LLM provides two advantages to users. On the one hand, an off-the-shelf LLM is already pretrained, usually on a web-scale data, with much knowledge and capabilities, including capabilities for producing fluent outputs. On the other hand, prompting gives a convenient interface to interact with a model, which allows users to specify and customize various generation tasks. Mollick and Mollick (2023) present a variety of exemplar LLM prompts for educational uses.

10.2 Generation

With the advances in generative AI, generating questions from text can be reduced in many cases to just writing a prompt for an LLM. A sample prompt is presented in Fig. 10.1.

Attali et al. (2022) described an interactive reading test that was designed for assessing adult students' reading comprehension. For this test, a GPT-3 model was used to generate reading texts and several kinds of assessment items. First, they used the LLM to generate short texts passages that would be used for the test. For this they use an instruction prompt, e.g. *"Generate short paragraphs from high school textbooks on the specified topic."* Each

---

Story:
Once upon a time there were three Bears, who lived together in a house of their own, in a wood. One of them was ... One day, after they prepared porridge for their breakfast, and poured it into their bowls, they went to the wood while the porridge was cooling ...
Instruction:
Read the above story and produce a question.
Question:
<LLM WILL FILL THIS SLOT>
Answer:
in a wood

Fig. 10.1 An example prompt for answer-aware question generation from text. This example, suited for GPT-3, was adapted from Yuan et al. (2023). The story is abbreviated for illustration

such prompt includes 3–5 examples (short texts) that exemplify the required characteristic for generation, as well as labels specifying the required format, style, and content. The authors reported generating over 14,000 passages that resemble news, expository texts, and narrative texts. However, they required considerable filtering of the resulting texts. They needed to remove texts that had repeating-text sections and eliminate passages that were too short or too long. In addition, generated texts were eliminated that had rather implausible or difficult sentences. In practice that was estimated with a negative log likelihood model. If a sentence had extremely high negative log likelihood (conditioned on the rest of the text), it was more likely to make less sense (being quite improbable) in the context. From the remaining texts, the authors sampled 800 passages and had educators review them for suitability, with 789 initially accepted.

The researchers then generated several item types based on those texts. One of the item types are text-based comprehension questions with multiple-choice answers. To generate such questions for a given passage, the researchers used a prompt that included the passage text, and some examples of questions and answers (this is a few-shot training). GPT-3 was then able to generate similar questions for the given target passages. To ensure item quality, the researchers needed to filter out extremely long questions (longer than 25 words), questions that had very short answers (1–2 words), and questions that were considered as unanswerable based on the passage. The low answerability likelihood was estimated by using an external question-answering system (trained on the SQuAD dataset). After additional review, which included fairness and cultural appropriateness human review, only 454 passages were retained. This aspect of their research exemplifies that even with the advanced capabilities of LLMs, considerable filtering and adjustment of generation results is needed when the task has significant quality requirements. The items were administered to students in a pilot study and have achieved good psychometric properties, with the authors stating that this is a viable and promising method of item generation.

Cheung et al. (2023) reported on a comparative study for generation of medical examination multiple-choice items. Fifty items were generated by medical experts, with reference to well-known medical textbooks. Fifty items were generated by ChatGPT, with excerpts from the same textbooks. For generation with ChatGPT, a prompt template was developed, as illustrated in Fig. 10.2. Note that this is an answer-unaware generation, where the model also automatically selects the target answer.

All one hundred items were randomized and presented to a panel of five medical experts for evaluation. Each item was rated for five aspects: Appropriateness, Clarity, Relevance, Quality of the alternatives, and estimated Discriminative power, using a 10-point scale (higher is better) for each aspect. On average, LLM-generated items achieved comparable evaluation scores to the human-authored items—in the 7–8 range of the 0–10 scale, on every aspect except 'Relevance', where the generated items had a statistically significant lower score (7.56 versus 7.88). For the combined score (0–50 scale), the generated items had a wider range of scores (about 27–47), while human-authored questions

10.2 Generation

> User:
> Can you write a multiple-choice question based on the following criteria, with the reference I am providing for you and your medical knowledge?
> 1. The questions were designed to meet the standard for a medical graduate exam.
> 2. Only four choices were allowed for each question.
> 3. The questions were limited to knowledge-based questions only.
> 4. Distractors were allowed to refer from sources other than the original reference provided.
> 5. An answer is required.
> 6. No explanation is required for the question.
>
> Reference:
> Acute pancreatitis
> Acute pancreatitis accounts for 3% of all cases of abdominal pain among patients...
> (*the full reference is a medical excerpt of about 1300 words*).
>
> ChatGPT:
> Which of the following is the most common cause of acute pancreatitis?
> a) Biliary calculi
> b) Alcohol abuse
> c) Tumours at the ampulla of Vater
> d) Hereditary pancreatitis
> Answer: a) Biliary calculi

Fig. 10.2 An example prompt for MCQ item generation from text. Parts "User" and "Reference" constitute the prompt. Part "ChatGPT" is the ChatGPT-generated item. Adapted from examples by Cheung et al. (2023)

were more consistent (range 32–44), but there was no statistically significant difference of the mean scores. In addition, for each item, each rater was asked to guess who wrote the item—human or machine. The average correct-guess rate was 58.4%. This study exemplifies two important aspects. First it demonstrates one typical approach to evaluation of AQG—comparing generated and human-authored questions/items in a multi-aspect human rating study. Second, it demonstrates that an advanced LLM, ChatGPT in this case, was able to generate multiple-choice items in a specialized domain, with quality on a par with human experts.

> **Context (Psychology):** Sleep debt and sleep deprivation have significant negative psychological and physiological consequences. As mentioned earlier, lack of sleep can result in decreased mental alertness and cognitive function. In addition, sleep deprivation often results in depression-like symptoms. These effects can occur as a function of accumulated sleep debt or in response to more acute periods of sleep deprivation. It may surprise you to know that sleep deprivation is associated with obesity, increased blood pressure, increased levels of stress hormones, and reduced immune functioning.
> **Target:** sleep deprivation
> **Reference human-authored question:** Which animal would be most likely to die from a lack of sleep?
> **Machine-generated question:** Sleep debt and sleep deprivation are associated with significant negative psychological and physiological consequences. What are some of the potential consequences of a person having less than optimal sleep?

Fig. 10.3 An illustration of context, target concept, example question and LLM-produced question, from Wang et al. (2022)

10.3 Prompt-Engineering for QG

Wang et al. (2022) investigated question generation via prompting a GPT-3 model. They focused on generating content-specific questions from introductory college-level textbooks. An example of their prompt is presented in Fig. 10.3. Their goal was to evaluate the quality of such automatically generated questions. They investigated the following aspects that may influence the generation task: (a) the number of examples supplied to the model, (b) the length of context and question in the examples, (c) source of data for the examples, (d) components included in the examples. The researchers produced 75 questions for each condition for each of those influence factors. To evaluate the quality of resulting questions, the researchers used several metrics with measures supplied by automated tools. The number of grammatical errors in each question was estimated with an automated grammar checker. The overall coherence of a question was estimated by computing its perplexity score (using a different language model). The preference is to have questions of better coherence. i.e. lower perplexity. Diversity of generated questions was estimated with the *distinct-3* measure, which counts the average number of distinct trigrams in the questions. The presence of profanity or inappropriate language was estimated with an online tool Perspective API.[2] The aspect of inappropriate language is an important one when a model trained on web-scale data is used for producing educational content. The fifth metric was acceptability of the questions by human raters.

With regard to the source of question examples, the researchers compared two conditions—providing example questions from the same specialized content domain (biology

---

[2] https://www.perspectiveapi.com.

10.3 Prompt-Engineering for QG

textbook) or from a general domain (using questions from the SQuAD dataset). The results indicated that using examples from the same domain produced questions that have lower perplexity (64.6 versus 102.8), slightly better diversity (0.895 versus 0.884), lower index of inappropriate language (0.153 versus 0.201), with not much difference in grammaticality (0.053 versus 0.093). Most importantly, using examples from the same content domain led to higher acceptability rate of generated questions (26.7 versus 18.0%), though overall acceptability was still rather low.

For the aspect of structural components in a prompt, the researchers compared two conditions. In one condition, termed CAQ, the example included the context (snippet of text for which the question is related), the specific answer, and the example question. In another condition, termed CTQA, the example includes an additional component, a specification of the conceptual target for the question. The CTQA condition led to lower perplexity (29.8 versus 64.6) of questions, and considerably larger proportion of acceptable questions (55 versus 27%).

With regard to the length of examples, the researchers investigated separately the length of example context and the length of example questions. The basic assumptions were that a short context or example question *"may limit the diversity and complexity of the generated questions"*, while a long context or question *"may contain irrelevant information ... leading to generated questions that are irrelevant or off-topic"*. The experiments used short contexts (2 sentences), medium contexts (4–5 sentences), and large contexts (a paragraph or more). Shorter example contexts resulted in generated questions with lower rate of grammar errors (0.380 versus 0.410 and 0.420 for medium and long contexts). However, there was not much difference in acceptability rates (22, 24 and 24% respectively). The length of example questions did have more pronounced effects. Three length sizes were used—short example questions (about 15 words long), medium (about 25 words), and long (about 40 words). Shorter example questions resulted in generated questions with lower rate of grammar errors (0.377 versus 0.487 versus 0.610). Shorter example questions also led to generated questions of better acceptability (30 versus 23.7 and 14.7% respectively). There was very little difference in question perplexity. Overall, having short example contexts and short example questions provided with better results.

With regard to the number of examples, the researchers investigated supplying the model with one, three, five, or seven examples. For the one- and three-examples conditions, the acceptability rates were 25 and 38%. Providing more examples led to better acceptability, 55% with five examples and 45% with seven. Inappropriate language decreased from 0.384 for one-example condition to 0.208 and 0.176 for five- and seven-examples conditions respectively. The proportion of grammatical errors dropped from 0.182 for one example condition to 0.076 for the seven-example condition. Overall, the researchers concluded that five or seven examples was preferable to fewer examples.

From the above evaluations, Wang et al. (2022) concluded that the optimal QG prompt design for college-level text is to use five to seven examples in CTQA format, use domain-specific examples, with relatively short example contexts and questions. In the second stage of evaluation, the researchers evaluated LLM-generated questions for several content domains. Human subject-matter experts (SMEs) were engaged in judging the question acceptability. Using optimal prompt configuration, the researchers generated questions for texts from biology, psychology, and history textbooks, 50 questions in total. They added 5 reference human-authored questions and gave the collection to the evaluators. The raters provided two ratings: (a) whether each question was machine-generated or human-authored, and (b) whether they would use the question for assessment in their class. The results were that about 70% of LLM-produced questions in biology were judged as human-authored, but that percentage was only about 50% for history and psychology. This may indicate that greater quality of formulation is needed for questions in the humanities. For the second aspect, about 70% of LLM-produced questions in biology were marked as OK for use in class-assessment, about 50% history questions were acceptable, but over 60% of questions is psychology were acceptable. Overall, those results indicate quite successful LLM-based AQG. However, the study also demonstrated that much filtering and adjustment is needed for obtaining good quality results.

10.4 Question Selection

The work by Yuan et al. (2023) addressed some very important aspects of utilizing LLMs for QG. They start with the notion that to obtain high quality AQG results, there are generally two approaches—improve the generation algorithms, or overgenerate and select only the best questions/items. With LLMs, some improvement of generation can be achieved by experimentally tweaking the prompts (as shown by Wang et al. 2022). However, prompt-engineering may have its limits. Many potential users of LLMs, including many researchers, have to deal with an LLM as a "black-box"—it can be accessed via API, but the LLM cannot be fine-tuned or adapted. In such cases the only option is to have the system generate (or overgenerate) questions and then select the better ones. This can be seen as a resurgence of the "overgenerate, rank, and select" approach that was introduced in AQG research by Heilman and Smith (2010a). Yuan et al. (2023) were interested which different automatic-selection strategies might be useful in some quite different cases. They used GPT-3 to generate questions and evaluated several automated-selection approaches. The basic setting was that the LLM could generate several different questions for a given query/prompt (using temperature[3] setting 0.7), but it was not specifically tuned to the QG task.

Yuan et al. (2023) proposed three different approaches to question selection. The first method was called n-gram similarity. The idea is to use n-gram similarity between the

---

[3] The notion 'temperature' refers to the probability in selecting the next token for generation. Low temperature means select only the most probable token, higher temperature allows a larger range of probabilities and thus more variability of the outputs.

10.4 Question Selection

question and the original text (context) to which it pertains. This is based on the assumption that a favorable question should be closely related to the information provided by the context. For each context and question, they computed the number of unique n-grams from the context that are also found in the question, and normalized that by the total count of unique n-grams in the question.

The second selection method was called "round-trip" (RT). It can be used when the answer to the question is known in advance (before or during the QG process). The idea is that a generated question could be fed to a good QA system and the resulting answer compared to the original (ground-truth) answer. If the two answers are considerably similar (indicating consistency), the question might be considered a good one. If the two answers are not similar, this may indicate that the question is inadequate. Questions can be ranked on such metrics (which actually compare the answers). Notably, the authors used the same GPT-3 model as a question-answering system. This relates well to scenarios where users do minimal NLP (just similarity comparisons) and the bulk of work is done via the LLM API.

The third selection method was called "prompt-based score". For this method, the authors designed prompts for the LLM to rate (score) the generated question on several aspects. The average score from those ratings was called 'averaged prompt-based score' (APS) and was used to rank questions for selection. The aspects for rating were grammatical correctness, offensiveness, clarity, relevance, importance, specificity, and answerability (with a 1–2–3 scale for each, higher is better). Those aspects were designed for a human (crowdsourced) evaluation. However, the authors demonstrated that with a sophisticated prompting technique, they could obtain question ratings from the LLM. This illustrates a remarkable capability of LLMs to perform rating/scoring tasks. We can note that additional methods of similarity-based selection could be employed, such as BERTScore, or directly computing the cosine between embedding of the context and the embedding of the generated question.

For the experiments, the researchers used subsets from two different datasets that have human-authored texts, questions, and answers—SQuAD (Rajpurkar et al. 2016) and FairytaleQA (Xu et al. 2022). The two datasets contrast on some key aspects. SQuAD was developed for expository texts (Wikipedia articles), it has sentence-level questions where the answers are explicit in the text and are usually proper substrings of the sentences. FairytaleQA texts are children's stories (narrative genre), it has paragraph-level questions, and the answers are typically not explicitly stated in the texts.

The texts (snippets) from those datasets were used as contexts for question generation with GPT-3. In each case (text), 5 questions were generated and one of them was selected—using different selection methods outlined above. In addition, the researchers also tried combinations of those selection methods. The selected questions were then evaluated in two ways. One evaluation was automated, reference-based, comparing the selected questions to the corresponding original questions from the datasets (using BLEU-4 for SQuAD and ROUGE-L for FairytaleQA). The idea of such evaluation is that a 'better' selection method would select questions that are closer (more similar on average) to the original refence questions. For SQuAD-based data, RT was the best performing selection method, with a score of 0.392, while the other methods were not far behind, with 0.382 for n-grams and 0.380 for APS. For FairytaleQA data, RT was again the best performing selection method, with a score of 0.434, while the other methods were not far behind, with 0.403 for n-grams and 0.406 for APS. A combination of all three methods achieved a score of 0.435, but just APS + RT was the best overall, with 0.439.

Those results illustrate some important points. The results of automated evaluation for SQuAD data were better than many previous tuned AQG systems (where the best was about 0.26, see Table 7.2). For FairytaleQA, the results (0.439) were somewhat lower than previously obtained with a tuned BART system (score 0.527, from Xu et al. 2022). Yuan et al. showed that, by combining non-tuned-LLM AQG with a selection strategy, one can obtain questions that are considerably similar (on average) to the original human-authored questions. However, such evaluation has limitations. Similarity-based metrics can indicate relative merits of the different selection methods, but their results do not clarify whether the generated-and-selected questions are really any good. As pointed by Yuan et al. (2023), human evaluation is needed for that. Indeed, the researchers conducted such an evaluation, with crowdsourced raters, who evaluated each question on eight aspects (see above). Raters' scores were averaged across aspects and across several raters into a single average human rating for each question. For the SQuAD data, the questions selected with the n-grams method had an average rating of 0.943, for the RT method the rating was 0.934, and with the APS method the rating was 0.913. The best rating, 0.951, was achieved by a combined method of n-grams with RT. For the FairytaleQA data, the best single selection method was APS, with rating of 0.959, while n-grams (0.943) and RT (0.926) were not far behind. The best combined selection method was n-grams with APS (0.948). Overall, the selected generated questions were rated very highly by human evaluators. The authors included an additional aspect in this evaluation—they included not only the selected LLM-generated questions, but also the original 'ground-truth' reference questions form the respective datasets. In the human evaluation, the reference questions rated 0.933 (SQuAD data) and 0.927 (FairytaleQA data), which is slightly lower than the 'best' generated questions. The finding that generated questions can be as good or even a bit better than human-authored questions illustrates that a reference-based evaluation for AQG can be misleading. The model-generated questions may be quite different from the human-authored questions, they can even ask about different information, but they can be quite good.

A novel method to include additional constraints on question generation is via utilizing the LLM to plan its own production/output. The Chain-of-Thought (CoT) is a prompting method for LLMs to explicitly generate a step-by-step explanation or blueprint of the desired output; such a plan is then fed into the LLM to generate the final results (Wei et al. 2022; Feng et al. 2023). This introduces intermediate tasks into the process, which can help constrain the output in the desired 'direction'. Li and Zhang (2024) utilized

LLM CoT-based planning capabilities for generating questions constrained by question type and difficulty. They used the FairytaleQA dataset of children's stories (Xu et al. 2022). The dataset includes gold-standard questions that are pre-annotated (by experts) with attributes (what the question is generally about, such as events, feelings, etc.) and labels for question locality (answer is in one place or is distributed in text, i.e. summative) and whether the question is implicit or explicit vis-à-vis the text (the latter being taken as a proxy for difficulty). The authors used LLaMa2 model (Touvron et al. 2023) to first train the model to generate initial plans, based on the annotated attribute labels. This stage just prepares the model to focus on (or retrieve) segments whose contents are thematically similar to those that had specific labels. In the next stage, the authors created prompts (templates of prompts) that ask the system to find or generate sentences (potential answers) according to type. For local explicit questions the prompt would just ask to use single sentences. For local implicit questions the prompt would ask to use single sentences and paraphrase them (thus, subsequently, questions generated from a paraphrase are not quite explicit). For summative explicit questions, the prompt asks the system to find sequences of sentences. For summative implicit questions, the prompt asks the system to find sequences of sentences and paraphrase them. Finally, question generation is performed by combining the thematic attribute plan generator with the question-type plan generator. The authors compared their AQG system with several previous systems using the FairytaleQA dataset, and reported that their generated questions were more similar to gold-standard questions than previous results (improvements Rouge-L $0.254 \rightarrow 0.413$, BERTScore $0.878 \rightarrow 0.897$). That experiment necessitated having a large pre-annotated dataset, which is not always available for various text types, but it also exemplified how generation-planning prompts can be utilized for AQG with LLMs.

10.5 Summary

With the advances in generative AI and availability of large language models, the task of generating questions from text became largely reduced to just writing a suitable prompt for an LLM. LLMs can generate various kinds of questions and multiple-choice items. Prompt engineering is now a common approach for generating questions, rather than coding NLP pipelines or training models. This aspect also allows more users, even those not experts in NLP, to experiment with AQG. Evaluations of LLM-generated questions often show that such questions are of rather good quality, achieving same ratings as human-authored questions, even for specialized content areas like medical texts. LLM-generated questions are also often indistinguishable from human generated questions, being quite fluent and related to the context. This advancement opens the door to working on specialized AQG that can make question difficulty and specific content-requirements of the users an integral part of the question generation.

Conclusion 11

Automatic Question Generation has come a long way in about 20 years. In that, it has followed the general trajectory of the whole field of computational linguistics. From linguistically inspired approaches, supported by statistical computations, the whole field, and AQG with it, have moved to deep learning neural approaches, and then increasingly relying on larger and larger models. This was in part enabled by the increasing computation power of available hardware. The phenomenal success of large language models was not an obvious outcome when considered even circa the year 2018.

The research agenda in AQG has developed as well. In the beginning, the basic research issue was how to automatically generate fluent and well-formed questions from arbitrary texts, usually from single sentences. The solutions were adopted from the general developments in linguistically-motivated contemporary NLP. Those included developments in syntactic parsing technologies, with availability of constituent and dependency parsers, and tools for handling morphology. Developments in semantic analysis were also adapted, specifically semantic-role parsers. This was closely followed by introduction of discourse parsers, which allowed generating questions across sentences. In addition, the development of template-based AQG approaches allowed greater control over the generation process, especially when combined with syntactic and semantic analyses.

The major potential use for AQG is often considered to be in educational applications. The educational field has a wide need for various types of questions, including interrogative forms and gap-filling items, and the ever-popular multiple-choice questions bring the need for generating good distractors. The demand for questions/items in education spans multiple aspects. One goal for automatic generation is improved supply and replenishment of question/item repositories. Automated generation promises to relieve the burden of manual question authoring, making questions more abundant and cheaper to produce.

In addition, as questions/items can be generated on demand, it allows integrating them for new learning objects and for formative practice situations. Such potential uses have also broadened the scope of AQG research. Researchers started looking not just for the capability of generating questions automatically, but also for additional requirements. They stared looking toward generating more diverse questions, and deeper questions, beyond the surface levels of the text, questions that may be used for supporting critical and reflective thinking, clarification and analysis of writing, and more engaging learning experience in general. While early research was largely focused on informational texts, such as textbooks, news, and Wikipedia articles, where questioning stresses knowledge assessment, later AQG research also expanded to narrative texts.

In parallel with the interest in AQG from text, there is a whole area of research on question generation from structured knowledge representations, i.e., ontologies, knowledge bases and knowledge graphs. One of the advantages of such resources is their curated nature, which is very useful for generating questions that assess knowledge, especially in highly technical domains where ontologies represent domain-specific content (e.g., biology, geography). Ontologies and knowledge bases are especially conducive for generating multiple-choice questions, since relevant distractors can be obtained from the same resource as the core of the question. Basing AQG on formal knowledge resources also enables integrating formal reasoning tools in the question generation process.

Different approaches to question generation have also proceeded to new applications for questions, in rather unexpected ways. Generation of questions from ontologies and knowledge bases has sparked an interest in using questions as a tool for validating knowledge bases (Ben Abacha et al. 2016). Deep learning methods in NLP rely on large training corpora. In the field of Question Answering (QA), the SQuAD corpus was one of the early and most prominent corpora that included texts, questions, and answers. While initially it was developed for research on question answering, it was soon also used for AQG. Once neural AQG was established, AQG quickly became utilized in the reverse direction: generating new questions for the purpose of creating new corpora for training neural QA systems (Reddy et al. 2017; Serban et al. 2016). Another interesting use of AQG was proposed by Woo et al. (2016), an application of AQG for generating personalized authentication questions for verifying user identity for accessing online accounts.

Some aspects of AQG were not covered in this book. One such aspect is question generation for interactive situations, such as conversations and dialogs, where the basis for questions changes dynamically as the conversation proceeds (Nakanishi et al. 2019; Wang et al. 2018b; Shen et al. 2021). This can be useful, for example, for equipping chatbots and virtual assistants with the ability to pose conversation-relevant questions. Another emerging area is AQG for fact checking. That involves generating questions for (textual) claims where the answer might not be in the text, but where the question needs to cover relevant aspects for seeking additional information (Ousidhoum et al. 2022; Fan et al. 2020). Yet another area is multimodal question generation, where information from multiple modalities may be integrated for generating questions. Visual QG, with integration of image information, is already an established area that connects vision research and NLP (Sarrouti et al. 2021; Li et al. 2018). On the language perspective, this book focused solely on question generation for English, based on English texts or knowledge resources. There is a growing body of AQG research for various other natural languages, such as French (Bernhard et al. 2012), Basque (Aldabe and Maritxalar 2014), Arabic (Bousmaha et al. 2020), Chinese (Liu et al. 2017), Indonesian (Muis and Purwarianti 2020), and isiZulu (Gilbert and Keet 2018).

Some aspects of AQG were barely touched in this book. One prolific research area is generation of good distractors for multiple-choice questions (Gierl et al. 2017), which spans various content domains, from assessing children's reading comprehension (Mostow et al. 2017), to professional medical exams (Yaneva et al. 2021; Ha and Yaneva 2018). Another prolific research area is prediction of question/item difficulty by using NLP tools (Benedetto et al. 2023; AlKhuzaey et al. 2021). A related aspect is difficulty control. It refers to the ability to generate questions at different levels of difficulty (or complexity). This is often motivated by educational considerations, such as providing questions with difficulty levels suited for different learner abilities or exam specifications. There is already considerable research literature on integrating difficulty control in the question generation process (Uto et al. 2023; Gao et al. 2019).

Question generation is an open-ended process, as multiple and different questions can be asked about the same input. This includes two aspects—which parts of the text are question-worthy, and what questions should be asked about the potential question targets. Those considerations where at the heart of AQG for a long time and different solutions were proposed. One of the solutions is to identify the most important parts of a text (like in summarization), another solution is to learn question preferences from a corpus, and yet another is to focus on a-priory known important aspects (like cause-effect relations). While those approaches can be useful in many cases, content-control often depends on the specific goals of an AQG project. Thus, developing new methods of content control remains an important area of research in AQG. The issue of content control also brought an important distinction between answer-aware AQG, where the potential answer is marked in advance, and answer-unaware AQG, where the system needs to pick a target automatically. A useful general approach that emerged in research is 'overgenerate, rank and filter', which can be utilized for content control, difficulty control and quality control of generated questions.

With the advances in generative AI, large language models (LLMs) revolutionized many aspects of NLP, including question generation. The task of generating questions from text became largely reduced to just writing suitable prompts for LLMs. This makes AQG more accessible, as even people who are not NLP-experts can interact with systems that provide impressive AQG outputs. Prompt engineering emerges as a new professional specialization in many areas, and that will probably include AQG for education and for other applications.

The advanced capabilities of LLM-based AQG have brought with them a new urgency to the evaluation of AQG. Automatic evaluation approaches, such as the classic BLEU and ROUGE metrics, and even newer metrics like BERTScore, rely on comparing newly generated questions to some reference questions. This approach provides only relative estimation of generated questions and is useful during AQG system development, to indicate relative progress of newer algorithms. However, such approach does not indicate the absolute quality of generated questions—are they good enough for the intended uses? New questions can be quite different from reference questions, and also be quite good (or bad). Multi-faceted evaluation by human raters, preferably subject-matter experts, is still the preferred method for question quality evaluation. Quality and suitability evaluation would become even more important when AQG outputs are increasingly used in practical applications, such as educational assessment. Human evaluation is usually expensive and time-consuming. A new and emerging trend is adapting LLMs to evaluate generated questions (Maity and Deroy 2024; Yuan et al. 2023; Khademi 2023). This can be done via just prompt-engineering, which opens new horizons for the evaluation line of research.

References

David Adamson, Divyanshu Bhartiya, Biman Gujral, Radhika Kedia, Ashudeep Singh, and Carolyn P. Rosé (2013). Automatically Generating Discussion Questions. In: H.C. Lane, K. Yacef, K., J. Mostow, and P. Pavlik (eds.) *Artificial Intelligence in Education, AIED 2013*, pp. 81–90. Lecture Notes in Computer Science, vol 7626. Springer-Verlag Berlin Heidelberg.

Naveed Afzal and Ruslan Mitkov (2014). Automatic generation of multiple choice questions using dependency-based semantic relations. *Soft Computing*, 18, 1269–1281. https://doi.org/10.1007/s00500-013-1141-4

Manish Agarwal and Prashanth Mannem (2011). Automatic Gap-fill Question Generation from Text Books. In *Proceedings of the Sixth Workshop on Innovative Use of NLP for Building Educational Applications*, pp. 56–64, Portland, Oregon, ACL. https://aclanthology.org/W11-1407

Manish Agarwal, Rakshit Shah, and Prashanth Mannem (2011). Automatic Question Generation using Discourse Cues. In *Proceedings of the Sixth Workshop on Innovative Use of NLP for Building Educational Applications*, pp. 1–9, Portland, Oregon, ACL. https://aclanthology.org/W11-1401

Renlong Ai, Sebastian Krause, Walter Kasper, Feiyu Xu, and Hans Uszkoreit (2015). Semi-automatic Generation of Multiple-Choice Tests from Mentions of Semantic Relations. In *Proceedings of the 2nd Workshop on Natural Language Processing Techniques for Educational Applications*, pp. 26–33, Beijing, China. ACL. https://aclanthology.org/W15-4405

Zakariae Alami Merrouni, Bouchra Frikh, and Brahim Ouhbi (2020). Automatic keyphrase extraction: a survey and trends. *Journal of Intelligent Information Systems*, 54, 391–424. https://doi.org/10.1007/s10844-019-00558-9

Itziar Aldabe and Montse Maritxalar (2014). Semantic Similarity Measures for the Generation of Science Tests in Basque. IEEE Transactions On Learning Technologies, 7 (4), pp. 375–387. https://doi.org/10.1109/TLT.2014.2355831

Husam Ali, Yllias Chali, and Sadid A. Hasan (2010). Automation of question generation from sentences. In Proceedings of QG2010: The Third Workshop on Question Generation, pp. 58–67. https://aclanthology.org/2010.jeptalnrecital-court.36.pdf

Samah AlKhuzaey, Floriana Grasso, Terry R. Payne, and Valentina Tamma (2021). A Systematic Review of Data-Driven Approaches to Item Difficulty Prediction. In: I. Roll, D., McNamara, S., Sosnovsky, R., Luckin, and V., Dimitrova, (eds.) *Artificial Intelligence in Education, AIED 2021*. LNCS, vol. 12748. Springer, Cham. https://doi.org/10.1007/978-3-030-78292-4_3

Tahani Alsubait, Bijan Parsia, and Ulrike Sattler (2016). Ontology-Based Multiple Choice Question Generation. *Künstliche Intelligenz*, 30, 183–188. https://doi.org/10.1007/s13218-015-0405-9

Tahani Alsubait, Bijan Parsia, and Ulrike Sattler (2014). Measuring similarity in ontologies: a new family of measures. In *Proceedings of the 19th international conference on knowledge engineering and knowledge management (EKAW 2014)*, pp. 13–25. Springer Nature. https://doi.org/10.1007/978-3-319-13704-9_2

Yigal Attali, Andrew Runge, Geoffrey T. LaFlair, Kevin Yancey, Sarah Goodwin, Yena Park and Alina A. von Davier (2022). The interactive reading task: Transformer-based automatic item generation. *Frontiers in Artificial Intelligence*, (5:903077). https://doi.org/10.3389/frai.2022.903077

Maha Al-Yahya (2014). Ontology-Based Multiple Choice Question Generation. *The Scientific World Journal*. https://doi.org/10.1155/2014/274949

Maha Al-Yahya (2011). OntoQue: a question generation engine for educational assessment based on domain ontologies. In *Proceedings of the 11th IEEE International Conference on Advanced Learning Technologies (ICALT '11)*, pp. 393–395, Athens, Ga, USA.

Jay Alammar (2018). The Illustrated Transformer [Blog post]. Accessed November 17, 2023. https://jalammar.github.io/illustrated-transformer

Bengt Altenberg (1984). Causal linking in spoken and written English. *Studia Linguistica*, 38(1), 20–69.

Jacopo Amidei, Paul Piwek, and Alistair Willis (2018a). Rethinking the Agreement in Human Evaluation Tasks. In *Proceedings of the 27th International Conference on Computational Linguistics*, pp. 3318–3329, Santa Fe, New Mexico, USA. ACL. https://aclanthology.org/C18-1281

Jacopo Amidei, Paul Piwek, and Alistair Willis (2018b). Evaluation methodologies in Automatic Question Generation 2013–2018. In *Proceedings of the 11th International Conference on Natural Language Generation*, pp. 307–317, Tilburg University, The Netherlands. ACL https://aclanthology.org/W18-6537

Lorin W. Anderson, David R. Krathwohl, Peter W. Airasian, Kathleen A. Cruikshank, Richard E. Mayer, Paul R. Pintrich, James Raths, and Merlin C. Wittrock (2001). A taxonomy for learning, teaching and assessing: A revision of Bloom's Taxonomy of Educational Objectives. New York, Longman.

Thomas Andre (1979). Does answering higher-level questions while reading facilitate productive learning? *Review of Educational Research*, 49, 280-31.

Ion Androutsopoulos, Gerasimos Lampouras, and Dimitrios Galanis (2013). Generating natural language descriptions from OWL ontologies: the natural OWL system. *Journal of Artificial Intelligence Research*, 48(1) ,671–715

Grigoris Antoniou, Enrico Franconi, and Frank van Harmelen (2005). Introduction to Semantic Web Ontology Languages. In: N. Eisinger, and J., Małuszyński (eds.) *Reasoning Web*. LNCS, vol. 3564. Springer, Berlin. https://doi.org/10.1007/11526988_1

Jun Araki, Dheeraj Rajagopal, Sreecharan Sankaranarayanan, Susan Holm, Yukari Yamakawa, and Teruko Mitamura (2016). Generating Questions and Multiple-Choice Answers using Semantic Analysis of Texts. In *Proceedings of the 26th International Conference on Computational Linguistics (COLING 2016): Technical Papers*, pp. 1125–1136, Osaka, Japan. The COLING 2016 Organizing Committee. https://aclanthology.org/C16-1107

Ron Artstein and Massimo Poesio (2008). Inter-coder agreement for computational linguistics. *Computational Linguistics*, 34(4), 555–596. https://aclanthology.org/J08-4004

Dzmitry Bahdanau, Kyunghyun Cho, and Yoshua Bengio (2014). Neural machine translation by jointly learning to align and translate. In *Proceedings of ICLR 2015*. http://arxiv.org/abs/1409.0473

Xiaoyu Bai and Manfred Stede (2022). A Survey of Current Machine Learning Approaches to Student Free-Text Evaluation for Intelligent Tutoring. *International Journal of Artificial Intelligence in Education*. https://doi.org/10.1007/s40593-022-00323-0

Satanjeev Banerjee and Alon Lavie (2005). METEOR: An Automatic Metric for MT Evaluation with Improved Correlation with Human Judgments. In *Proceedings of the ACL Workshop on Intrinsic and Extrinsic Evaluation Measures for Machine Translation and/or Summarization*, pp. 65–72. https://aclanthology.org/W05-0909

Hangbo Bao, Li Dong, Furu Wei, Wenhui Wang, Nan Yang, Xiaodong Liu, Yu Wang, Songhao Piao, Jianfeng Gao, Ming Zhou, and Hsiao-Wuen Hon (2020). Unilmv2: Pseudomasked language models for unified language model pre-training. In *Proceedings of the 37th International Conference on Machine Learning (ICML'20)*, pp. 642–652. https://doi.org/10.5555/3524938.3524998

Lee Becker, Sumit Basu, and Lucy Vanderwende (2012). Mind the Gap: Learning to Choose Gaps for Question Generation. In *Proceedings of the 2012 Conference of the North American Chapter of the Association for Computational Linguistics: Human Language Technologies*, pp. 742–751, Montréal, Canada. https://aclanthology.org/N12-1092

Iz Beltagy, Matthew E. Peters, and Arman Cohan (2020). Longformer: The Long-Document Transformer.

Asma Ben Abacha, Julio Cesar Dos Reis, Yassine Mrabet, Cédric Pruski, and Marcos Da Silveira (2016). Towards natural language question generation for the validation of ontologies and mappings. *Journal of Biomedical Semantics*, 2016, 7–48. https://doi.org/10.1186/s13326-016-0089-6

Emily M Bender, Timnit Gebru, Angelina McMillan-Major, and Shmargaret Shmitchell (2021). On the dangers of stochastic parrots: Can language models be too big? In *Proceedings of the 2021 ACM Conference on Fairness, Accountability, and Transparency*, pp. 610–623. https://doi.org/10.1145/3442188.3445922

Luca Benedetto, Paolo Cremonesi, Andrew Caines, Paula Buttery, Andrea Cappelli, Andrea Giussani, and Roberto Turrin (2023). A Survey on Recent Approaches to Question Difficulty Estimation from Text. *ACM Computing Surveys*, 55, 9, Article 178. https://doi.org/10.1145/3556538

Jonathan Berant, Andrew Chou, Roy Frostig, and Percy Liang (2013). Semantic Parsing on Freebase from Question-Answer Pairs. In *Proceedings of the 2013 Conference on Empirical Methods in Natural Language Processing (EMNLP 2013)*, pp. 1533–1544, Seattle, Washington, USA. ACL. https://aclanthology.org/D13-1160

Jonathan Berant, Vivek Srikumar, Pei-Chun Chen, Abby Vander Linden, Brittany Harding, Brad Huang, Peter Clark, and Christopher D. Manning (2014). Modeling Biological Processes for Reading Comprehension. In *Proceedings of the 2014 Conference on Empirical Methods in Natural Language Processing (EMNLP 2014)*, pp. 1499–1510, Doha, Qatar. ACL. https://aclanthology.org/D14-1159

Delphine Bernhard, Louis de Viron, Véronique Moriceau, and Xavier Tannier (2012). Question Generation for French: Collating Parsers and Paraphrasing Questions. *Dialogue and Discourse*, 3(2), pp. 43–74.

Benjamin S. Bloom, Max D. Engelhart, Edward J. Furst, Walker H. Hill, and David R. Krathwohl (1956). Taxonomy of educational objectives: The classification of educational goals. Vol. Handbook I: Cognitive domain. New York: David McKay Company.

Miroslav Blšták and Viera Rozinajová (2022). Automatic question generation based on sentence structure analysis using machine learning approach. *Natural Language Engineering*, 28(4), 487-517. https://doi.org/10.1017/S1351324921000139

Miroslav Blšták and Viera Rozinajová (2016). Automatic Question Generation Based on Analysis of Sentence Structure. In P. Sojka, A. Horák, I. Kopeček, and K. Pala (eds.) *Text, Speech, and Dialogue (TSD 2016)*. Lecture Notes in Computer Science, vol 9924. Springer, Cham. https://doi.org/10.1007/978-3-319-45510-5_26

Rishi Bommasani et al. (2021). On the Opportunities and Risks of Foundation Models. Stanford Institute for Human-Centered Artificial Intelligence (HAI). https://crfm.stanford.edu/assets/report.pdf

Kheira Z. Bousmaha, Nour H. Cherguin, Mahfoud Sid Ali Mbarek, and Lamia Belguith Hadrich (2020). AQG: Arabic Question Generator. *Revue d'Intelligence Artificielle*, 34(6), 721–729. https://doi.org/10.18280/ria.340606

Kristy Boyer, William Lahti, Robert Phillips, Michael Wallis, Mladen Vouk, and James Lester (2009). An Empirically-Derived Question Taxonomy for Task-Oriented Tutorial Dialogue. In *Proceedings of the 2nd Workshop on Question Generation*, held in conjunction with the 14th International Conference on Artifical Intelligence in Education.

Kristy Boyer and Paul Piwek (2010). Proceedings of QG2010: The Third Workshop on Question Generation. Available at https://oro.open.ac.uk/22343

Jonathan Brown, Gwen Frishkoff, and Maxine Eskenazi (2005). Automatic Question Generation for Vocabulary Assessment. In Proceedings of Human Language Technology Conference and Conference on Empirical Methods in Natural Language Processing, pp. 819–826, Vancouver, British Columbia, Canada. ACL. https://aclanthology.org/H05-1103

Tom B. Brown, Benjamin Mann, Nick Ryder, Melanie Subbiah, Jared Kaplany, Prafulla Dhariwal, Arvind Neelakantan, Pranav Shyam, Girish Sastry, Amanda Askell, Sandhini Agarwal, Ariel Herbert-Voss, Gretchen Krueger, Tom Henighan, Rewon Child, Aditya Ramesh, Daniel M. Ziegler, Jeffrey Wu, Clemens Winter, Christopher Hesse, Mark Chen, Eric Sigler, Mateusz Litwin, Scott Gray, Benjamin Chess, Jack Clark, Christopher Berner, Sam McCandlish, Alec Radford, Ilya Sutskever, Dario Amodei. (2020). Language Models are Few-Shot Learners. In *Advances in Neural Information Processing Systems, 33 (NeurIPS 2020)*. https://proceedings.neurips.cc/paper_files/paper/2020/hash/1457c0d6bfcb4967418bfb8ac142f64a-Abstract.html

Lorenz Bühmann, Ricardo Usbeck, and Axel-Cyrille Ngonga Ngomo (2015). ASSESS – Automatic Self-Assessment Using Linked Data. In M. Arenas et al. (eds.), *Proceedings of the International Semantic Web Conference (ISWC 2015)*, Part II, LNCS 9367, pp. 76–89. Springer International Publishing, Switzerland. https://doi.org/10.1007/978-3-319-25010-6_5

Chris Callison-Burch, Miles Osborne, and Philipp Koehn (2006). Re-evaluating the Role of Bleu in Machine Translation Research. In Proceedings of the 11th Conference of the European Chapter of the Association for Computational Linguistics (EACL 2006), pp. 249–256, Trento, Italy. ACL. https://aclanthology.org/E06-1032

Mengyun Cao, Xiaoping Sun, and Hai Zhuge (2016). The role of cause-effect link within scientific paper. In *12th International Conference on Semantics, Knowledge and Grids (SKG)*, Beijing, China, 2016, pp. 32–39. https://doi.org/10.1109/SKG.2016.013

Jaime R. Carbonell (1970). AI in CAI: an artificial-intelligence approach to computer-assisted instruction. *IEEE Transactions on Man-Machine Systems*, 11(4), 190–202.

Lynn Carlson, Daniel Marcu, and Mary Ellen Okurovsky (2001). Building a Discourse-Tagged Corpus in the Framework of Rhetorical Structure Theory. In *Proceedings of the Second SIGdial Workshop on Discourse and Dialogue*. https://aclanthology.org/W01-1605

Carol A. Carrier and Terri Fautsch-Patridge (1981). Levels of questions: A Framework for the Exploration of Processing Activities. *Contemporary Educational Psychology*, 6, 365–382.

Asli Celikyilmaz, Elizabeth Clark, and Jianfeng Gao (2020). Evaluation of text generation: A survey. *ArXiv preprint* arXiv:2006.14799. https://doi.org/10.48550/arXiv.2006.14799

Yllias Chali and Sadid A. Hasan (2012). Towards Topic-to-Question Generation. in *Proceedings of COLING 2012: Technical Papers*, pp. 475–492. Mumbai, India. The COLING 2012 Organizing Committee. https://aclanthology.org/C12-1030

Yllias Chali and Sadid A. Hasan (2015). Towards Topic-to-Question Generation. *Computational Linguistics*, 41(1), 1–20. https://aclanthology.org/J15-1001

References

Ying-Hong Chan and Yao-Chung Fan (2019). A Recurrent BERT-based Model for Question Generation. In *Proceedings of the 2nd Workshop on Machine Reading for Question Answering*, pp. 154–162, Hong Kong, China. https://aclanthology.org/D19-5821

Boxing Chen and Colin Cherry (2014). A Systematic Comparison of Smoothing Techniques for Sentence-Level BLEU. In *Proceedings of the Ninth Workshop on Statistical Machine Translation*, pp. 362–367, Baltimore, Maryland, USA. ACL. https://aclanthology.org/W14-3346

Guanliang Chen, Jie Yang, Claudia Hauff, and Geert-Jan Houben (2018). LearningQ: a large-scale dataset for educational question generation. In *Proceedings of the International AAAI Conference on Web and Social Media*, 12(1). https://doi.org/10.1609/icwsm.v12i1.14987

Guanliang Chen, Jie Yang, and Dragan Gasevic (2019). A comparative study on question-worthy sentence selection strategies for educational question generation. In S. Isotani, E. Millán, A. Ogan, P. Hastings, B. McLaren, and R. Luckin (eds.), *Proceedings of the 20th international conference on artificial intelligence in education, AIED 2019*. LNCS (LNAI), vol. 11625, pp. 59–70. Springer, Cham. https://doi.org/10.1007/978-3-030-23204-7_6

Billy Ho Hung Cheung, Gary Kui Kai Lau, Gordon Tin Chun Wong, Elaine Yuen Phin Lee, Dhananjay Kulkarni, Choon Sheong Seow, Ruby Wong, and Michael Tiong-Hong Co (2023). ChatGPT versus human in generating medical graduate exam multiple choice questions — A multinational prospective study (Hong Kong S.A.R., Singapore, Ireland, and the United Kingdom). *PLoS ONE*, 18(8): e0290691. https://doi.org/10.1371/journal.pone.0290691

Ethan A. Chi, John Hewitt, and Christopher D. Manning (2020). Finding Universal Grammatical Relations in Multilingual BERT. In *Proceedings of the 58th Annual Meeting of the Association for Computational Linguistics (ACL 2020)*, pp. 5564–5577, Online. ACL. https://aclanthology.org/2020.acl-main.493

Maria Chinkina and Detmar Meurers (2017). Question generation for language learning: From ensuring texts are read to supporting learning. In *Proceedings of the 12th Workshop on Innovative Use of NLP for Building Educational Applications (BEA)*, pp. 334–344. https://aclanthology.org/W17-5038

Kyunghyun Cho, Bart van Merriënboer, Caglar Gulcehre, Dzmitry Bahdanau, Fethi Bougares, Holger Schwenk, and Yoshua Bengio (2014). Learning Phrase Representations using RNN Encoder–Decoder for Statistical Machine Translation. In *Proceedings of the 2014 Conference on Empirical Methods in Natural Language Processing (EMNLP 2014)*, pp. 1724–1734, Doha, Qatar. ACL. https://aclanthology.org/D14-1179

Eunsol Choi, He He, Mohit Iyyer, Mark Yatskar, Wen-tau Yih, Yejin Choi, Percy Liang, and Luke Zettlemoyer (2018). QuAC: Question Answering in Context. In *Proceedings of the 2018 Conference on Empirical Methods in Natural Language Processing*, pp. 2174–2184, Brussels, Belgium. ACL. https://aclanthology.org/D18-1241

Noam Chomsky (1973). Conditions on transformations. In Stephen R. Anderson and Paul Kiparsky (eds.), *A Festschrift for Morris Halle*. New York: Holt, Rinehart and Winston.

Peter Christen, David J. Hand, and Nishadi Kirielle (2023). A Review of the F-Measure: Its History, Properties, Criticism, and Alternatives. ACM Computing Surveys, 56(3), Article 73. https://doi.org/10.1145/3606367

Jacob Cohen (1960). A coefficient of agreement for nominal scales. *Educational and Psychological Measurement*, 20(1), 37–46.

Jacob Cohen (1968). Weighted kappa: Nominal scale agreement with provision for scaled disagreement or partial credit. *Psychological Bulletin*, 70(4), 213–220.

Alison Crowe, Clarissa Dirks, and Mary Pat Wenderoth (2008). Biology in Bloom: implementing Bloom's Taxonomy to enhance student learning in biology. *CBE Life Sciences Education*, 7(4) 368–381. https://doi.org/10.1187/cbe.08-05-0024

Marija Cubric and Milorad Tosic (2011). Towards automatic generation of e-assessment using semantic web technologies. *International Journal of e-Assessment*. http://hdl.handle.net/2299/7785

Maria Josep Cuenca (1997). Form-Use Mappings for Tag Questions. In W.-A. Liebert, G, Redeker, and L.R. Waugh (eds.), *Discourse and Perspective in Cognitive Linguistics*, 3–19. Amsterdam: John Benjamins. https://doi.org/10.1075/cilt.151.04cue

Sergio Curto, Ana Cristina Mendes, and Luisa Coheur (2012). Question Generation based on Lexico-Syntactic Patterns Learned from the Web. *Dialogue and Discourse*, 3(2), 147–175. https://doi.org/10.5087/dad.2012.207

Sérgio Curto, Ana Cristina Mendes, and Luísa Coheur (2011). Exploring linguistically-rich patterns for question generation. In P*roceedings of the UCNLG+Eval: Language Generation and Evaluation Workshop*, pp. 33–38. Edinburgh, Scotland. https://aclanthology.org/W11-2705

Veneeta Dayal (2016). Questions. Oxford University Press. Oxford, UK.

Bidyut Das, Mukta Majumder, Santanu Phadikar, and Arif Ahmed Sekh (2021). Automatic question generation and answer assessment: a survey. *Research and Practice in Technology Enhanced Learning*, 16:5. https://doi.org/10.1186/s41039-021-00151-1

Bidyut Das and Mukta Majumder (2017). Factual open cloze question generation for assessment of learner's knowledge. *International Journal of Educational Technology in Higher Education*, 14:24. https://doi.org/10.1186/s41239-017-0060-3

Richard R. Day and Jeong-suk Park (2005). Developing reading comprehension questions. *Reading in a Foreign Language*, 17:1.

Wim De Mulder, Steven Bethard, and Marie-Francine Moens (2015). A survey on the application of recurrent neural networks to statistical language modeling. *Computer Speech and Language*, 30, 61–98. https://doi.org/10.1016/j.csl.2014.09.005

Takshak Desai, Parag Dakle, and Dan Moldovan (2018). Generating Questions for Reading Comprehension using Coherence Relations. In *Proceedings of the 5th Workshop on Natural Language Processing Techniques for Educational Applications*, pp. 1–10, Melbourne, Australia. ACL. https://aclanthology.org/W18-3701

Jacob Devlin, Ming-Wei Chang, Kenton Lee, and Kristina Toutanova (2019). BERT: Pre-training of Deep Bidirectional Transformers for Language Understanding. In *Proceedings of the 2019 Conference of the North American Chapter of the Association for Computational Linguistics: Human Language Technologies, Volume 1 (Long and Short Papers)*, pp. 4171–4186, Minneapolis, Minnesota. ACL. https://aclanthology.org/N19-1423

Kaustubh Dhole and Christopher D. Manning (2020). Syn-QG: Syntactic and Shallow Semantic Rules for Question Generation. In *Proceedings of the 58th Annual Meeting of the Association for Computational Linguistics (ACL 2020)*, pp. 752–765. Online. ACL. https://aclanthology.org/2020.acl-main.69

J.T. Dillon (1982). The Multidisciplinary Study of Questioning. *Journal of Educational Psychology*, 74:2, 147-168.

George Doddington (2002). Automatic Evaluation of Machine Translation Quality. Using N-gram Co-Occurrence Statistics. In *Proceedings of the second international conference on Human Language Technology Research (HLT'02)*, pp. 138–145. https://doi.org/10.5555/1289189.1289273

Chenhe Dong, Yinghui Li, Haifan Gong, Miaoxin Chen, Junxin Li, Ying Shen, and Min Yang (2022). A Survey of Natural Language Generation. *ACM Computing Surveys*, 55(8), pp 1–38. https://doi.org/10.1145/3554727

Li Dong, Nan Yang, Wenhui Wang, Furu Wei, Xiaodong Liu, Yu Wang, Jianfeng Gao, Ming Zhou, and Hsiao-Wuen Hon (2019). Unified language model pre-training for natural language understanding and generation. In *Advances in Neural Information Processing Systems (NIPS'19)*, pp. 13042–13054. https://doi.org/10.5555/3454287.3455457

Xinya Du and Claire Cardie (2018). Harvesting Paragraph-Level Question-Answer Pairs from Wikipedia. In *Proceedings of the 56th Annual Meeting of the Association for Computational Linguistics (Volume 1: Long Papers)*, pp. 1907–1917, Melbourne, Australia. ACL. https://aclanthology.org/P18-1177

Xinya Du and Claire Cardie (2017). Identifying where to focus in reading comprehension for neural question generation. In *Proceedings of the Conference on Empirical Methods in Natural Language Processing (EMNLP 2017)*, pp. 2067–2073, Copenhagen, Denmark. ACL. https://aclanthology.org/D17-1219

Xinya Du, Junru Shao, and Claire Cardie (2017). Learning to ask: Neural question generation for reading comprehension. In *Proceedings of the 55th Annual Meeting of the Association for Computational Linguistics (Volume 1: Long Papers)*, pp. 1342–1352, Vancouver, Canada. ACL. https://aclanthology.org/P17-1123

Nan Duan, Duyu Tang, Peng Chen, and Ming Zhou (2017). Question generation for question answering. In *Proceedings of the 2017 Conference on Empirical Methods in Natural Language Processing (EMNLP 2017)*, pp. 866–874, Copenhagen, Denmark. ACL. https://aclanthology.org/D17-1090

Jesse Dunietz, Greg Burnham, Akash Bharadwaj, Owen Rambow, Jennifer Chu-Carroll, and Dave Ferrucci (2020). To Test Machine Comprehension, Start by Defining Comprehension. In *Proceedings of the 58th Annual Meeting of the Association for Computational Linguistics (ACL 2020)*, pp. 7839–7859, Online. ACL. https://aclanthology.org/2020.acl-main.701

Ondřej Dušek, David M. Howcroft, and Verena Rieser (2019). Semantic Noise Matters for Neural Natural Language Generation. In *Proceedings of The 12th International Conference on Natural Language Generation (INLG)*, pp. 421–426, Tokyo, Japan. ACL. https://aclanthology.org/W19-8652

Nouha Dziri, Andrea Madotto, Osmar Zaïane, and Avishek Joey Bose (2021). Neural Path Hunter: Reducing Hallucination in Dialogue Systems via Path Grounding. In *Proceedings of the 2021 Conference on Empirical Methods in Natural Language Processing (EMNLP 2021)*, pp. 2197–2214, Online and Punta Cana, Dominican Republic. ACL. https://aclanthology.org/2021.emnlp-main.168

Daniel Edmiston (2020) A Systematic Analysis of Morphological Content in BERT Models for Multiple Languages. *ArXiv preprint* arXiv:2004.03032. https://doi.org/10.48550/arXiv.2004.03032

Gunes Erkan and Dragomir Radev (2004). LexRank: graph-based lexical centrality as salience in text summarization. *Journal of Artificial Intelligence Research*, 22:1, pp 457–479. https://doi.org/10.1613/jair.1523

Angela Fan, Aleksandra Piktus, Fabio Petroni, Guillaume Wenzek, Marzieh Saeidi, Andreas Vlachos, Antoine Bordes, and Sebastian Riedel (2020). Generating Fact Checking Briefs. In *Proceedings of the 2020 Conference on Empirical Methods in Natural Language Processing (EMNLP)*, pp. 7147–7161, Online. ACL. https://aclanthology.org/2020.emnlp-main.580

Wenqi Fan, Yujuan Ding, Liangbo Ning, Shijie Wang, Hengyun Li, Dawei Yin, Tat-Seng Chua, and Qing Li (2024). A Survey on RAG Meeting LLMs: Towards Retrieval-Augmented Large Language Models. In *Proceedings of the 30th ACM SIGKDD Conference on Knowledge Discovery and Data Mining (KDD'24)*, 6491–6501. https://doi.org/10.1145/3637528.3671470

Guhao Feng, Bohang Zhang, Yuntian Gu, Haotian Ye, Di He, and Liwei Wang. (2023). Towards revealing the mystery behind chain of thought: a theoretical perspective. In *Proceedings of the*

37th International Conference on Neural Information Processing Systems (NIPS'23), article 3100, pp. 70757–70798.

Patrick J. Finn (1975). A Question Writing Algorithm: The Value of Explicitly Specified Processes in Test Construction. *Journal of Reading Behavior*, 7:4, 341-367. https://doi.org/10.1080/10862967509547153

Joseph L. Fleiss (1971). Measuring nominal scale agreement among many raters. *Psychological Bulletin*, 76(5), 378–382.

Michael Flor and Brian Riordan (2018). A Semantic Role-based Approach to Open-Domain Automatic Question Generation. In *Proceedings of the Thirteenth Workshop on Innovative Use of NLP for Building Educational Applications (BEA)*, pp. 254–263. New Orleans, Louisiana. ACL. https://aclanthology.org/W18-0530

Yingxue Fu (2022). Towards Unification of Discourse Annotation Frameworks. In *Proceedings of the 60th Annual Meeting of the Association for Computational Linguistics (ACL 2022): Student Research Workshop*, pp. 132–142, Dublin, Ireland. ACL. https://aclanthology.org/2022.acl-srw.12

Yin-Chun Fung, Jason Chun-Wai Kwok, Lap-Kei Lee, Kwok Tai Chui, and Leong Hou U (2020). Automatic Question Generation System for English Reading Comprehension. In: L.K. Lee, L.H. U, F.L. Wang, S.K.S. Cheung, O. Au, and K.C. Li, (eds.) *Technology in Education. Innovations for Online Teaching and Learning (ICTE 2020)*. Communications in Computer and Information Science, vol 1302. Springer, Singapore. https://doi.org/10.1007/978-981-33-4594-2_12

Meredith D. Gall (1970). The Use of Questions in Teaching. *Review of Educational Research*, 40, 707-721.

Isabel O. Gallegos, Ryan A. Rossi, Joe Barrow, Md Mehrab Tanjim, Sungchul Kim, Franck Dernoncourt, Tong Yu, Ruiyi Zhang, and Nesreen K. Ahmed (2024). Bias and Fairness in Large Language Models: A Survey. *Computational Linguistics*, 50(3):1097–1179.

Julia R. Galliers and Karen Sparck Jones. K. (1993). Evaluating natural language processing systems. Technical Report TR-291, Computer Laboratory, University of Cambridge.

Michel Galley, Chris Brockett, Alessandro Sordoni, Yangfeng Ji, Michael Auli, Chris Quirk, Margaret Mitchell, Jianfeng Gao, and Bill Dolan (2015). deltaBLEU: A Discriminative Metric for Generation Tasks with Intrinsically Diverse Targets. In *Proceedings of the 53rd Annual Meeting of the Association for Computational Linguistics and the 7th International Joint Conference on Natural Language Processing (ACL-IJCNLP, Volume 2: Short Papers)*, pp. 445–450, Beijing, China. ACL. https://aclanthology.org/P15-2073

Lingyu Gao, Debanjan Ghosh, Kevin Gimpel (2022). "What makes a question inquisitive?" A Study on Type-Controlled Inquisitive Question Generation. In *Proceedings of the 11th Joint Conference on Lexical and Computational Semantics,* pp. 240–257, Seattle, Washington. ACL. https://aclanthology.org/2022.starsem-1.22

Yifan Gao, Lidong Bing, Wang Chen, Michael Lyu, and Irwin King (2019). Difficulty Con-trollable Generation of Reading Comprehension Questions. In *Proceedings of the Twenty-Eighth International Joint Conference on Artificial Intelligence (IJCAI 2019)*, pp. 4968–4974. https://doi.org/10.24963/ijcai.2019/690

Yunfan Gao, Yun Xiong, Xinyu Gao, Kangxiang Jia, Jinliu Pan, Yuxi Bi, Yi Dai, Jiawei Sun, Meng Wang, Haofen Wang (2024). Retrieval-Augmented Generation for Large Language Models: A Survey. arXiv:2312.10997v5. https://arxiv.org/abs/2312.10997

Muskan Garg (2021). A survey on different dimensions for graphical keyword extraction techniques. *Artificial Intelligence Review*, 54(6): 4731–4770. https://doi.org/10.1007/s10462-021-10010-6

Donna Gates (2008). Generating Look-Back Strategy Questions from Expository Texts. Technical Report. Carnegie-Mellon University.

Donna Gates, Greg Aist, Jack Mostow, Margaret McKeown, and Juliet Bey (2011). How to Generate Cloze Questions from Definitions: A Syntactic Approach. In *Proceedings of the 2011 AAAI Fall Symposium Series, Question Generation Papers*. https://www.cs.cmu.edu/~listen/pdfs/gates-2011-aaai-qg.pdf

Albert Gatt and Emiel Krahmer (2018). Survey of the State of the Art in Natural Language Generation: Core tasks, applications and evaluation. *Journal of Artificial Intelligence Research*, 61(1), pp. 65–170. https://doi.org/10.5555/3241691.3241693

Gemma Team (2024). Gemma: Open Models Based on Gemini Research and Technology. E-reprint, arXiv:2403.08295v4. https://arxiv.org/abs/2403.08295

Nikolaos Giarelis, Charalampos Mastrokostas, and Nikos Karacapilidis (2023). Abstractive vs. Extractive Summarization: An Experimental Review. *Applied Sciences*, 13, 7620. https://doi.org/10.3390/app13137620

Mark J. Gierl, Okan Bulut, and Xinxin Zhang (2017). Developing, Analyzing, and Using Distractors for Multiple-Choice Tests in Education: A Comprehensive Review. *Review of Educational Research*, 87(6), pp. 1082–1116. https://doi.org/10.3102/0034654317726529

Nikhil Gilbert and C. Maria Keet (2018). Automating Question Generation and Marking of Language Learning Exercises for isiZulu. In Brian Davis, C. Maria Keet, and Adam Wyner (eds), *Controlled Natural Language*, pp. 31–40. IOS Press. https://doi.org/10.3233/978-1-61499-904-1-31

Arnold L. Glass and Neha Sinha (2013). Multiple-Choice Questioning Is an Efficient Instructional Methodology That May Be Widely Implemented in Academic Courses to Improve Exam Performance. *Current Directions in Psychological Science*, 22(6) 471–477. https://doi.org/10.1177/0963721413495870

Tobias Glasmachers (2017). Limits of End-to-End Learning. *Proceedings of Machine Learning Research*, 77:17–32. http://proceedings.mlr.press/v77/glasmachers17a/glasmachers17a.pdf

Kathleen Godfrey (2001). Teacher Questioning Techniques, Student Responses and Critical Thinking. Master's Thesis, Portland State University.

Keith Godwin and Paul Piwek (2016). Collecting Reliable Human Judgements on Machine-Generated Language: The Case of the QG-STEC Data. In *Proceedings of the 9th International Natural Language Generation conference*, pp. 212–216, Edinburgh, UK. ACL. https://aclanthology.org/W16-6634

Adele Goldberg (2006). Constructions at Work: The Nature of Generalization in Language. New York: Oxford University Press.

Takuya Goto, Tomoko Kojiri, Toyohide Watanabe, Tomoharu Iwata, and Takeshi Yamada (2010). Automatic Generation System of Multiple-Choice Cloze Questions and its Evaluation. *Knowledge Management & E-Learning: An International Journal*, 2 (3), 210–224.

Art Graesser, Vasile Rus, and Zhiqiang Cai (2008). Question Classification Schemes. In *Proceedings of the Workshop on Question Generation*. https://www.cs.memphis.edu/~vrus/questiongeneration/16-GraesserEtAl-QG08.pdf

Arthur C. Graesser and Natalie Person (1994). Question Asking During Tutoring. *American Educational Research Journal*, 31(1), 104–137.

Arthur C. Graesser, Kathy Lang, and Dianne Horgan (1988). A Taxonomy for Question Generation. *Questioning Exchange*, 2(1), 3–15.

Yvette Graham (2015). Re-evaluating automatic summarization with BLEU and 192 shades of ROUGE. In *Proceedings of the 2015 Conference on Empirical Methods in Natural Language Processing (EMNLP 2015)*, pp. 128–137, Lisbon, Portugal. ACL. https://aclanthology.org/D15-1013

Thomas Gruber (1995). Toward principles for the design of ontologies used for knowledge sharing. *International Journal of Human-Computer Studies*, 43, 907–928.

Jiatao Gu, Zhengdong Lu, Hang Li, and Victor O.K. Li. (2016). Incorporating Copying Mechanism in Sequence-to-Sequence Learning. In *Proceedings of the 54th Annual Meeting of the Association for Computational Linguistics* (Volume 1: Long Papers), pages 1631–1640, Berlin, Germany. Association for Computational Linguistics. https://aclanthology.org/P16-1154

Caglar Gulcehre, Sungjin Ahn, Ramesh Nallapati, Bowen Zhou, and Yoshua Bengio (2016). Pointing the Unknown Words. In *Proceedings of the 54th Annual Meeting of the Association for Computational Linguistics* (Volume 1: Long Papers), pages, 140–149, Berlin, Germany. ACL. https://aclanthology.org/P16-1014

Kilem Li Gwet (2014). Handbook of inter-rater reliability: The definitive guide to measuring the extent of agreement among raters. Advanced Analytics, LLC, Gaithersburg, MD.

Le An Ha and Victoria Yaneva (2018). Automatic Distractor Suggestion for Multiple-Choice Tests Using Concept Embeddings and Information Retrieval. In *Proceedings of the Thirteenth Workshop on Innovative Use of NLP for Building Educational Applications*, pp. 389–398, New Orleans, Louisiana. ACL. https://aclanthology.org/W18-0548

Kevin A. Hallgren (2012). Computing inter-rater reliability for observational data: An overview and tutorial. *Tutorials in quantitative methods for psychology*, 8(1), 23–34.

Christiaan Hamaker (1986). The effect of adjunct questions on prose learning. *Review of Educational Research*, 56(2):212–242.

Xu Han, Tianyu Gao, Yankai Lin, Hao Peng, Yaoliang Yang, Chaojun Xiao, Zhiyuan Liu, Peng Li, Jie Zhou, and Maosong Sun (2020). More Data, More Relations, More Context and More Openness: A Review and Outlook for Relation Extraction. In *Proceedings of the 1st Conference of the Asia-Pacific Chapter of the Association for Computational Linguistics and the 10th International Joint Conference on Natural Language Processing*, pp. 745–758, Suzhou, China. ACL. https://aclanthology.org/2020.aacl-main.75

Michael Hanna and Ondřej Bojar (2021). A Fine-Grained Analysis of BERTScore. In *Proceedings of the Sixth Conference on Machine Translation*, pp. 507–517, Online. ACL. https://aclanthology.org/2021.wmt-1.59

Sanda M. Harabagiu, Steven J. Maiorano, and Marius A. Pasca (2003). Open-domain question answering techniques. *Natural Language Engineering*, 9(3), 1–38.

Vrindavan Harrison and Marilyn Walker (2018). Neural Generation of Diverse Questions using Answer Focus, Contextual and Linguistic Features. *arXiv preprint* arXiv:1809.02637v2 https://doi.org/10.48550/arXiv.1809.02637

Kimihiro Hasegawa, Takaaki Matsumoto, and Teruko Mitamura (2019). Anaphora Reasoning Question Generation Using Entity Coreference. In 25th Annual Conference of the Association for Natural Language Processing (NLP2019). https://anlp.jp/proceedings/annual_meeting/2019/pdf_dir/P5-18.pdf

Andrew F. Hayes and Klaus Krippendorff (2007). Answering the call for a standard reliability measure for coding data. *Communication methods and measures*, 1(1), 77–89. https://doi.org/10.1080/19312450709336664

Michael Heilman (2011). Automatic factual question generation from text. Carnegie Mellon University, PhD thesis.

Michael Heilman and Noah A. Smith (2010a). Good question! Statistical ranking for question generation. In *Proceedings of the 2010 Annual Conference of the North American Chapter of the Association for Computational Linguistics (NAACl-HLT 2010)*, pp.609–617, Los Angeles, California. ACL. https://www.aclweb.org/anthology/N10-1086

Michael Heilman and Noah A. Smith (2010b). Rating computer-generated questions with Mechanical Turk. In Chris Callison-Burch and Mark Dredze (eds.), *Proceedings of the NAACL HLT 2010 Workshop on Creating Speech and Language Data with Amazon's Mechanical Turk,* pages 35–40,

Los Angeles, California. Los Angeles. Association for Computational Linguistics. https://aclanthology.org/W10-0705/

Michael Heilman and Noah A. Smith (2010c). Extracting simplified statements for factual question generation. In *Proceedings of QG2010: The Third Workshop on Question Generation*.

Michael Heilman and Noah A. Smith (2009). Question generation via overgenerating transformations and ranking. Technical Report CMU-LTI-09–013, Language Technologies Institute, Carnegie Mellon University.

Karl Moritz Hermann, Tomáš Kočiský, Edward Grefenstette, Lasse Espeholt, Will Kay, Mustafa Suleyman, and Phil Blunsom (2015). Teaching machines to read and comprehend. In *Proceedings of the 28th International Conference on Neural Information Processing Systems - Volume 1 (NIPS'15)*, pp. 1693–1701, Cambridge, MA, USA. MIT Press.

John Hewitt and Christopher D. Manning (2019). A Structural Probe for Finding Syntax in Word Representations. In *Proceedings of the 2019 Conference of the North American Chapter of the Association for Computational Linguistics: Human Language Technologies, Volume 1 (NAACL-HLT 2019)*, pp. 4129–4138, Minneapolis, Minnesota. ACL. https://aclanthology.org/N19-1419

Geoffrey E. Hinton, Simon Osindero, and Yee-Whye Teh (2006). A Fast Learning Algorithm for Deep Belief Nets. *Neural Computation*, 18(7):1527–1554.

Valentin Hofmann, Janet Pierrehumbert, and Hinrich Schütze (2020). DagoBERT: Generating Derivational Morphology with a Pretrained Language Model. In *Proceedings of the 2020 Conference on Empirical Methods in Natural Language Processing (EMNLP 2020)*, pp. 3848–3861, Online. ACL. https://aclanthology.org/2020.emnlp-main.316

Edmond Holohan, Mark Melia, Declan McMullen, and Claus Pahl (2005). Adaptive E-learning content generation based on semantic web technology. In *Proceedings of the International Workshop on Applications of Semantic Web Technologies for E-learning*, Amsterdam, Netherlands.

Andrea Horbach, Itziar Aldabe, Marie Bexte, Oier Lopez de Lacalle, and Montse Maritxalar (2020). Linguistic appropriateness and pedagogic usefulness of reading comprehension questions. In *Proceedings of the 12th Language Resources and Evaluation Conference (LREC 2020)*, pp. 1753–1762. https://aclanthology.org/2020.lrec-1.217

Sepp Hochreiter and Jürgen Schmidhuber (1997). Long short-term memory. *Neural Computation*, 9(8), 1735–1780. https://www.bioinf.jku.at/publications/older/2604.pdf

Ian Horrocks (2013). What Are Ontologies Good For? In: Küppers, B.O., Hahn, U., Artmann, S. (eds.) *Evolution of Semantic Systems*. Springer, Berlin, Heidelberg. https://doi.org/10.1007/978-3-642-34997-3_9

Ian Horrocks (2008). Ontologies and the semantic web. *Communications of the ACM*, 51(12), 58–67. https://doi.org/10.1145/1409360.1409377

Ayako Hoshino and Hiroshi Nakagawa (2005). A Realtime Multiple-choice Question Generation for Language Testing: A Preliminary Study. In *Proceedings of the 2nd Workshop on Building Educational Applications Using NLP (BEA)*, pp. 17–20, Ann Arbor, MI. ACL. https://aclanthology.org/W05-0203

Eduard Hovy, Ulf Hermjakob, and Deepak Ravichandran (2002). A question/answer typology with surface text patterns. In *Proceedings of the second international conference on Human Language Technology Research (HLT'02)*, pp. 247–251. https://doi.org/10.5555/1289189.1289206

David M. Howcroft, Anya Belz, Miruna-Adriana Clinciu, Dimitra Gkatzia, Sadid A. Hasan, Saad Mahamood, Simon Mille, Emiel van Miltenburg, Sashank Santhanam, and Verena Rieser (2020). Twenty Years of Confusion in Human Evaluation: NLG Needs Evaluation Sheets and Standardised Definitions. In *Proceedings of the 13th International Conference on Natural Language Generation*, pp. 169–182, Dublin, Ireland. ACL. https://aclanthology.org/2020.inlg-1.23

Yan Huang and Lianzhen He (2016). Automatic generation of short answer questions for reading comprehension assessment. *Natural Language Engineering*, 22, pp. 457-489. https://doi.org/10.1017/S1351324915000455

Md Asadul Islam and Enrico Magnani (2021). Is this the end of the gold standard? A straightforward reference-less grammatical error correction metric. In *Proceedings of the 2021 Conference on Empirical Methods in Natural Language Processing (EMNLP 2021)*, pp. 3009–3015, Online and Punta Cana, Dominican Republic. ACL. https://aclanthology.org/2021.emnlp-main.239

Ganesh Jawahar, Benoît Sagot, Djamé Seddah (2019). What Does BERT Learn about the Structure of Language? In *Proceedings of the 57th Annual Meeting of the Association for Computational Linguistics (ACL 2019)*, pp. 3651–3657, Florence, Italy. ACL. https://aclanthology.org/P19-1356

Taino Ji, Chenyang Lyu, Gareth Jones, Liting Zhou, and Yvette Graham (2022). QAScore—An Unsupervised Unreferenced Metric for the Question Generation Evaluation. *Entropy*, 24, 1514. https://doi.org/10.3390/e24111514

Ziwei Ji, Nayeon Lee, Rita Frieske, Tiezheng Yu, Dan Su, Yan Xu, Etsuko Ishii, Yejin Bang, Delong Chen, Ho Shu Chan, Wenliang Dai, Andrea Madotto, and Pascale Fung (2023). Survey of Hallucination in Natural Language Generation. *ACM Computing Surveys*, 55(12), pp. 1-38. https://doi.org/10.1145/3571730

Albert Jiang, Alexandre Sablayrolles, Arthur Mensch, Chris Bamford, Devendra Singh Chaplot, Diego de las Casas, Florian Bressand, Gianna Lengyel, Guillaume Lample, Lucile Saulnier, Lélio Renard Lavaud, Marie-Anne Lachaux, Pierre Stock, Teven Le Scao, Thibaut Lavril, Thomas Wang, Timothée Lacroix, and William El Sayed (2023). Mistral 7B. E-print, arXiv:2310.06825v1. https://doi.org/10.48550/arXiv.2310.06825

Mandar Joshi, Eunsol Choi, Daniel Weld, and Luke Zettlemoyer (2017). TriviaQA: A Large Scale Distantly Supervised Challenge Dataset for Reading Comprehension. In *Proceedings of the 55th Annual Meeting of the Association for Computational Linguistics* (Volume 1: Long Papers), pp. 1601–1611, Vancouver, Canada. ACL. https://aclanthology.org/P17-1147

Dan Jurafsky and James H. Martin (2023). Speech and Language Processing (3rd ed. Draft). https://web.stanford.edu/~jurafsky/slp3/

Saidalavi Kalady, Ajeesh Elikkottil, and Rajarshi Das (2010). Natural language question generation using syntax and keywords. In Proceedings of QG2010: The Third Workshop on Question Generation, pp. 1–10.

Jared Kaplan, Sam McCandlish, Tom Henighan, Tom B. Brown, Benjamin Chess, Rewon Child, Scott Gray, Alec Radford, Jeffrey Wu, and Dario Amodei [2020]. Scaling Laws for Neural Language Models.

Aniruddha Kembhavi, Minjoon Seo, Dustin Schwenk, Jonghyun Choi, Ali Farhadi, and Hannaneh Hajishirzi (2017). Are You Smarter Than a Sixth Grader? Textbook Question Answering for Multimodal Machine Comprehension. In *Proceedings of the IEEE Conference on Computer Vision and Pattern Recognition (CVPR 2017)*. pp. 5376–5384.

Pia Keukeleire, Tom Viering, Stavros Makrodimitris, Arman Naseri Jahfari, Marco Loog, David Tax (2020). Correspondence Between Perplexity Scores and Human Evaluation of Generated TV-Show Scripts. Delft University of Technology. http://resolver.tudelft.nl/uuid:ab543db3-f285-477c-b4ce-b6ac57507554

Abdolvahab Khademi (2023). Can ChatGPT and Bard generate aligned assessment items? A reliability analysis against human performance. *Journal of Applied Learning & Teaching*, 6(1). https://doi.org/10.37074/jalt.2023.6.1.28

Payal Khullar, Konigari Rachna, Mukul Hase, Manish Shrivastava (2018). Automatic Question Generation using Relative Pronouns and Adverbs. In *Proceedings of the Association for Computational Linguistics (ACL 2018), Student Research Workshop*, pp. 153–158, Melbourne, Australia. ACL. https://aclanthology.org/P18-3022

John Kirchenbauer, Jonas Geiping, Yuxin Wen, Jonathan Katz, Ian Miers, and Tom Goldstein (2023). A Watermark for Large Language Models. In *Proceedings of the 40th International Conference on Machine Learning, PMLR*, 202:17061–17084. https://proceedings.mlr.press/v202/kirchenbauer23a.html

Nikita Kitaev, Lukasz Kaiser, Anselm Levskaya (2020). Reformer: The Efficient Transformer. In Proceedings of ICLR2020. https://iclr.cc/virtual_2020/poster_rkgNKkHtvB.html

Wei-Jen Ko, Te-yuan Chen, Yiyan Huang, Greg Durrett, Junyi Jessy Li (2020). Inquisitive question generation for high level text comprehension. In *Proceedings of the 2020 Conference on Empirical Methods in Natural Language Processing (EMNLP 2020)*, pp. 6544–6555. Online. ACL. https://aclanthology.org/2020.emnlp-main.530

Tomáš Kočiský, Jonathan Schwarz, Phil Blunsom, Chris Dyer, Karl Moritz Hermann, Gábor Melis, and Edward Grefenstette (2018). The NarrativeQA Reading Comprehension Challenge. *Transactions of the Association for Computational Linguistics*, 6:317–328. https://aclanthology.org/Q18-1023.pdf

Ioannis Konstas and Mirella Lapata (2013). A global model for concept-to-text generation. *Journal of Artificial Intelligence Research*. 48(1), 305–346.

René Knaebel (2021). discopy: A Neural System for Shallow Discourse Parsing. In *Proceedings of the 2nd Workshop on Computational Approaches to Discourse*, pp. 128–133, Punta Cana, Dominican Republic and Online. ACL. https://aclanthology.org/2021.codi-main.12

Colin Knight, Dragan Gašević, and Griff Richard (2006). An Ontology-Based Framework for Bridging Learning Design and Learning Content. *Educational Technology & Society*, 9 (1), 23–37.

David R. Krathwohl (2002). A revision of Bloom's taxonomy: An overview. *Theory into Practice*, 41(4), 212–218.

Kettip Kriangchaivech and Artit Wangperawong (2019). Question Generation by Transformers. *arXiv preprint* arXiv:1909.05017. https://doi.org/10.48550/arXiv.1909.05017

Manfred Krifka (2011). Questions. In K. von Heusinger, C. Maienborn, and P. Portner (eds.), *Semantics. An International Handbook of Natural Language Meaning*. Vol. 2., pp. 1742–1785. De Gruyter Mouton.

Hidenobu Kunichika, Tomoki Katayama, Tsukasa Hirashima, and Akira Takeuchi (2004). Automated question generation methods for intelligent English learning systems and its evaluation. In *Proceedings of the International Conference on Computers in Education (ICCE 2002)*, pp. 97–101.

Ghader Kurdi, Jared Leo, Bijan Parsia, Uli Sattler, and Salam Al-Emari (2020). A Systematic Review of Automatic Question Generation for Educational Purposes. *International Journal of Artificial Intelligence in Education*, 30, 121–204. https://doi.org/10.1007/s40593-019-00186-y

Artur Kulmizev, Vinit Ravishankar, Mostafa Abdou, Joakim Nivre (2020). Do Neural Language Models Show Preferences for Syntactic Formalisms?. In *Proceedings of the 58th Annual Meeting of the Association for Computational Linguistics (ACL 2020)*, pp. 4077–4091, Online. ACL. https://aclanthology.org/2020.acl-main.375

Tom Kwiatkowski, Jennimaria Palomaki, Olivia Redfield, Michael Collins, Ankur Parikh, Chris Alberti, Danielle Epstein, Illia Polosukhin, Jacob Devlin, Kenton Lee, Kristina Toutanova, Llion Jones, Matthew Kelcey, Ming-Wei Chang, Andrew M. Dai, Jakob Uszkoreit, Quoc Le, and Slav Petrov (2019). Natural Questions: A Benchmark for Question Answering Research. *Transactions of the Association for Computational Linguistics*, 7:452–466. https://aclanthology.org/Q19-1026

Igor Labutov, Sumit Basu, and Lucy Vanderwende (2015). Deep questions without deep understanding. In *Proceedings of the 53rd Annual Meeting of the Association for Computational Linguistics and the 7th International Joint Conference on Natural Language Processing (ACL-IJCNLP, Volume 1: Long Papers)*, pp. 889–898. Beijing, China. ACL. http://www.aclweb.org/anthology/P15-1086

Guokun Lai, Qizhe Xie, Hanxiao Liu, Yiming Yang, and Eduard Hovy (2017). RACE: Large-scale ReAding Comprehension Dataset From Examinations. In *Proceedings of the 2017 Conference on Empirical Methods in Natural Language Processing* (EMNLP 2017), pp. 785–794, Copenhagen, Denmark. ACL. https://aclanthology.org/D17-1082

Richard Landis and Gary G. Koch (1977). The measurement of observer agreement for categorical data. *Biometrics*, 33(1), 159–74.

Alon Lavie and Abhaya Agarwal (2007). METEOR: An Automatic Metric for MT Evaluation with High Levels of Correlation with Human Judgments. In *Proceedings of the Second Workshop on Statistical Machine Translation*, pp. 228–231, https://aclanthology.org/W07-0734

Nuyen-Thinh Le, Tomoko Kojiri, and Niels Pinkwart (2014a). Automatic question generation for educational applications–the state of art. In T. Do, H.A. Le Thi, and N.T. Nguyen (eds.), *Advanced computational methods for knowledge engineering*, pp. 325–338. Springer. Cham. https://doi.org/10.1007/978-3-319-06569-4_24

Nguyen-Thinh Le, Nhu-Phuong Nguyen, Kazuhisa Seta, and Niels Pinkwart (2014b). Automatic question generation for supporting argumentation. *Vietnam Journal of Computer Science*, 1:117–127. https://doi.org/10.1007/s40595-014-0014-9

Seungjun Lee, Jungseob Lee, Hyeonseok Moon, Chanjun Park, Jaehyung Seo, Sugyeong Eo, Seonmin Koo, and Heuiseok Lim (2023). A Survey on Evaluation Metrics for Machine Translation. *Mathematics*, 11, 1006. https://doi.org/10.3390/math11041006

Wendy Lehnert (1978). The Process of Question Answering. Hillsdale, NJ: Erlbaum.

Wendy Lehnert, Claire Cardie, and Ellen Riloff (1990). Analyzing Research Papers Using Citation Sentences. In *Proceedings of the Twelfth Annual Conference of the Cognitive Science Society*, pp. 511–518. Cambridge, MA.

Roger Levy and Galen Andrew (2006). Tregex and Tsurgeon: tools for querying and manipulating tree data structures. In *Proceedings of the Fifth International Conference on Language Resources and Evaluation (LREC'06)*. Genoa, Italy. ELRA. https://aclanthology.org/L06-1311

Patrick Lewis, Ethan Perez, Aleksandra Piktus, Fabio Petroni, Vladimir Karpukhin, Naman Goyal, Heinrich Küttler, Mike Lewis, Wen-tau Yih, Tim Rocktäschel, Sebastian Riedel, and Douwe Kiela (2020). Retrieval-augmented generation for knowledge-intensive NLP tasks. In *Proceedings of the 34th International Conference on Neural Information Processing Systems (NIPS'20)*, article 793, pp. 9459–9474.

Jiwei Li, Michel Galley, Chris Brockett, Jianfeng Gao, Bill Dolan (2016). A Diversity-Promoting Objective Function for Neural Conversation Models. In *Proceedings of the 2016 Conference of the North American Chapter of the Association for Computational Linguistics: Human Language Technologies (NAACL2016)*, pp. 110–119. San Diego, California. ACL. https://aclanthology.org/N16-1014

Kunze Li and Yu Zhang (2024). Planning first, question second: An LLM-guided method for controllable question generation. In *Findings of the Association for Computational Linguistics ACL 2024*, pp. 4715–4729, Bangkok, Thailand. Association for Computational Linguistics. https://aclanthology.org/2024.findings-acl.280

Xin Li and Dan Roth (2002). Learning Question Classifiers. In *Proceedings of the 19th International Conference on Computational Linguistics (COLING 2002)*. https://aclanthology.org/C02-1150

Yikang Li, Nan Duan, Bolei Zhou, Xiao Chu, Wanli Ouyang, Xiaogang Wang, and Ming Zhou (2018). Visual Question Generation as Dual Task of Visual Question Answering. In *2018 IEEE/CVF Conference on Computer Vision and Pattern Recognition*, pp. 6116–6124. IEEE. https://doi.org/10.1109/CVPR.2018.00640

Chin-Yew Lin (2004). ROUGE: A Package for Automatic Evaluation of Summaries. In *Text Summarization Branches Out*, pp. 74–81. Barcelona, Spain. ACL. https://aclanthology.org/W04-1013

David Lindberg, Fred Popowich, John Nesbit, and Phil Winne (2013). Generating Natural Language Questions to Support Learning On-Line. In *Proceedings of the 14th European Workshop on Natural Language Generation*, pp. 105–114. Sofia, Bulgaria. ACL. https://aclanthology.org/W13-2114

Chia-Wei Liu, Ryan Lowe, Iulian Serban, Mike Noseworthy, Laurent Charlin, and Joelle Pineau (2016). How NOT To Evaluate Your Dialogue System: An Empirical Study of Unsupervised Evaluation Metrics for Dialogue Response Generation. In *Proceedings of the 2016 Conference on Empirical Methods in Natural Language Processing (EMNLP 2016)*, pp. 2122–2132. Austin, TX. ACL. https://aclanthology.org/D16-1230

Dayiheng Liu, Yu Yan, Yeyun Gong, Weizhen Qi, Hang Zhang, Jian Jiao, Weizhu Chen, Jie Fu, Linjun Shou, Ming Gong, Pengcheng Wang, Jiusheng Chen, Daxin Jiang, Jiancheng Lv, Ruofei Zhang, Winnie Wu, Ming Zhou, and Nan Duan (2021). GLGE: A New General Language Generation Evaluation Benchmark. In *Findings of the Association for Computational Linguistics: ACL-IJCNLP 2021*, pp. 408–420, Online. ACL. https://aclanthology.org/2021.findings-acl.36

Ming Liu, Rafael A. Calvo, and Vasile Rus (2014). Automatic Generation and Ranking of Questions for Critical Review. *Educational Technology & Society*, 17 (2), 333–346.

Ming Liu, Rafael A. Calvo, and Vasile Rus (2012). G-Asks: An intelligent automatic question generation system for academic writing support. *Dialogue & Discourse*, 3:2, 101–124.

Ming Liu, Rafael A. Calvo, and Vasile Rus (2010). Automatic Question Generation for Literature Review Writing Support. In *Proceedings of The Tenth International Conference on Intelligent Tutoring Systems*, pp. 45–54, LNCS 6094. Pittsburgh, USA. Springer.

Qi Liu, Matt J. Kusner, and Phil Blunsom (2020). A Survey on Contextual Embeddings. *arXiv preprint* arXiv:2003.07278. https://doi.org/10.48550/arXiv.2003.07278

Tianyu Liu, Bingzhen Wei, Baobao Chang, and Zhifang Sui (2018). Large-Scale Simple Question Generation by Template-Based Seq2seq Learning. In X. Huang, J. Jiang, D. Zhao, Y. Feng, and Y. Hong (eds.), *Natural Language Processing and Chinese Computing (NLPCC 2017)*. LNCS, vol 10619. Springer, Cham. https://doi.org/10.1007/978-3-319-73618-1_7

Babak Loni (2011). A survey of state-of-the-art methods on question classification. Delft University of Technology, Technical report. https://repository.tudelft.nl/islandora/object/uuid%3A8e57caa8-04fc-4fe2-b668-20767ab3db92

Birte Lönneker-Rodman and Colin F. Barker (2009). The FrameNet model and its applications. *Natural Language Engineering*, 15(3), 415–453. https://doi.org/10.1017/S1351324909005117

Luis Enrico Lopez, Diane Kathryn Cruz, Jan Christian Blaise Cruz, and Charibeth Cheng (2020). Transformer-based End-to-End Question Generation. *arXiv preprint* arXiv:2005.01107. https://doi.org/10.48550/arXiv.2005.01107

Luis Enrico Lopez, Diane Kathryn Cruz, Jan Christian Blaise Cruz, and Charibeth Cheng (2021). Simplifying Paragraph-Level Question Generation via Transformer Language Models. In D.N. Pham, T. Theeramunkong, G. Governatori, and F. Liu (eds.) *PRICAI 2021: Trends in Artificial Intelligence.* LNCS, vol 13032. Springer, Cham. https://doi.org/10.1007/978-3-030-89363-7_25

Renze Lou, Kai Zhang, and Wenpeng Yin (2024). Large Language Model Instruction Following: A Survey of Progresses and Challenges. *Computational Linguistics*, 50(3):1053–1095.

Holy Lovenia, Felix Limanta, and Agus Gunawan (2018). Automatic question-answer pairs generation from text. Technical Report. Bandung Institute of Technology, Indonesia. https://doi.org/10.13140/RG.2.2.33776.92162

Chao-Yi Lu and Sin-En Lu (2021). A Survey of Approaches to Automatic Question Generation: from 2019 to Early 2021. In *Proceedings of the 33rd Conference on Computational Linguistics and Speech Processing (ROCLING 2021)*, pp. 151–162. Taoyuan, Taiwan. ACL and Chinese Language Processing. https://aclanthology.org/2021.rocling-1.21

Nitin Madnani, Beata Beigman Klebanov, Anastassia Loukina, Binod Gyawali, Patrick Lange, John Sabatini, and Michael Flor (2019). My Turn To Read: An Interleaved E-book Reading Tool for Developing and Struggling Readers. In *Proceedings of the 57th Annual Meeting of the Association for Computational Linguistics: System Demonstrations*, pages 141–146, Florence, Italy. Association for Computational Linguistics. https://aclanthology.org/P19-3024

Sedigheh Mahdavi, Aijun An, Heidar Davoudi, Marjan Delpisheh, and Emad Gohari (2020). Question-Worthy Sentence Selection for Question Generation. In C. Goutte, and X. Zhu (eds.), *Advances in Artificial Intelligence, Canadian AI 2020*. LNCS, vol 12109. Springer, Cham. https://doi.org/10.1007/978-3-030-47358-7_40

William C. Mann and Sandra A. Thompson (1988). Rhetorical structure theory: Toward a functional theory of text organization. *Text*, 8(3):243–281.

Prashanth Mannem, Rashmi Prasad, and Aravind Joshi (2010). Question generation from paragraphs at UPenn: QGSTEC system description. In K.E. Boyer and P. Piwek (eds.), *Proceedings of QG2010: The Third Workshop on Question Generation*, pp. 84–91. Pittsburgh, PA. http://www.cs.ecu.edu/gudivada/research/papers/Third%20Workshop%20on%20Question%20Generation%20QG2010-Proceedings.pdf

Marianna Martindale, Marine Carpuat, Kevin Duh, and Paul McNamee (2019). Identifying Fluently Inadequate Output in Neural and Statistical Machine Translation. In *Proceedings of Machine Translation Summit XVII: Research Track*, pp. 233–243. Dublin, Ireland. European Association for Machine Translation. https://aclanthology.org/W19-6623

Vaibhav Mavi, Anubhav Jangra, and Adam Jatowt (2023). A Survey on Multi-hop Question Answering and Generation. A survey on multi-hop question answering. *Foundations and Trends in Information Retrieval*, 17(5), 457–586. https://doi.org/10.1561/1500000102

Joshua Maynez, Shashi Narayan, Bernd Bohnet, and Ryan McDonald (2020). On Faithfulness and Factuality in Abstractive Summarization. In *Proceedings of the 58th Annual Meeting of the Association for Computational Linguistics (ACL 2020)*, pp. 1906–1919, Online. ACL. https://aclanthology.org/2020.acl-main.173

Karen Mazidi and Paul Tarau (2016). Infusing NLU into Automatic Question Generation. In *Proceedings of The 9th International Natural Language Generation conference (INLG)*, pp. 51–60. Edinburgh, UK. ACL. https://aclanthology.org/W16-6609

Karen Mazidi and Rodney D. Nielsen (2015). Leveraging multiple views of text for automatic question generation. In C. Conati, N. Heffernan, A. Mitrovic, and M.F Verdejo (eds.), *Articial Intelligence in Education (AIED 2015)*. pp. 257–266. LNCS, LNAI volume 9112. Springer International Publishing, Cham.

Karen Mazidi and Rodney D. Nielsen (2014a). Linguistic considerations in automatic question generation. In *Proceedings of the 52nd Annual Meeting of the Association for Computational Linguistics (ACL 2014, Volume 2: Short Papers)*, pp. 321–326. Baltimore, Maryland. ACL. https://aclanthology.org/P14-2053

Karen Mazidi and Rodney D. Nielsen (2014b). Pedagogical Evaluation of Automatically Generated Questions. In S. Trausan-Matu, K.E. Boyer, M. Crosby, and K. Panourgia (eds.), *Intelligent Tutoring Systems (ITS 2014)*. LNCS, vol 8474. Springer, Cham. https://doi.org/10.1007/978-3-319-07221-0_36

Johanna Melly, Gabriel Luthier, and Andrei Popescu-Belis (2020). Consolidated Dataset for Knowledge-based Question Generation using Predicate Mapping of Linked Data. In *Proceedings of the 16th Joint ACL-ISO Workshop on Interoperable Semantic Annotation (ISA-16)*, pp. 59–66. Language Resources and Evaluation Conference (LREC 2020), Marseille, France. ELRA. https://aclanthology.org/2020.isa-1.7

Clara Meister and Ryan Cotterell (2021). Language Model Evaluation Beyond Perplexity. In Proceedings of the 59th Annual Meeting of the Association for Computational Linguistics and the

11th International Joint Conference on Natural Language Processing (ACL-IJCNLP, Volume 1: Long Papers), pp. 5328–5339, Online. ACL. https://aclanthology.org/2021.acl-long.414

Ana Cristina Mendes, Sérgio Curto, and Luísa Coheur (2011). Bootstrapping Multiple-Choice Tests with The-Mentor. In Alexander F. Gelbukh (ed.) *Computational Linguistics and Intelligent Text Processing (CICLing 2011)*, pp 451–462. LNCS, vol. 6608. Springer, Berlin. https://doi.org/10.1007/978-3-642-19400-9_36

Heidi Anne Mesmer, and M.M. Rose-McCully (2017). A Closer Look at Close Reading: Three Under-the-Radar Skills Needed to Comprehend Sentences. *The Reading Teacher*, 71, 4, 451–461. https://doi.org/10.1002/trtr.1639

Adam Meyers, Ruth Reeves, Catherine Macleod, Rachel Szekely, Veronika Zielinska, Brian Young, and Ralph Grishman (2004). The NomBank Project: An Interim Report. In *Proceedings of the Workshop Frontiers in Corpus Annotation at HLT-NAACL 2004*, pp. 24–31. Boston, MA, USA. ACL. https://aclanthology.org/W04-2705

Stéphane Meystre and Peter J Haug (2005). Evaluation of Medical Problem Extraction from Electronic Clinical Documents Using MetaMap Transfer (MMTx). *Studies in Health Technology and Informatics*, 116, 823–828.

Rada Mihalcea and Paul Tarau (2004). TextRank: Bringing Order into Text. In *Proceedings of the 2004 Conference on Empirical Methods in Natural Language Processing (EMNLP 2004)*, pp. 404–411. Barcelona, Spain. ACL. https://aclanthology.org/W04-3252

Tomas Mikolov, Ilya Sutskever, Kai Chen, Greg Corrado, and Jeffrey Dean (2013). Distributed representations of words and phrases and their compositionality. In *Proceedings of the 26th Conference on Neural Information Processing Systems (NIPS 2013)*, Vol 2 , pp. 3111–3119.

Ruslan Mitkov, Le An Ha., and Nikiforos Karamanis (2006). A computer-aided environment for generating multiple-choice test items. *Natural Language Engineering*, 12 (2), 177–194. https://doi.org/10.1017/S1351324906004177

Ruslan Mitkov, Le An Ha, Andrea Varga, and Luz Rello (2009). Semantic similarity of distracters in multiple-choice tests: extrinsic evaluation. In *Proceedings of the EACL 2009 Workshop on GEMS: GEometical Models of Natural Language Semantics*, pp. 49–56, Athens, Greece. ACL. https://aclanthology.org/W09-0207

Melanie Mitchell (2024). Large Language Models. In M. C. Frank & A. Majid (eds.), *Open Encyclopedia of Cognitive Science*. MIT Press. https://doi.org/10.21428/e2759450.2bb20e3c

Manal Mohammed and Nazlia Omar (2020). Question classification based on Bloom's taxonomy cognitive domain using modified TF-IDF and word2vec. *PLoS ONE*, 15(3): e0230442. https://doi.org/10.1371/journal.pone.0230442

Ethan R. Mollick and Lilach Mollick (2023). Assigning AI: Seven Approaches for Students, with Prompts. The Wharton School Research Paper. https://doi.org/10.2139/ssrn.4475995

Jack Mostow and Wei Chen (2009). Generating instruction automatically for the reading strategy of self-questioning. In *Proceedings of the 2009 conference on Artificial Intelligence in Education: Building Learning Systems that Care: From Knowledge Representation to Affective Modelling*, pp. 465–472. IOS Press.

Nikahat Mulla, and Prach Gharpure (2023). Automatic question generation: a review of methodologies, datasets, evaluation metrics, and applications. *Progress in Artificial Intelligence*, 12:1–32. https://doi.org/10.1007/s13748-023-00295-9

Stefan Müller (2018). Grammatical theory. From transformational grammar to constraint-based approaches. Language Science Press, Berlin, Germany.

Ferdiant Joshua Muis and Ayu Purwarianti (2020). Sequence-to-Sequence Learning for Indonesian Automatic Question Generator. In *7th International Conference on Advance Informatics: Concepts, Theory and Applications (ICAICTA)*, pp. 1–6, Tokoname, Japan. IEEE. https://doi.org/10.1109/icaicta49861.2020.9429032

Lidiya Murakhovs'ka, Chien-Sheng Wu, Philippe Laban, Tong Niu, Wenhao Liu, and Caiming Xiong (2022). MixQG: Neural Question Generation with Mixed Answer Types. In *Findings of the Association for Computational Linguistics: NAACL 2022*, pp. 1486–1497, Seattle, WA, USA. ACL. https://aclanthology.org/2022.findings-naacl.111

Mao Nakanishi, Tetsunori Kobayashi, and Yoshihiko Hayashi (2019). Towards Answer-unaware Conversational Question Generation. In *Proceedings of the 2nd Workshop on Machine Reading for Question Answering*, pp. 63–71, Hong Kong, China. ACL. https://aclanthology.org/D19-5809

Shashi Narayan and Claire Gardent (2020). Deep Learning Approaches to Text Production. Morgan & Claypool (Synthesis Lectures on Human Language Technologies). https://doi.org/10.2200/s00979ed1v01y201912hlt044

Annamaneni Narendra, Manish Agarwal, and Rakshit Shah (2013). Automatic Cloze-Questions Generation. In *Proceedings of the International Conference Recent Advances in Natural Language Processing (RANLP 2013)*, pp. 511–515. Shoumen, Bulgaria. INCOMA Ltd. https://aclanthology.org/R13-1067

Preksha Nema and Mitesh M. Khapra (2018). Towards a Better Metric for Evaluating Question Generation Systems. In *Proceedings of the 2018 Conference on Empirical Methods in Natural Language Processing (EMNLP 2018)*, pp. 3950–3959. https://aclanthology.org/D18-1429

Ani Nenkova, Lucy Vanderwende, and Kathleen McKeown (2006). A Compositional Context Sensitive Multidocument Summarizer. In *Proceedings of the 29th annual international ACM SIGIR conference on Research and development in information retrieval (SIGIR 2006)*, pp. 573–580. https://doi.org/10.1145/1148170.1148269

Cornelia Neuert, Katharina Meitinger, Dorothée Behr, and Matthias Schonlau. (2021). The use of open-ended questions in surveys. *Methods, data, analyses: a journal for quantitative methods and survey methodology (mda)*, 15(1): 3–6.

Lynn D. Newton (2013). Teachers' Questions: can they support understanding and higher-level thinking? *Research Journal* (Ecole Internationale de Genève, Ecolint Institute of Learning and Teaching), 1, 6-17.

Tri Nguyen, Mir Rosenberg, Xia Song, Jianfeng Gao, Saurabh Tiwary, Rangan Majumder, and Li Deng (2016). MS MARCO: A human generated machine reading comprehension dataset. In *CEUR Workshop Proceedings Coco@NIPS*, volume 1773. http://ceur-ws.org/Vol-1773/CoCoNIPS_2016_paper9.pdf

Rodney D. Nielsen, Jason Buckingham, Gary Knoll, Ben Marsh, and Leysia Palen (2008). A Taxonomy of Questions for Question Generation. In *Proceedings of the Workshop on Question Generation.* http://www.cs.ecu.edu/gudivada/research/papers/A%20Taxonomy%20of%20Questions%20for%20Question%20Generation.pdf

Irina Nikishina, Mikhail Tikhomirov, Varvara Logacheva, Yuriy Nazarov, Alexander Panchenko, and Natalia Loukachevitch (2022). Taxonomy Enrichment with Text and Graph Vector Representations. *Semantic Web Journal*, 13 (3). https://www.semantic-web-journal.net/content/taxonomy-enrichment-text-and-graph-vector-representations-1

Jingcheng Niu and Gerald Penn (2020). Grammaticality and Language Modelling. In *Proceedings of the First Workshop on Evaluation and Comparison of NLP Systems*, pp. 110–119, Online. ACL. https://aclanthology.org/2020.eval4nlp-1.11

Andrew M. Olney, Arthur C. Graesser, and Natalie K. Person (2012). Question Generation from Concept Maps. *Dialogue and Discourse*, 3(2), 75–99.

Riccardo Orlando, Simone Conia, and Roberto Navigli (2023). Exploring Non-Verbal Predicates in Semantic Role Labeling: Challenges and Opportunities. In *Findings of the Association for Computational Linguistics: ACL 2023*, pp. 12378–12388. Toronto, Canada. ACL. https://aclanthology.org/2023.findings-acl.783

Nedjma Ousidhoum, Zhangdie Yuan, and Andreas Vlachos (2022). Varifocal Question Generation for Fact-checking. In *Proceedings of the 2022 Conference on Empirical Methods in Natural Language Processing (EMNLP 2022)*, pp. 2532 – 2544. Abu Dhabi. UAE. ACL. https://aclanthology.org/2022.emnlp-main.163

Long Ouyang, Jeff Wu, Xu Jiang, Diogo Almeida, Carroll L. Wainwright, Pamela Mishkin, Chong Zhang, Sandhini Agarwal, Katarina Slama, Alex Ray, John Schulman, Jacob Hilton, Fraser Kelton, Luke Miller, Maddie Simens, Amanda Askell, PeterWelinder, Paul Christiano, Jan Leike, and Ryan Lowe (2022). Training language models to follow instructions with human feedback. In *Proceedings of the 36th Conference on Neural Information Processing Systems (NeurIPS 2022)*.

Frank R. Palmer (1987). The English Verb. 2nd edition. Longman, London, UK.

Martha Palmer, Dan Gidea, and Nianwen Xue (2010). Semantic Role Labeling. Morgan & Claypool.

Martha Palmer, Daniel Gildea, and Paul Kingsbury (2005). The Proposition Bank: A Corpus Annotated with Semantic Roles. *Computational Linguistics*, 31(1), 71–106. https://aclanthology.org/J05-1004

Boyuan Pan, Hao Li, Ziyu Yao, Deng Cai, and Huan Sun (2019). Reinforced Dynamic Reasoning for Conversational Question Generation. In *Proceedings of the 57th Annual Meeting of the Association for Computational Linguistics (ACL 2019)*, pp. 2114–2124. Florence, Italy. ACL. https://aclanthology.org/P19-1203

Liangming Pan, Wenqiang Lei, Tat-Seng Chua, and Min-Yen Kan (2019). Recent Advances in Neural Question Generation. *arXiv preprint* arXiv:1905.08949v3. https://doi.org/10.48550/arXiv.1905.08949

Andreas Papasalouros, Konstantinos Kanaris and Konstantinos I. Kotis (2008). Automatic generation of multiple choice questions from domain ontologies. In *Proceedings of the IADIS e-Learning Conference*, pp. 427–434, Amsterdam, The Netherlands.

Kishore Papineni, Salim Roukos, Todd Ward, and Wei-Jing Zhu (2002). Bleu: a Method for Automatic Evaluation of Machine Translation. In *Proceedings of the 40th Annual Meeting of the Association for Computational Linguistics (ACL 2002)*, pp. 311–318, Philadelphia, PA, USA. ACL. https://aclanthology.org/P02-1040

Narendra Patwardhan, Stefano Marrone, and Carlo Sansone (2023). Transformers in the Real World: A Survey on NLP Applications. *Information*, 14, 242. https://doi.org/10.3390/info14040242

Jeffrey Pennington, Richard Socher, and Christopher Manning (2014). GloVe: Global Vectors for Word Representation. In *Proceedings of the 2014 Conference on Empirical Methods in Natural Language Processing (EMNLP 2014)*, pp. 1532–1543. Doha, Qatar. ACL. https://aclanthology.org/D14-1162

Gabrijela Perković, Antun Drobnjak, and Ivica Botički (2024). Hallucinations in LLMs: Understanding and Addressing Challenges. In *47th MIPRO ICT and Electronics Convention*, pp. 2084–2088, Opatija, Croatia. IEEE. https://doi.org/10.1109/MIPRO60963.2024.10569238

Natalie Person, Arthur C. Graesser, and The Tutoring Research Group (2002). Human or Computer? AutoTutor in a Bystander Turing Test. In *Proceedings of the 6th International Conference on Intelligent Tutoring Systems*, pp. 821–830. London, UK. https://link.springer.com/chapter/https://doi.org/10.1007/3-540-47987-2_82

Paul Piwek and Kristy Boyer (2012). Varieties of question generation: introduction to this special issue. *Dialogue and Discourse*, 3(2): 1–9.

Jeffrey Pomerantz (2005). A Linguistic Analysis of Question Taxonomies. *Journal of the American Society for Information Science and Technology*, 56(7), 715–728.

Sameer Pradhan, Julia Bonn, Skatje Myers, Kathryn Conger, Tim O'Gorman, James Gung, Kristin Wright-Bettner, and Martha Palmer (2022). PropBank Comes of Age—Larger, Smarter, and more Diverse. In *Proceedings of the 11th Joint Conference on Lexical and Computational Semantics*, pp. 278–288, Seattle, WA, USA. ACL. https://aclanthology.org/2022.starsem-1.24

Rashmi Prasad, Nikhil Dinesh, Alan Lee, Eleni Miltsakaki, Livio Robaldo, Aravind Joshi and Bonnie Webber. (2008). The Penn Discourse TreeBank 2.0. In *Proceedings of the Sixth International Conference on Language Resources and Evaluation (LREC'08)*, Marrakech, Morocco. European Language Resources Association (ELRA). http://www.lrec-conf.org/proceedings/lrec2008/pdf/754_paper.pdf

Rashmi Prasad and Aravind Joshi (2008). A Discourse-based Approach to Generating Why-Questions from Texts. In *Proceedings of the Workshop on the Question Generation Shared Task and Evaluation Challenge*, pp. 1–3. Arlington, VA, USA.

Weizhen Qi, Yu Yan, Yeyun Gong, Dayiheng Liu, Nan Duan, Jiusheng Chen, Ruofei Zhang, and Ming Zhou (2020). ProphetNet: Predicting Future N-gram for Sequence-to-SequencePre-training. In *Findings of the Association for Computational Linguistics: EMNLP 2020*, pp. 2401–2410. Online. ACL. https://aclanthology.org/2020.findings-emnlp.217

Alec Radford, Jeff Wu, Rewon Child, David Luan, Dario Amodei, and Ilya Sutskever (2019). Language Models are Unsupervised Multitask Learners. *OpenAI blog*. https://cdn.openai.com/better-language-models/language_models_are_unsupervised_multitask_learners.pdf

Andrew Radford (2009). An Introduction to English Sentence Structure. Cambridge: Cambridge University Press.

Andrew Radford (1988). Transformational Grammar: A First Course. Cambridge: Cambridge University Press.

Colin Raffel, Noam Shazeer, Adam Roberts, Katherine Lee, Sharan Narang, Michael Matena, Yanqi Zhou, Wei Li, and Peter J. Liu (2020). Exploring the Limits of Transfer Learning with a Unified Text-to-Text Transformer. *Journal of Machine Learning Research*, 21, 1–67. https://jmlr.org/papers/v21/20-074.html

Pranav Rajpurkar, Robin Jia, and Percy Liang (2018). Know What You Don't Know: Unanswerable Questions for SQuAD. In *Proceedings of the 56th Annual Meeting of the Association for Computational Linguistics (ACL 2018, Volume 2: Short Papers)*, pp. 784–789, Melbourne, Australia. ACL. https://aclanthology.org/P18-2124

Pranav Rajpurkar, Jian Zhang, Konstantin Lopyrev, and Percy Liang (2016). Squad: 100,000+ questions for machine comprehension of text. In *Proceedings of the 2016 Conference on Empirical Methods in Natural Language Processing (EMNLP 2016)*, pp. 2383–2392. Austin, Texas. ACL. https://aclweb.org/anthology/D16-1264

Lance Ramshaw and Mitch Marcus (1995). Text Chunking using Transformation-Based Learning. In *Third Workshop on Very Large Corpora*. https://aclanthology.org/W95-0107

Earl F. Rankin Jr. (1959). The Cloze Procedure – Its Validity and Utility. In Oscar S. Causey and William Eller (eds.), *Starting and Improving College Reading Programs*, the Eighth Yearbook of the National Reading Conference, pp.131–144. Milwaukee, Wisconsin: National Reading Conference. Fort Worth, Texas: The Texas Christian University Press.

Sathish Reddy, Dinesh Raghu, Mitesh M. Khapra, and Sachindra Joshi (2017). Generating Natural Language Question-Answer Pairs from a Knowledge Graph Using a RNN Based Question Generation Model. In *Proceedings of the 15th Conference of the European Chapter of the ACL: Volume 1, Long Papers (EACL 2017)*, pp. 376–385, Valencia, Spain. ACL. https://aclanthology.org/E17-1036

Siva Reddy, Danqi Chen, and Christopher D. Manning (2019). CoQA: A Conversational Question Answering Challenge. *Transactions of the Association for Computational Linguistics*, 7:249–266. https://aclanthology.org/Q19-1016

Ehud Reiter (2018a). A Structured Review of the Validity of BLEU. *Computational Linguistics*, 44(3):393–401. https://doi.org/10.1162/coli_a_00322

Ehud Reiter (2018b). Hallucination in Neural NLG. *Ehud Reiter's Blog*. https://ehudreiter.com/2018/11/12/hallucination-in-neural-nlg

Ehud Reiter and Anja Belz (2009). An investigation into the validity of some metrics for automatically evaluating natural language generation systems. *Computational Linguistics*, 35(4):529–558. https://aclanthology.org/J09-4008

Matthew Richardson, Christopher J.C. Burges, and Erin Renshaw (2013). MCTest: A Challenge Dataset for the Open-Domain Machine Comprehension of Text. In *Proceedings of the 2013 Conference on Empirical Methods in Natural Language Processing (EMNLP 2013)*, pp. 193–203, Seattle, Washington, USA. ACL. https://aclanthology.org/D13-1020

Adam Roberts and Colin Raffel (2020). Exploring Transfer Learning with T5: the Text-To-Text Transfer Transformer. Blog post entry, 24 Feb, 2020, https://ai.googleblog.com/2020/02/exploring-transfer-learning-with-t5.html

Anna Rogers, Matt Gardner, and Isabelle Augenstein (2023). QA Dataset Explosion: A Taxonomy of NLP Resources for Question Answering and Reading Comprehension. *ACM Computing Surveys*, 55(10), article 197, pp 1–45. https://doi.org/10.1145/3560260

Anna Rohrbach, Lisa Anne Hendricks, Kaylee Burns, Trevor Darrell, and Kate Saenko (2018). Object Hallucination in Image Captioning. In *Proceedings of the 2018 Conference on Empirical Methods in Natural Language Processing*, pp. 4035–4045, Brussels, Belgium. ACL. https://aclanthology.org/D18-1437

John Robert Ross (1967). Constraints on Variables in Syntax. Ph.D. thesis, Massachusetts Institute of Technology, Cambridge, MA, USA.

Denis Rothman (2021). Transformers for Natural Language Processing. Packt Publishing.

Vasile Rus and Mihai Lintean (2012). A Comparison of Greedy and Optimal Assessment of Natural Language Student Input Using Word-to-Word Similarity Metrics. In *Proceedings of the Seventh Workshop on Building Educational Applications Using NLP*, pp. 157–162, Montréal, Canada. ACL. https://aclanthology.org/W12-2018

Vasile Rus, Brendan Wyse, Paul Piwek, Mihai Lintean, Svetlana Stoyanchev, and Cristian Moldovan (2012). A detailed account of the First Question Generation Shared Task Evaluation Challenge. *Dialogue & Discourse*, 3(2), pp. 177–204.

Vasile Rus, Brendan Wyse, Paul Piwek, Mihai Lintean, Svetlana Stoyanchev, and Cristian Moldovan (2011). Question Generation Shared Task and Evaluation Challenge – Status Report. In *Proceedings of the 13th European Workshop on Natural Language Generation (ENLG)*, pp. 318–320. Nancy, France. ACL. https://aclanthology.org/W11-2853

Vasile Rus, Brendan Wyse, Paul Piwek, Mihai Lintean, Svetlana Stoyanchev, and Cristian Moldovan (2010). The First Question Generation Shared Task Evaluation Challenge. In *Proceedings of the 6th International Natural Language Generation Conference (INLG)*. ACL. https://aclanthology.org/W10-4234

Vasile Rus and James Lester (2009). The 2nd Workshop on Question Generation. In Dimitrova, V., Mizoguchi, R., du Boulay, B., and Graesser, A. (eds.), *Proceedings of the 2009 conference on Artificial Intelligence in Education*. https://doi.org/10.3233/978-1-60750-028-5-808.

Mobashir Sadat, Zhengyu Zhou, Lukas Lange, Jun Araki, Arsalan Gundroo, Bingqing Wang, Rakesh Menon, Md Parvez, and Zhe Feng (2023). DelucionQA: Detecting Hallucinations in Domain-specific Question Answering. In *Findings of the Association for Computational Linguistics: EMNLP 2023*, pp. 822–835, Singapore. Association for Computational Linguistics. https://aclanthology.org/2023.findings-emnlp.59

Mourad Sarrouti, Asma Ben Abacha, and Dina Demner-Fushman (2021). Goal-Driven Visual Question Generation from Radiology Images. *Information*, 12, 334. https://doi.org/10.3390/info12080334

Maximilian Schreiner (2023). GPT-4 architecture, datasets, costs and more leaked. The Decoder, blogpost July 11, 2023. https://the-decoder.com/gpt-4-architecture-datasets-costs-and-more-leaked

Darina Scully (2017). Constructing Multiple-Choice Items to Measure Higher-Order Thinking. Practical Assessment. *Research & Evaluation,* 22(4). https://doi.org/10.7275/swgt-rj52

Abigail See, Aneesh Pappu, Rohun Saxena, Akhila Yerukola, and Christopher D. Manning (2019). Do Massively Pretrained Language Models Make Better Storytellers?. In *Proceedings of the 23rd Conference on Computational Natural Language Learning (CoNLL),* pp. 843–861, Hong Kong, China. ACL. https://aclanthology.org/K19-1079

Thibault Sellam, Dipanjan Das, and Ankur Parikh (2020). BLEURT: Learning robust metrics for text generation. In *Proceedings of the 58th Annual Meeting of the Association for Computational Linguistics (ACL 2020),* pp. 7881–7892. Online. ACL. https://aclanthology.org/2020.acl-main.704

Iulian Vlad Serban, Alberto García-Durán, Caglar Gulcehre, Sungjin Ahn, Sarath Chandar, Aaron Courville, and Yoshua Bengio (2016). Generating Factoid Questions With Recurrent Neural Networks: The 30M Factoid Question-Answer Corpus. In *Proceedings of the 54th Annual Meeting of the Association for Computational Linguistics (ACL 2016, Volume 1: Long Papers),* pp. 588–598. Berlin, Germany. ACL. https://aclanthology.org/P16-1056

Andrew Shen, Fajri Koto, Jey Han Lau, and Timothy Baldwin (2022). Easy-First Bottom-Up Discourse Parsing via Sequence Labelling. In *Proceedings of the 3rd Workshop on Computational Approaches to Discourse,* pp. 35–41, Gyeongju, Republic of Korea and Online. International Conference on Computational Linguistics. https://aclanthology.org/2022.codi-1.5

Lei Shen, Fandong Meng, Jinchao Zhang, Yang Feng, and Jie Zhou (2021). GTM: A Generative Triple-wise Model for Conversational Question Generation. In *Proceedings of the 59th Annual Meeting of the Association for Computational Linguistics and the 11th International Joint Conference on Natural Language Processing (ACL-IJCNLP),* Volume 1: Long Papers, pp. 3495–3506, Online. ACL. https://aclanthology.org/2021.acl-long.271

Hiroki Shimanaka, Tomoyuki Kajiwara, and Mamoru Komachi (2018). RUSE: Regressor Using Sentence Embeddings for Automatic Machine Translation Evaluation. In *Proceedings of the Third Conference on Machine Translation: Shared Task Papers,* pp. 751–758. Belgium, Brussels. ACL. https://aclanthology.org/W18-6456

Miguel-Ángel Sicilia and Elena García Barriocanal (2005). On the convergence of formal ontologies and standardized e-learning. *International Journal of Distance Education Technologies,* 3(2), 13–29.

Ben Snyder, Marius Moisescu, and Muhammad Bilal Zafar (2024). On Early Detection of Hallucinations in Factual Question Answering. In *Proceedings of the 30th ACM SIGKDD Conference on Knowledge Discovery and Data Mining (KDD'24),* pp. 2721–2732. https://doi.org/10.1145/3637528.3671796

C. Srihari, Shivanand Sunagar, Ramadas K. Kamat, K. S. Raghavendra, and Merin Meleet (2023). Question and Answer Generation from Text Using Transformers. In: S.M. Thampi, J. Mukhopadhyay, M. Paprzycki, and K.C. Li (eds.), *International Symposium on Intelligent Informatics, ISI 2022.* Smart Innovation, Systems and Technologies, vol 333. Springer, Singapore. https://doi.org/10.1007/978-981-19-8094-7_15

Katherine Stasaski and Marti A. Hearst (2017). Multiple Choice Question Generation Utilizing An Ontology. In *Proceedings of the 12th Workshop on Innovative Use of NLP for Building Educational Applications (BEA),* pp. 303–312, Copenhagen, Denmark. ACL. https://aclanthology.org/W17-5034\

Katherine Stasaski, Manav Rathod, Tony Tu, Yunfang Xiao, and Marti A. Hearst (2021). Automatically Generating Cause-and-Effect Questions from Passages. In *Proceedings of the 16th Workshop on Innovative Use of NLP for Building Educational Applications (BEA),* pp. 158–170, Online. ACL. https://aclanthology.org/2021.bea-1.17

Tim Steuer, Anna Filighera, Tobias Meuser, and Christoph Rensing (2021). I Do Not Understand What I Cannot Define: Automatic Question Generation With Pedagogically-Driven Content Selection. *arXiv preprint* arXiv:2110.04123. https://doi.org/10.48550/arXiv.2110.04123

Tim Steuer, Anna Filighera, Thomas Tregel, and André Miede (2022). Educational Automatic Question Generation Improves Reading Comprehension in Non-native Speakers: A Learner-Centric Case Study. *Frontiers in Artificial Intelligence*, 5:900304. https://doi.org/10.3389/frai.2022.900304

Dan Su, Xiaoguang Li, Jindi Zhang, Lifeng Shang, Xin Jiang, Qun Liu, and Pascale Fung (2022). Read before Generate! Faithful Long Form Question Answering with Machine Reading. *arXiv preprint* arXiv:2203.00343. https://doi.org/10.48550/arXiv.2203.00343

Sandeep Subramanian, Tong Wang, Xingdi Yuan, Saizheng Zhang, Adam Trischler, and Yoshua Bengio. (2018). Neural Models for Key Phrase Extraction and Question Generation. In *Proceedings of the Workshop on Machine Reading for Question Answering*, pp. 78–88. Melbourne, Australia. ACL. https://aclanthology.org/W18-2609

Ilya Sutskever, Oriol Vinyals, and Quoc Le (2014). Sequence to sequence learning with neural networks. In *Proceedings of the 27th International Conference on Neural Information Processing Systems (NIPS'14)*, Volume 2, pp. 3104–3112. http://papers.nips.cc/paper/5346-sequence-to-sequence-learning-with-neural-networks.pdf

Rohail Syed, Kevyn Collins-Thompson, Paul N. Bennett, Mengqiu Teng, Shane Williams, Wendy W. Tay, and Shamsi Iqbal (2020). Improving Learning Outcomes with Gaze Tracking and Automatic Question Generation, In *WWW'20: Proceedings of The Web Conference 2020*, pp. 1693–1703. https://doi.org/10.1145/3366423.3380240

Maite Taboada (2009). Implicit and explicit coherence relations. In J. Renkema (ed.), *Discourse, of course: an overview of research in discourse studies* pp. 127–140. Amsterdam; Philadelphia: John Benjamins Publishing Company. https://doi.org/10.1075/z.148.13tab

Maite Taboada and William C. Mann (2006). Applications of Rhetorical Structure Theory. *Discourse Studies*, 8(4), 567–588. https://doi.org/10.1177/1461445606064836

Bin Tan, Nour Armoush, Elisabetta Mazzullo, Okan Bulut, and Mark J. Gierl (2024). A Review of Automatic Item Generation Techniques Leveraging Large Language Models. *EdArXiv* Preprint, https://osf.io/preprints/edarxiv/6d8tj

Chongyang Tao, Lili Mou, Dongyan Zhao, and Rui Yan (2018), RUBER: An Unsupervised Method for Automatic Evaluation of Open-Domain Dialog Systems. In *Proceedings of the AAAI Conference on Artificial Intelligence (AAAI 2018)*, 32(1). https://doi.org/10.1609/aaai.v32i1.11321

Wilson L. Taylor (1953). 'Cloze Procedure': A New Tool for Measuring Readability, J*ournalism Quarterly*, 30, 414–438.

Hugo Touvron, Thibaut Lavril, Gautier Izacard, Xavier Martinet, Marie-Anne Lachaux, Timothée Lacroix, Baptiste Rozière, Naman Goyal, Eric Hambro, Faisal Azhar, Aurelien Rodriguez, Armand Joulin, Edouard Grave, and Guillaume Lample (2023). LLaMA: Open and Efficient Foundation Language Models. E-print, arXiv:2302.13971. https://arxiv.org/abs/2302.13971

Adam Trischler, Tong Wang, Xingdi Yuan, Justin Harris, Alessandro Sordoni, Philip Bachman, and Kaheer Suleman (2017). NewsQA: A Machine Comprehension Dataset. In *Proceedings of the 2nd Workshop on Representation Learning for NLP*, pages 191–200, Vancouver, Canada. ACL. https://aclanthology.org/W17-2623

Lewis Tunstall, Leandro von Werra, and Thomas Wolf (2022). Natural Language Processing with Transformers. O'Reilly Media, Inc., Sebastopol, CA.

Richard E. Turner (2023). An Introduction to Transformers. *arXiv preprint* arXiv:2304.10557. https://doi.org/10.48550/arXiv.2304.10557

Masaki Uto, Yuto Tomikawa, and Ayaka Suzuki (2023). Difficulty-Controllable Neural Question Generation for Reading Comprehension using Item Response Theory. In *Proceedings of the 18th*

Workshop on Innovative Use of NLP for Building Educational Applications, pp. 119–129, Toronto, Canada. ACL. https://aclanthology.org/2023.bea-1.10

Rachel van Campenhout, Marth Hubertz, and Benny G. Johnson (2022). Evaluating AI-Generated Questions: A Mixed-Methods Analysis Using Question Data and Student Perceptions. In M.M. Rodrigo, N. Matsuda, A.I. Critea, and V. Dimitrova (eds), *AIED 2022*, pp. 344–353. LNCS, vol. 13355. Springer Nature Switzerland. https://doi.org/10.1007/978-3-031-11644-5_28

Chris van der Lee, Albert Gatt, Emiel van Miltenburg, and Emiel Krahmer (2021). Human evaluation of automatically generated text: Current trends and best practice guidelines. *Computer Speech & Language*, 67, 101151. https://doi.org/10.1016/j.csl.2020.101151

Emiel van Miltenburg, Miruna Clinciu, Ondřej Dušek, Dimitra Gkatzia, Stephanie Inglis, Leo Leppänen, Saad Mahamood, Emma Manning, Stephanie Schoch, Craig Thomson, and Luou Wen (2021). Underreporting of errors in NLG output, and what to do about it. In *Proceedings of the 14th International Conference on Natural Language Generation (INLG)*, pp. 140–153, Aberdeen, Scotland, UK. https://aclanthology.org/2021.inlg-1.14

Cornelius J. Van Rijsbergen (1979). *Information Retrieval*. Butterworth and Co., London.

Stalin Varanasi, Saadullah Amin, and Guenter Neumann (2020). CopyBERT: A Unified Approach to Question Generation with Self-Attention. In *Proceedings of the 2nd Workshop on Natural Language Processing for Conversational AI*, pp. 25–31, Online. ACL. https://aclanthology.org/2020.nlp4convai-1.3

Andrea Varga and Le An Ha (2010). WLV: A question generation system for the QGSTEC 2010 task B. In *Proceedings of QG2010: The Third Workshop on Question Generation*, pp. 80–83. https://www.researchgate.net/publication/256662093_WLV_A_Question_Generation_System_for_the_QGSTEC_2010_Task_B

Ashish Vaswani, Noam Shazeer, Niki Parmar, Jakob Uszkoreit, Llion Jones, Aidan N. Gomez, Łukasz Kaiser, and Illia Polosukhin (2017). Attention is all you need. In *Advances in Neural Information Processing Systems*, pp. 6000–6010. https://papers.nips.cc/paper/7181-attention-is-all-you-need

Marc Verhagen, Roser Saurí, Tommaso Caselli, and James Pustejovsky (2010). SemEval-2010 Task 13: TempEval-2. In *Proceedings of the 5th International Workshop on Semantic Evaluation*, pp. 57–62. Uppsala, Sweden. ACL. https://aclanthology.org/S10-1010

Oriol Vinyals and Quoc Le (2015). A Neural Conversational Model. *arXiv preprint* arXiv:1506.05869. https://doi.org/10.48550/arXiv.1506.05869

Oriol Vinyals, Meire Fortunato, and Navdeep Jaitly (2015). Pointer networks. In *Advances in Neural Information Processing Systems 28 (NIPS 2015)*, pp. 2692–2700. https://papers.nips.cc/paper_files/paper/2015/file/29921001f2f04bd3baee84a12e98098f-Paper.pdf

Vinu Ellampallil Venugopal, and P. Sreenivasa Kumar (2019). Improving ontology verbalization using semantic-level refinement. In Proceedings of the 32nd International Workshop on Description Logics, CEUR volume 2373. https://ceur-ws.org/Vol-2373/paper-44.pdf

Vinu Ellampallil Venugopal, and P. Sreenivasa Kumar (2018). Automated Generation of Assessment Tests from Domain Ontologies. *Semantic Web Journal*, 8 (6), 1023–1047. https://www.semantic-web-journal.net/content/automated-generation-assessment-tests-domain-ontologies-1

Vinu Ellampallil Venugopal and P. Sreenivasa Kumar (2015). A novel approach to generate MCQs from domain ontology: Considering DL semantics and open-world assumption. *Journal of Web Semantics*, 34, 40-54. https://doi.org/10.1016/j.websem.2015.05.005

Ivan Vulić, Edoardo Maria Ponti, Robert Litschko, Goran Glavaš, and Anna Korhonen (2020). Probing Pretrained Language Models for Lexical Semantics. In *Proceedings of the 2020 Conference on Empirical Methods in Natural Language Processing (EMNLP 2020)*, pp. 7222–7240. Online. ACL. https://aclanthology.org/2020.emnlp-main.586

Baoxun Wang, Bingquan Liu, Chengjie Sun, Xiaolong Wang, and Deyuan Zhang (2012). Generating Questions from Web Community Contents. In *Proceedings of COLING 2012: Demonstration Papers*, pp. 467–474. Mumbai, India. The COLING 2012 Organizing Committee. https://aclanthology.org/C12-3059

Chaojun Wang and Rico Sennrich (2020). On Exposure Bias, Hallucination and Domain Shift in Neural Machine Translation. In *Proceedings of the 58th Annual Meeting of the Association for Computational Linguistics (ACL 2020)*, pp. 3544–3552, Online. ACL. https://aclanthology.org/2020.acl-main.326

Siyuan Wang, Zhongyu Wei, Zhihao Fan, Yang Liu, and Xuanjing Huang (2019). A Multi-Agent Communication Framework for Question-Worthy Phrase Extraction and Question Generation. In *Proceedings of the The Thirty-Third AAAI Conference on Artificial Intelligence (AAAI-19)*, 33(01), pp. 7168–7175. https://doi.org/10.1609/aaai.v33i01.33017168

Weiming Wang, Tianyong Hao, and Wenyin Liu (2008). Automatic Question Generation for Learning Evaluation in Medicine. In H. Leung, F. Li, R. Lau, and Q. Li (eds.), *Advances in Web Based Learning – ICWL 2007*. LNCS, vol. 4823, pp 242–251. Springer, Berlin. https://doi.org/10.1007/978-3-540-78139-4_22

Alex Wang, Amanpreet Singh, Julian Michael, Felix Hill, Omer Levy, Samuel Bowman (2018a). GLUE: A Multi-Task Benchmark and Analysis Platform for Natural Language Understanding. In *Proceedings of the 2018 EMNLP Workshop BlackboxNLP: Analyzing and Interpreting Neural Networks for NLP*, pp. 353–355. Brussels, Belgium. ACL. https://aclanthology.org/W18-5446

Yansen Wang, Chenyi Liu, Minlie Huang, Liqiang Nie. (2018b). Learning to Ask Questions in Open-domain Conversational Systems with Typed Decoders. In *Proceedings of the 56th Annual Meeting of the Association for Computational Linguistics (ACL 2018, Volume 1: Long Papers)*, pp. 2193–2203, Melbourne, Australia. ACL. https://aclanthology.org/P18-1204

Zichao Wang, Kyle Manning, Debshila Basu Mallick, and Richard G. Baraniuk (2021). Towards Blooms Taxonomy Classification Without Labels. In: I. Roll, D. McNamara, S. Sosnovsky, R. Luckin, and V. Dimitrova, (eds.) *Artificial Intelligence in Education, AIED 2021*. LNCS, vol. 12748. Springer, Cham. https://doi.org/10.1007/978-3-030-78292-4_35

Zichao Wang, Jakob Valdez, Debshila Basu Mallick, and Richard G. Baraniuk (2022). Towards Human-Like Educational Question Generation with Large Language Models. In *Proceedings of the 23rd Artificial Intelligence in Education International Conference (AIED 2022)*, Durham, UK. Springer.

Jason Wei, Xuezhi Wang, Dale Schuurmans, Maarten Bosma, Brian Ichter, Fei Xia, Ed H. Chi, Quoc V. Le, and Denny Zhou (2022). Chain-of-thought prompting elicits reasoning in large language models. In *Proceedings of the 36th International Conference on Neural Information Processing Systems (NIPS'22)*, article 1800, pp. 24824–24837.

Ian A.G. Wilkinson, and Eun Hye Son (2009). Questioning. In E.M. Anderman, and L.H. Anderman (Eds.), *Psychology of Classroom Learning: An Encyclopedia*, pp. 723-728. Detroit, MI: Gale Cengage.

Alexander Williams (2015). Arguments in Syntax and Semantics. Cambridge: Cambridge University Press.

Angelica Willis, Glenn Davis, Sherry Ruan, Lakshmi Manoharan, James Landay, and Emma Brunskill (2019). Key Phrase Extraction for Generating Educational Question-Answer Pairs. In *L@S '19: Proceedings of the Sixth (2019) ACM Conference on Learning @ Scale*, pp. 1–10. https://doi.org/10.1145/3330430.3333636

Jules White, Quchen Fu, Sam Hays, Michael Sandborn, Carlos Olea, Henry Gilbert, Ashraf Elnashar, Jesse Spencer-Smith, and Douglas C. Schmidt (2023). A Prompt Pattern Catalog to Enhance Prompt Engineering with ChatGPT. E-print arXiv:2302.11382v1. https://doi.org/10.48550/arXiv.2302.11382

Thomas Wolf et al. (2020). Transformers: State-of-the-Art Natural Language Processing. In *Proceedings of the 2020 Conference on Empirical Methods in Natural Language Processing (EMNLP 2020): System Demonstrations*, pp. 38–45, Online. ACL. https://aclanthology.org/2020.emnlp-demos.6

John H. Wolfe (1975). An aid to independent study through automatic question generation (AUTOQUEST). Report NPRDC TR 76–18. Navy Personnel Research and Development Center, San Diego, California.

Ka Wong, Praveen Paritosh, and Lora Aroyo (2021). Cross-replication Reliability – An Empirical Approach to Interpreting Inter-rater Reliability. In *Proceedings of the 59th Annual Meeting of the Association for Computational Linguistics and the 11th International Joint Conference on Natural Language Processing (ACL-IJCNLP, Volume 1: Long Papers)*, pp. 7053–7065. Online. ACL. https://aclanthology.org/2021.acl-long.548

Simon Woo, Zuyao Li, and Jelena Mirkovic (2016). Good automatic authentication question generation. In *Proceedings of the 9th International Natural Language Generation Conference (INLG)*, pp. 203–206. Edinburgh, UK. ACL. https://aclanthology.org/W16-6632

Peter Worley (2015). Open thinking, closed questioning: Two kinds of open and closed question. *Journal of Philosophy in Schools*, 2(2), 17-29.

Zichen Wu, Xin Jia, Fanyi Qu, and Yunfang Wu (2022). Enhancing Pre-trained Models with Text Structure Knowledge for Question Generation. In *Proceedings of the 29th International Conference on Computational Linguistics (COLING)*, pp. 6564–6574. Gyeongju, Republic of Korea. International Committee on Computational Linguistics. https://aclanthology.org/2022.coling-1.571

Dongling Xiao, Han Zhang, Yukun Li, Yu Sun, Hao Tian, Hua Wu, and Haifeng Wang (2020). ERNIE-GEN: An Enhanced Multi-Flow Pre-training and Fine-tuning Framework for Natural Language Generation. In *Proceedings of the Twenty-Ninth International Joint Conference on Artificial Intelligence (IJCAI-20)*, pp. 3997–4003. Yokohama, Japan. https://doi.org/10.24963/ijcai.2020/553

Binbin Xie, Jia Song, Liangying Shao, Suhang Wu, Xiangpeng Wei, Baosong Yang, Huan Lin, Jun Xie, and Jinsong Su (2023). From Statistical Methods to Deep Learning, Automatic Keyphrase Prediction: A Survey. Information *Processing &Management*, 60, 4, 103382. https://doi.org/10.1016/j.ipm.2023.103382

Ying Xu, Dakuo Wang, Mo Yu, Daniel Ritchie, Bingsheng Yao, Tongshuang Wu, Zheng Zhang, Toby Li, Nora Bradford, Branda Sun, Tran Hoang, Yisi Sang, Yufang Hou, Xiaojuan Ma, Diyi Yang, Nanyun Peng, Zhou Yu, and Mark Warschauer (2022). Fantastic Questions and Where to Find Them: FairytaleQA – An Authentic Dataset for Narrative Comprehension. In *Proceedings of the 60th Annual Meeting of the Association for Computational Linguistics* (Volume 1: Long Papers), pp. 447–460, Dublin, Ireland. ACL. https://aclanthology.org/2022.acl-long.34

Victoria Yaneva, Daniel Jurich, Le An Ha, and Peter Baldwin (2021). Using Linguistic Features to Predict the Response Process Complexity Associated with Answering Clinical MCQs. In *Proceedings of the 16th Workshop on Innovative Use of NLP for Building Educational Applications*, pp. 223–232, Online. ACL. https://aclanthology.org/2021.bea-1.23

Zhilin Yang, Peng Qi, Saizheng Zhang, Yoshua Bengio, William Cohen, Ruslan Salakhutdinov, and Christopher D. Manning (2018). HotpotQA: A Dataset for Diverse, Explainable Multi-hop Question Answering. In *Proceedings of the 2018 Conference on Empirical Methods in Natural Language Processing*, pp. 2369–2380, Brussels, Belgium. ACL. https://aclanthology.org/D18-1259

Xingdi Yuan, Tong Wang, Yen-Hsiang Wang, Emery Fine, Rania Abdelghani, Hélène Sauzéon, and Pierre-Yves Oudeyer (2023). Selecting Better Samples from Pre-trained LLMs: A Case Study on

Question Generation. In *Findings of the Association for Computational Linguistics, ACL 2023*, pp. 12952–12965, Toronto, Canada. ACL. https://aclanthology.org/2023.findings-acl.820

Lishan Zhang and Kurt VanLehn (2016). How do machine-generated questions compare to human-generated questions? *Research and Practice in Technology Enhanced Learning*, 11(7): 1–28. https://doi.org/10.1186/s41039-016-0031-7

Ruqing Zhang, Jiafeng Guo, Lu Chen, Yixing Fan, and Xueqi Cheng (2021). A Review on Question Generation from Natural Language Text. *ACM Transactions on Information Systems*, 40 (1), Article 14. https://doi.org/10.1145/3468889

Shiyue Zhang and Mohit Bansal (2019). Addressing Semantic Drift in Question Generation for Semi-Supervised Question Answering. In *Proceedings of the 2019 Conference on Empirical Methods in Natural Language Processing and the 9th International Joint Conference on Natural Language Processing (EMNLP-IJCNLP)*, pp. 2495–2509, Hong Kong, China. https://aclanthology.org/D19-1253

Tianyi Zhang, Varsha Kishore, Felix Wu, Kilian Q. Weinberger, and Yoav Artzi (2020). BERTScore: Evaluating Text Generation with BERT. In *Proceedings of ICLR2020*. https://iclr.cc/virtual_2020/poster_SkeHuCVFDr.html

Shiqi Zhao, Haifeng Wang, Chao Li, Ting Liu, and Yi Guan (2011). Automatically generating questions from queries for community-based question answering. In *Proceedings of the 5th International Joint Conference on Natural Language Processing*, pp. 929–937. Chiang Mai, Thailand. Asian Federation of Natural Language Processing. https://aclanthology.org/I11-1104

Wei Zhao, Maxime Peyrard, Fei Liu, Yang Gao, Christian M. Meyer, and Steffen Eger (2019). MoverScore: Text Generation Evaluating with Contextualized Embeddings and Earth Mover Distance. In *Proceedings of the 2019 Conference on Empirical Methods in Natural Language Processing and the 9th International Joint Conference on Natural Language Processing (EMNLP-IJCNLP)*, pp. 563–578, Hong Kong, China. ACL. https://aclanthology.org/D19-1053

Wayne Xin Zhao, Kun Zhou, Junyi Li, Tianyi Tang, Xiaolei Wang, Yupeng Hou, Yingqian Min, Beichen Zhang, Junjie Zhang, Zican Dong, Yifan Du, Chen Yang, Yushuo Chen, Zhipeng Chen, Jinhao Jiang, Ruiyang Ren, Yifan Li, Xinyu Tang, Zikang Liu, Peiyu Liu, Jian-Yun Nie, and Ji-Rong Wen (2023). A Survey of Large Language Models. E-print, arXiv:2303.18223v14. https://doi.org/10.48550/arXiv.2303.18223

Yao Zhao, Xiaochuan Ni, Yuanyuan Ding, and Qifa Ke (2018). Paragraph-level neural question generation with maxout pointer and gated self-attention networks. In *Proceedings of the 2018 Conference on Empirical Methods in Natural Language Processing (EMNLP 2018)*, pp. 3901–3910, Brussels, Belgium. https://aclanthology.org/D18-1424

Youwen Zhao, Xiangbo Yuan, Ye Yuan, Shaoxiong Deng, and Jun Quan (2023). Relation extraction: advancements through deep learning and entity-related features. *Social Network Analysis and Mining*, 13:92. https://doi.org/10.1007/s13278-023-01095-8

Chunting Zhou, Graham Neubig, Jiatao Gu, Mona Diab, Francisco Guzmán, Luke Zettlemoyer, Marjan Ghazvininejad (2021). Detecting Hallucinated Content in Conditional Neural Sequence Generation. In *Findings of the Association for Computational Linguistics: ACL-IJCNLP 2021*, pp. 1393–1404, Online. ACL. https://aclanthology.org/2021.findings-acl.120

Qingyu Zhou, Nan Yang, Furu Wei, Chuanqi Tan, Hangbo Bao, and Ming Zhou (2017). Neural Question Generation from Text: A Preliminary Study. In: X. Huang, J. Jiang, D. Zhao, Y. Feng, and Y. Hong (eds.), *Natural Language Processing and Chinese Computing. NLPCC 2017*. LNCS, vol. 10619. Springer, Cham. https://doi.org/10.1007/978-3-319-73618-1_56

Derui Zhu, Dingfan Chen, Qing Li, Zongxiong Chen, Lei Ma, Jens Grossklags, and Mario Fritz (2024). PoLLMgraph: Unraveling Hallucinations in Large Language Models via State Transition

Dynamics. In *Findings of the Association for Computational Linguistics: NAACL 2024*, pp. 4737–4751, Mexico City, Mexico. Association for Computational Linguistics. https://aclanthology.org/2024.findings-naacl.294

Yukun Zhu, Ryan Kiros, Rich Zemel, Ruslan Salakhutdinov, Raquel Urtasun, Antonio Torralba, and Sanja Fidler (2015). Aligning Books and Movies: Towards Story-Like Visual Explanations by Watching Movies and Reading Books. In *2015 IEEE International Conference on Computer Vision (ICCV)*, pp. 19–27. Santiago, Chile. IEEE. https://doi.org/10.1109/ICCV.2015.11

Branko Žitko, Slavomir Stankov, Marki Rosić, and Ani Grubišić (2009). Dynamic test generation over ontology-based knowledge representation in authoring shell. *Expert Systems with Applications*, 36, 8185–8196. https://doi.org/10.1016/j.eswa.2008.10.028

Nomi Erteschik-Shir (1986). Wh-questions and Focus. Linguistics and Philosophy, 9, 117–149.

Subhankar Maity and Aniket Deroy (2024). The Future of Learning in the Age of Generative AI: Automated Question Generation and Assessment with Large Language Models. ArXiv preprint. https://doi.org/10.48550/arXiv.2410.09576

Ming Liu, Vasile Rus, and Li Liu (2017). Automatic Chinese Factual Question Generation. IEEE Transactions on Learning Technologies, 10(2), 194–204.

Jack Mostow, Yi-Ting Huang, Hyeju Jang, Anders Weinstein, Joe Valeri, and Donna Gates (2017). Developing, evaluating, and refining an automatic generator of diagnostic multiple choice cloze questions to assess children's comprehension while reading. Natural Language Engineering, 3(2):245–294. https://doi.org/10.1017/S1351324916000024

Allyson Ettinger (2020). What BERT Is Not: Lessons from a New Suite of Psycholinguistic Diagnostics for Language Models. Transactions of the Association for Computational Linguistics, 8:34–48. https://aclanthology.org/2020.tacl-1.3/

GPSR Compliance

The European Union's (EU) General Product Safety Regulation (GPSR) is a set of rules that requires consumer products to be safe and our obligations to ensure this.

If you have any concerns about our products, you can contact us on

ProductSafety@springernature.com

In case Publisher is established outside the EU, the EU authorized representative is:

Springer Nature Customer Service Center GmbH
Europaplatz 3
69115 Heidelberg, Germany

www.ingramcontent.com/pod-product-compliance
Lightning Source LLC
Chambersburg PA
CBHW081553280725
30249CB00006B/527